W9-BTZ-059

CLASSIFICATION IN MENTAL RETARDATION

Editor:
Herbert J. Grossman, M.D.

Contributors:
Michael J. Begab, Ph.D.
Dennis P. Cantwell, M.D.
James D. Clements, M.D.
Richard K. Eyman, Ph.D.
C. Edward Meyers, Ph.D.
George Tarjan, M.D.
Sue Allen Warren, Ph.D.

Production Editor:
Yvette Taylor, M.A.

DISCARDED
JENKS LRC
GORDON COLLEGE

Published by
American Association on Mental Deficiency
1719 Kalorama Road, NW
Washington, DC 20009

JENKS L.R.C.
GORDON COLLEGE
255 GRAPEVINE RD.
WENHAM, MA 01984-1895

The American Association on Mental Deficiency, founded in 1876, is a large national organization of professionals from many different disciplines who are concerned with mental retardation; its purposes include the development of a body of scientific literature about mental retardation and dissemination of information, as well as a variety of other activities on behalf of mentally retarded persons.

Copyright © 1983 by the American Association on Mental Deficiency

Published by
American Association on Mental Deficiency
1719 Kalorama Road, NW
Washington, DC 20009

Library of Congress Catalog Card Number: 83–8779
International Standard Book Number: 0–940898–12–8

Library of Congress Cataloging in Publication Data
Main entry under title:

Classification in mental retardation.

Includes index.
1. Mental deficiency—Classification. I. Grossman, Herbert J., 1923–   II. Begab, Michael J. (Michael Jay), 1918–   III. American Association on Mental Deficiency, [DNLM: 1. Mental retardation—Classification. WM 15 A509c]
RC570.C515 1983   616.85'88'0012   83–8779
ISBN 0–940898–12–8

Printed in the United States of America

First printing: May, 1983
Second printing: September, 1984

RC
570
.C515
1983

TABLE OF CONTENTS

CHAPTER 1: INTRODUCTION   1

Definitions   1
The 1983 Classification System   2
Revision Process   3

**CHAPTER 2: A BRIEF HISTORY OF CLASSIFICATION
                        AND TERMINOLOGY   5**

AAMD Manuals   5
Early Efforts   8

CHAPTER 3: DEFINITIONS   11

Definitions   11
Discussion   17

**CHAPTER 4: THE ASSESSMENT OF INTELLIGENCE,
                        ADAPTIVE BEHAVIOR, AND
                        SOCIAL–ENVIRONMENTAL FACTORS   27**

Intelligence   27
Psychological Assessment   38
Adaptive Behavior   42
Social–Environmental Measures of the Family   47
Safeguarding the Assessment Process   53

CHAPTER 5: TYPOLOGY OF MENTAL RETARDATION   59

Retardation of Biologic Origin   59
Social–Environmental Factors   70
Incidence and Prevalence   75

**CHAPTER 6: APPLICATIONS OF THIS CLASSIFICATION
                        SYSTEM TO THE DELIVERY OF SERVICES
                        AND RESEARCH   79**

Service-System Management   79
Planning   81
Evaluation of Services   82
Research   89

CHAPTER 7: CLINICAL APPLICATIONS 91

Medical Management 91
Emotional–Behavioral Disorders 98
Living Arrangements 110
Behavioral and Educational Management 111

CHAPTER 8: MEDICAL ETIOLOGICAL CLASSIFICATION 123

Revised AAMD Medical Classification System 126
Medical Etiological Classification 130
Definitions of Medical Etiologies 135
Concurrent Medical Problems 150

GLOSSARY 155

APPENDIX A: ILLUSTRATIONS OF HIGHEST LEVEL OF ADAPTIVE BEHAVIOR FUNCTIONING BY CHRONOLOGICAL AGE AND LEVEL 203

APPENDIX B: ILLUSTRATIONS OF DECISION-MAKING IN IDENTIFICATION AND LEVELS 208

ACKNOWLEDGEMENTS

We acknowledge our indebtedness to all of the individuals who worked so hard for many decades to pave the way for this work. We are also indebted to the leadership of the American Association on Mental Deficiency, who have been highly supportive of this current endeavor. Many hours have been contributed by thoughtful individuals who have influenced our writing. We are also grateful to the Executive Director, Albert J. Berkowitz, and the Central Office Staff, particularly the Director of Publications, Susan Yoder, for their outstanding help. We also acknowledge Diane Ulm for her many contributions during the deliberations and activities of the Committee.

CHAPTER 1
INTRODUCTION

DEFINITIONS

MENTAL RETARDATION REFERS TO SIGNIFICANTLY SUBAVERAGE GENERAL INTELLECTUAL FUNCTIONING EXISTING CONCURRENTLY WITH DEFICITS IN ADAPTIVE BEHAVIOR AND MANIFESTED DURING THE DEVELOPMENTAL PERIOD.

GENERAL INTELLECTUAL FUNCTIONING is defined as the results obtained by assessment with one or more of the individually administered general intelligence tests developed for the purpose of assessing intellectual functioning.

SIGNIFICANTLY SUBAVERAGE INTELLECTUAL FUNCTIONING is defined as approximately IQ 70 or below.

ADAPTIVE BEHAVIOR is defined as the effectiveness or degree with which individuals meet the standards of personal independence and social responsibility expected for age and cultural group.

DEVELOPMENTAL PERIOD is defined as the period of time between conception and the 18th birthday.

Note. All of these concepts are defined in detail in Chapters 3 and 4 and discussed throughout this publication.

1

THE 1983 CLASSIFICATION SYSTEM

Purposes

The purpose of any classification system is to provide a sense of order. More particularly, in this publication, the purposes include:

1. *Contribution toward an acceptable system to be used throughout the world.* Toward this end, efforts have been made to keep this system as compatible as possible with other published systems. Specifically, the developers of this classification have worked in cooperation with leaders of the World Health Organization and the American Psychiatric Association to ensure maximal compatibility between the three major classification schemes: World Health Organization's system of International Classification of Diseases, Clinical Modification (ICD-9 CM), the American Psychiatric Association's Diagnostic and Statistical Manual (DSM-III), and the American Association on Mental Deficiency's (AAMD's) Classification in Mental Retardation.
2. *Facilitation of communication for diagnostic, treatment, and research purposes.* Such communications include record keeping, epidemiology, program and curriculum planning, social issues, and other activities associated with concerns for mentally retarded persons.
3. *Facilitation of prevention efforts.* A major purpose of this classification system is to provide opportunities for the identification of cause, with implications for prevention.

Characteristics

Any useful classification system should be comprehensive and consistent with current knowledge in the field, with terms that are operationally defined to the maximal extent possible. It should have internal consistency, should not be labile, and should be easy to use. Systems of classification dealing with human beings will, of necessity, be imperfect, but we have kept in mind the characteristics described as guidelines for the development of this system.

Limitations

The narrative in this publication was designed to provide an approach for accurate identification and diagnosis. To understand this approach, readers must carefully study the narrative sections in which assessment, identification, and interpretation of data are discussed.

This publication is not intended to be a comprehensive textbook in mental retardation. It should serve, however, as a valuable supplementary resource for expansion of knowledge. This book is not intended to provide detailed instructions for treatment, management, education, habilitation, and rehabilitation but should serve useful purposes for persons involved in those activities.

Recognizing these limitations, we reiterate the purposes of the publication: (a) to provide for a world-wide use of a common nosology with definitional criteria; (b) to improve opportunities to gather more precise knowledge of epidemiology and prevalence, as well as to share more fully the results of experience and research; and (c) to facilitate efforts at prevention and treatment by identifying the causes of the mental retardation.

REVISION PROCESS

Since its earliest days, the AAMD has made significant contributions to the field of mental retardation in the areas of diagnosis and classification. This eighth revision represents the collective thinking of a large number of professionals. In addition to the members of the AAMD's Terminology and Classification Committee, many persons knowledgeable in the field have offered critiques and suggestions that we have incorporated. During the past 5 years, there have been helpful presentations at national and regional meetings of AAMD, national and local hearings, and discussions with representatives of many professional, social, and political action groups. The leadership of AAMD, including the Council, have been very beneficial to the Committee. As a result of all of those activities, very careful attention has been paid to clarification of important issues, including:

1. The recognition of the responsibility of clinicians using results of intelligence tests to take into consideration the fact that the standard error of measurement varies with different individual intelligence tests, depending on the reliability and the standard deviation of the test or tests being used.
2. The recognition of variability in individuals of similar intellectual functioning levels (as measured by tests) and the

knowledge that such variability precludes the setting of precise "numerical cut-off points" for assignment to the status of retardation or to any specific level of retardation.

3. The recognition that we must realize that available measures of adaptive behavior are necessarily somewhat imprecise. Since dual criteria of intellectual functioning and adaptive behavior define mental retardation, the determination of the presence or absence of mental retardation requires sound clinical judgment. Once the diagnosis or classification of mental retardation is made, adaptive behavior scales are useful in further specification. The illustrations of adaptive behavior levels by chronological age that appear in Appendix A may be used to provide a general estimate of adaptive behavior.

4. The recognition that no classification system in mental retardation can provide for the unique needs of individuals who require services. We believe that it is important to determine diagnosis prior to, and independent of, assessing the service needs of individuals.

Herbert J. Grossman, Chairman
Michael J. Begab
Dennis P. Cantwell
James D. Clements
Richard K. Eyman
C. Edward Meyers
George Tarjan
Sue Allen Warren

CHAPTER 2
A BRIEF HISTORY OF CLASSIFICATION AND TERMINOLOGY

AAMD MANUALS

Since the founding of the organization now known as the American Association on Mental Deficiency (AAMD), its members have been concerned about the differentiation of mental retardation from other handicapping conditions and about differences found within the population of retarded individuals. At the second meeting of the organization members, a paper was presented on the topic of differentiating medical conditions associated with the condition; throughout the years other evidence of the concern for development of a system of differentiation to aid in treatments, programs, and planning purposes has appeared in the publications of AAMD. In 1919, the Committee on Classification and Uniform Statistics was appointed to develop such a system. Collaborating with the National Committee for Mental Hygiene, the group developed a manual that was published in 1921. The second edition of that manual was published in 1933 and the third in 1941. An AAMD Committee on Nomenclature developed an etiological classification system that was published in 1957; that Committee recommended the development of a comprehensive manual on terminology and classification in mental retardation. The task was undertaken by the Project on Technical Planning in Mental Retardation of AAMD, and the fifth manual was published in 1959. That manual, with minor corrections, was reprinted in 1961.

The 1959 manual provided uniformity in terminology and presented a dual classification system, medical and behavioral. The medical system was subdivided into eight sections designed to be consistent with the medical knowledge of the time. The behavioral system was subdivided into two sections, measured intellectual levels and adaptive behavior levels. At that time, measured intelligence was used to define levels of retardation based on the stan-

5

dard deviations of the intelligence tests being used; the definition of intelligence in terms of intelligence testing was changed from the traditional one of "about 70 IQ" to one standard deviation below the mean of the test, which was approximately 85 IQ on the most commonly used tests; this change made it possible to include almost 15 percent of the total United States population in the group identified as retarded. The developers of the 1959 manual, however, were well aware that many individuals who obtained intelligence test scores between 70 and 85 did not function as retarded. That factor was not a major concern, however, because the definition of retardation developed by that group required that an individual should be retarded in both current intellectual functioning and in adaptive behavior. There was much concern among users of the 1959 manual about the inclusion of such a large segment of the general population as being potentially identifiable as retarded, and numerous debates took place at national conferences and in local staff conferences.

After long debate, serious consideration, and consultation with many leaders in the field of mental retardation, the AAMD Committee on Terminology that prepared the 1973 Manual on Terminology and Classification decided to abolish the cut-off score of *one* standard deviation below the mean (Borderline) and return to the more traditional cut-off point, which was approximately two standard deviations below the mean for the test used. The 1973 manual was different in a number of other ways, for it built upon experience with the earlier manuals. The definition of mental retardation in the 1959 manual was clarified to ensure that readers clearly understood that both adaptive behavior and measured intelligence must be present at the same time in order to designate an individual as retarded. The developmental period was defined as prior to the 18th birthday (rather than 16th birthday recommended in the 1959 manual). The 1973 manual provided a carefully developed extensive *Glossary*.

Since the introduction of the adaptive behavior criterion in the 1959 manual, there had been much concern about the measurement of that aspect of behavior. The AAMD had developed an Adaptive Behavior Scale, but by 1973 it was not widely available, and at that time it had no norms for children who lived outside residential facilities. The 1973 manual, therefore, included a table of illustrations of levels of adaptive behavior that had been developed and used by one of the committee members (S.A.W.); the table provided guidelines for estimating the level of adaptive functioning by age.

In the 1977 edition of the AAMD Manual on Terminology and Classification, new materials were added and clarifications were made of the procedures for diagnosing mental retardation in the behavioral system. The medical system and the Glossary were updated.

This 1983 AAMD classification system developed by the AAMD Committee on Terminology and Classification, has been changed to reflect current thinking in the field and to make it consistent with the International Classification of Diseases-9 (ICD-9) of the World Health Organization and the American Psychiatric Association's Diagnostic and Statistical Manual-III (DSM-III), particularly with reference to medical classification. The ICD-9 and DSM-III are also generally consistent in defining levels of retardation in the behavioral system. Clinicians using the system should be well aware that in determining whether a person is retarded and at what level of intellectual functioning the individual is operating, it is important to understand the concept of standard error of measurement and to use it when making a clinical determination of retardation and level of functioning. If the intelligence test being used has a large standard error of measurement, less confidence can be placed in the obtained IQ than is the case in which the standard error is small, for example, as is the case with the Wechsler scales.

This 1983 classification system represents an effort to take into consideration the need for a world-wide system that is consistent and useful. Consideration was also given to the large-scale attack on intelligence tests that has taken place in the 1960s and 1970s. Such criticisms have emerged in part from lack of understanding of test construction on the part of the lay public, as well as users of test results. The criticisms also reflected current widespread attacks on "labeling." Labeling has been equated with classification, and the advantages of classification have been lost in the attacks on labels as automatically stigmatizing; whether labels are more stigmatizing than advantageous is still a moot question. Nevertheless, there is a need for a comprehensive and consistent system of classification in mental retardation in order to facilitate communication of professional personnel working in the field, particularly research workers

who need such a system if they are to make progress toward the
ultimate goal of prevention of the condition. Such a system is also
needed to ensure that eligible persons are identified so that services
can be provided.

EARLY EFFORTS

The work of AAMD is not the earliest effort to gain precision in
defining retardation, which was first described in Thebes, Greece,
as early as 1500 B.C. Hippocrates, the father of medicine, mentioned it in about 500 B.C. and discussed certain deformities of the
skull associated with retarded behavior. The Roman physician
Galen wrote about differing levels of mental acuity. During the
Middle Ages (about 400 to 1500 A.D.), retarded persons were
sometimes tolerated as fools, favored as "innocents," or persecuted
as witches, the designation being based on observations of everyday
behavior of individuals and probably not at all consistent from
place to place. Furthermore, usually no differentiation was likely
made between mentally ill and mentally retarded persons.

Late in the Middle Ages, in England, efforts were made to
differentiate mental retardation and mental illness, and in the 16th
and 17th centuries, there were legal definitions proposed, such as
Fitz-Hebert's comment in 1534: "And he who shall be said to be a
sot (i.e., simpleton) and idiot from his birth is such a person who
cannot account or remember 20 pence, nor can he tell how old he
is, etc. so as it may appear that he hath no understanding or reason
of what shall be for his profit nor what for his loss." (In that era the
term *idiot* encompassed all levels of retardation.)

In 1672 in a medical textbook, Willis discussed the classification
of mental retardation and indicated differences within the group
with these words: "Some are unable to learn their letters but can
handle mechanical arts; others who fail at this can easily comprehend agriculture; others are unfit except to eat and sleep;
others merely dolts or driviling fools."

In the late 18th century, John Locke offered his classic differentiation between mental retardation and mental illness by indicating that mentally ill individuals put wrong ideas together and
reason from them, but "idiots" make few or no propositions and
reason scarce at all. At the end of the 19th century, the psychiatrist
Pinel identified as an idiot a wild boy found in the forest near Paris

and held the view that the child was incurable. (That idea of incurability of retardation persisted into the mid-20th century, but is clearly rejected in all recent AAMD manuals on identification and diagnosis.)

During the late 18th century and throughout the 19th century, a number of workers attempted to differentiate some of the medical conditions associated with retardation, particularly cretinism, gargoylism, and the condition known today as Down syndrome, which was described by Down in 1866. Down offered a medical classification system, as follows:

Congenital idiocy
  Microcephaly
  Hydrocephaly
  Paralysis and epilepsy
Developmental idiocy due to anxiety associated with
  Cutting teeth
  Puberty
Accidental injury due to
  Injury (mechanical)
  Illness

The classification system proposed by Down indicates the state of understanding of conditions associated with retardation in his day.

The end of the 19th century and beginning of the 20th century brought two related movements, the development of intelligence tests and concern for genetics as a factor in mental retardation. Both Dugdale and Goddard became interested in a group of persons in society who did not have obvious physical signs of disorders associated with retardation, and both did extensive family pedigree studies of persons who became known as "familial retarded" persons; these studies indicate an awareness of differing groups within the retarded population. The development of intelligence tests, which began in France and America at the turn of this century, made possible an objective and consistent procedure for measurement of abilities. These tests became useful in differentiating retarded persons behaviorally in addition to the medical differentiations that were in use. The terms *idiot, imbecile,* and *moron* were used to identify three levels of retarded behavior, and approximate cut-off scores on intelligence tests were devised: 25, 50, and 75. During World War I, extensive work was done on the development of intelligence tests, and by 1925, the 1916 version of the Stanford-Binet Intelligence Scale was in wide use to identify, classify, and plan for school children who were classified as retarded on the basis of this measure. The usefulness of these relatively brief, objective observations done in a standardized manner for predicting academic achievement led to the development of numerous other intelligence tests.

During the period from about 1920 to 1950, a number of workers (for example, Fernald, Edgar Doll, Porteus) became interested in the variability in everyday functioning of retarded persons of the same mental age or IQ. Porteus proposed a test of "planfulness," and Doll developed what he called "a measure of social maturity" (now called "adaptive behavior"). In addition, it became obvious that IQ was not immutable. After this was recognized, it became customary to be cautious in making long-term predictions from results of intelligence tests alone, particularly for individuals who were functioning in the upper range of retardation. The trend was toward emphasizing current level of intellectual and adaptive behavior functioning, and since the publication of the 1959 AAMD manual, it has been customary to view mental retardation in terms of current level of functioning in both intelligence and adaptive behavior.

Both the ICD-9 and the DSM-III medical classification systems have adopted the definition of mental retardation that was published in the 1973 AAMD manual. Many state laws now include variations of the AAMD definition of retardation in either their laws or regulations. Public Law (PL) 94–142 and other federal legislation now recognize the AAMD definition. The 1983 definition, slightly modified for clarity, was introduced in the 1959 manual; it is intended to represent the current status of scientific knowledge in the field and the current thinking about social issues associated with mental retardation. One may anticipate that as both knowledge and philosophy change, there will be modifications reflecting such changes in future manuals.

CHAPTER 3
DEFINITIONS

DEFINITIONS

Mental retardation refers to significantly subaverage general intellectual functioning existing concurrently with deficits in adaptive behavior and manifested during the developmental period.

General intellectual functioning is operationally defined as the results obtained by assessment with one or more of the individually administered standardized general intelligence tests developed for that purpose.

Significantly subaverage is defined as IQ of 70 or below on standardized measures of intelligence. This upper limit is intended as a guideline; it could be extended upward through IQ 75 or more, depending on the reliability of the intelligence test used. This particularly applies in schools and similar settings if behavior is impaired and clinically determined to be due to deficits in reasoning and judgment.

Deficits in adaptive behavior are defined as significant limitations in an individual's effectiveness in meeting the standards of maturation, learning, personal independence, and/or social responsibility that are expected for his or her age level and cultural group, as determined by clinical assessment and, usually, standardized scales.

Developmental period is defined as the period of time between conception and the 18th birthday. Developmental deficits may be manifested by slow, arrested, or incomplete development resulting from brain damage, degenerative processes in the central nervous system, or regression from previously normal states due to psychosocial factors.

Figure 1 illustrates possible combinations of measured intellectual functioning and adaptive behavior. Table 1 shows levels of mental retardation. Retardation may occur through physical

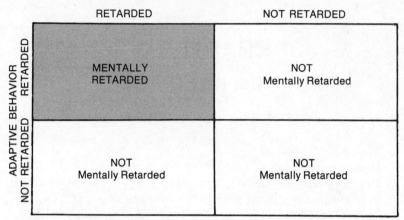

Figure 1. Possible combinations of measured intellectual functioning and adaptive behavior.

trauma or central nervous system deterioration at any age beyond the developmental period. When manifestations occur later, the condition is more properly classified as *dementia* (see DSM-III—Organic Mental Disorders).

The term *mental retardation,* as commonly used today, embraces a heterogeneous population, ranging from totally dependent to nearly independent people. Although all individuals so designated share the common attributes of low intelligence and inadequacies in adaptive behavior, there are marked variations in the degree of deficit manifested and the presence or absence of associated physical handicaps, stigmata, and psychologically disordered states. These variations greatly affect the needs of retarded individuals, the nature of the problems and services required by their families, and the burdens posed to community agencies and supportive systems. The differences are highly related to etiological factors, setting biologically damaged persons apart from psychosocially disadvantaged individuals on a number of significant dimensions: performance, problems, potentials, and prognosis.

Conceptually, the identifiable mentally retarded population can be divided into two distinct, albeit overlapping, groups. One group, approximately 25 percent of the total population, constitutes the "clinical types." Individuals of this group generally demonstrate

TABLE 1

LEVEL OF RETARDATION INDICATED BY IQ RANGE OBTAINED ON
MEASURE OF GENERAL INTELLECTUAL FUNCTIONING

Term	IQ range for level	(Code)
Mild mental retardation	50–55 to approx. 70	(317.0)
Moderate mental retardation	35–40 to 50–55	(318.0)
Severe mental retardation	20–25 to 35–40	(318.1)
Profound mental retardation	Below 20 or 25	(318.2)
Unspecified		(319.0)

Note. Levels of retardation are identified with the same terms as those used in previous AAMD manuals. The IQ ranges for levels are generally consistent with those suggested by the American Psychiatric Association in their *Diagnostic and Statistical Manual III*, but a narrow band at each end of each level was used to indicate that clinical judgment about all information, including the IQs, and more than one test, the information about intellectual functioning obtained from other sources, etc., is necessary in determining level. Thus, someone whose Full Scale Wechsler IQ is 53 might be diagnosed as either mild or moderate, depending on other factors, such as the relative difference in Performance and Verbal IQ or results of other tests. A psychometric explanation for the overlap in categories can be found in pages 56–57.

Procedure for determining level of retardation
1. Recognize that a problem exists (e.g., delay in developmental milestones).
2. Determine that an adaptive behavior deficit exists.
3. Determine measured general intellectual functioning.
4. Make decision about whether or not there is retardation of intellectual functioning.
5. Make decision about level of retardation as indicated by level of measured intellectual functioning.

some central nervous system pathology, usually have IQs in the moderate range or below, have associated handicaps or stigmata, and can often be diagnosed from birth or early childhood. Individuals of the second group, comprising the majority of the retarded population in the United States and elsewhere in the world, appear to be neurologically intact, have no readily detectable physical signs or clinical laboratory evidence related to retardation, function in the mildly retarded range of intelligence, and are heavily concentrated in the lowest socioeconomic segments of society. Often, they are identified as retarded only during the school years.

Neither of these groups represents "pure" entities. Children with central nervous system abnormalities can and do function within the mild range of intelligence, and many children from seriously disadvantaged homes are further handicapped by biological deficiencies. Nevertheless, the association of IQ and physical signs is very high, and the differentiation of the two groups by primary etiological agents of biological versus social-environmental origin has meaningful implications for prevention, planning, and treatment.

The complex of symptoms subsumed under the term *mental retardation* overlaps considerably with the legislative definition of *developmental disabilities* as contained in PL 94–103 and amended in PL 95–602, Title V. In the Developmental Disabilities Assistance and Bill of Rights Act, the term *developmental disabilities* refers to a severe, chronic disability that "is attributable to a mental or physical impairment or combination of mental and physical impairments" that are (a) manifested before age 22, (b) likely to continue indefinitely, and (c) result in substantial functional limitations in three or more areas of major life activity.

The areas of limitation clearly apply to the more severe forms of mental retardation and to some mildly retarded individuals during certain periods of their lives. For severely retarded people, nearly all of the defined areas of limitation are substantial and applicable: self-care, receptive and expressive language, learning, mobility, self-direction, capacity for independent living, and economic self-sufficiency. For mildly retarded individuals, many of whom achieve self-sufficiency in adulthood, the disability may be confined to impairments primarily in the areas of learning and possibly self-direction.

Other conditions embraced in the definitions of developmental disability that share some characteristics in common with mental retardation are cerebral palsy, epilepsy, and autism. Significant proportions of these populations function intellectually at retarded levels.

Developmental disabilities are therefore distinguishable from the milder forms of mental retardation and less severe conditions of cerebral palsy, epilepsy, and autism by the nature of the functional limitations described. In order to satisfy the definition, individuals must demonstrate *substantial* functional limitations that are age-specific. Although the term *substantial* is not explicitly defined, the requirement that these limitations reflect a need for services that are of life-long or extended duration and are individually planned and coordinated clearly delimits the target population.

The concepts of mental retardation and developmental disabilities, although parallel in many respects, reflect some marked differences. Both are developmental in origin and stress impairment in adaptive behavior. Most clinical types of retardation involving central nervous system pathology and IQs below approximately 55 fulfill both the physical and mental criteria of developmental disability. For this subgroup in retardation, the handicap is permanent and "substantial." The differences between the two categories occur primarily at the upper end of the retarded intellectual range. *The AAMD definition carries no connotation of chronicity or irreversibility and, on the contrary, applies only to levels of functioning.* "Significantly subaverage" is precisely defined, if not precisely measured, and imposes as a guideline a ceiling for performance that is clearly higher than inferred under the newly defined term *substantial handicap*. The fact that psychosocially disadvantaged mildly retarded children often are functionally impaired in the school years only, have no demonstrable neurological disorders, and achieve some level of adult independence indicates that they fall outside the definition of developmental disabilities.

Children with autism, in particular, share many attributes with severely and profoundly mentally retarded children. Although there is considerable variation in the behavior patterns of the latter, many of them, like autistic children, fail to develop interpersonal relationships, have serious communication and receptive language deficits, and engage in repetitive and compulsive behavior. Approximately 70 percent of autistic children have IQs within the retarded range, and all have behavioral impairments that are manifested before 30 months of age.

Learning disabilities are defined in federal legislation (PL 94–142) as referring to children:

... who exhibit a disorder in one or more of the basic psychological processes involved in understanding or in using spoken or written language. These may be manifested in disorders of listening, thinking, talking, reading, writing, or arithmetic. They include conditions which have been referred to as perceptual handicaps, brain injury, minimal brain dysfunction, dyslexia, developmental aphasia, etc. They do not include learning problems which are due primarily to visual, hearing, or motor handicap, to mental retardation, emotional disturbance, or to environmental disadvantage.

In empirical studies of children with learning disabilities, a number of frequently occurring, though not universal, characteristics have been identified. These include deficiencies in academic achievement, information-processing problems, attentional deficits, hyperactivity, uneven patterns of learning performance, and difficulties in social relationships. Since the latter have been noted especially in interactions with peers and teachers, these difficulties could stem from reactions to academic frustration and failure.

These characteristics do not discriminate learning disabled from mentally retarded populations. Both groups, for example, have a fairly high incidence of hyperactivity, an inability to modulate motor behavior appropriate to a given situation. Usually, such behavior is manifested when children are required to perform certain tasks in structured situations. Various subcategories of hyperactivity in learning-disabled children have been described, including: (a) aggressive, destructive, unpredictable, and impulsive behavior; (b) aimless and clumsy, but placid behavior; (c) highly verbal, talkative, and somewhat immature behavior. Mentally retarded children fall predominantly in the first category, reflecting perhaps their more extensive central nervous system pathology in relation to autistic children than to the learning-disabled group. Thus, on these traits, as in the others previously described, learning-disabled children are not readily distinguishable from children with other mentally handicapping conditions.

The most discriminating characteristic between learning disability and mental retardation is the level of measured intelligence. By definition, the former category specifically excludes mental retardation and, presumably, includes children of at least average intelligence. Conceptually, this difference is clear and significant. In practice, however, and in classification as well, this discriminating factor is not easily applied. Retarded children can be learning disabled, but the converse—by definition—is not possible.

The ambiguities of classification are particularly apparent with children whose measured intelligence is borderline or dull normal and who demonstrate the range of learning problems and characteristics alluded to in the discussion of learning disabilities. Under existing systems of classification and definition, these children, often called "slow learners," are neither mentally retarded nor learning disabled, yet their difficulties in school work and social relationships may be very comparable to these two groups. This classification dilemma remains to be resolved; the schools, however, classify many slow-learning children as learning disabled if they are not mentally retarded.

DISCUSSION

Uses and Misuses of Classification Systems

Uses of classification systems. The fundamental purpose of using classification systems is to provide an organized schema for the categorization of many kinds of phenomena relevant to the human condition. Such information, properly ordered and conceptualized, is essential (a) for the acquisition of knowledge in the prevention and control of disability and its manifestations and (b) in the promotion of physical, mental, and social well being. To satisfy these objectives as they relate to the complexities and origins of retarded mental performance, the system must include the identification of etiological agents and the specification of the psychological and cultural contexts influencing behavior and its measurement.

The 1983 classification system consciously addresses these two major objectives. The definition of mental retardation sets forth the criteria by which the target population can be identified, and the etiological section specifies the causes that, in most instances, are necessary precursors to studies in pathogenesis and ultimately to the development of preventive measures. The newly added axis on social-environmental variables not only takes cognizance of the important contributory role of these factors to impaired intellectual and behavioral functioning, but highlights areas for intervention and treatment in promoting a higher level of well being for retarded individuals.

The protection and promotion of the health and welfare of our citizens—including those who are mentally retarded—is an important function and responsibility of government. This function has been afforded even greater prominence in recent years as a consequence of judicial actions affirming the rights of mentally retarded persons to treatment and education. The classification of individuals and their environments is a tool of government, indispensable to the fulfillment of this responsibility. It is basic to the processes for acquiring data needed by human-service-delivery systems for planning and administering programs for the treatment and rehabilitation of affected persons for removing barriers to service utilization and for program evaluation.

In our prevailing system of categorical funding, the classification of persons is an essential process in determining eligibility for

various health, social, economic, educational, and training services
as well as benefits under federal, state, and local laws. Commercial
health insurance companies, too, apply classification criteria in
assessing eligibility and evaluating claims for reimbursement. Even
primitive societies apply some form of classification, largely informal, through class or caste structures, role assignment, status, and
division of labor in influencing the lives of their citizens. Thus,
classification of persons may be properly viewed as inherent in the
regulation of societal activities.

Classification systems depend upon research, are fundamental to
the definition of subject populations, and are a fruitful source for
the generation of research hypotheses. The reliance on research in
stipulating the properties of intelligence and behavior and in the
discovery and description of clinical syndromes would seem to be
fully supportable; however, in the classification of human populations in general, and mentally retarded persons in particular,
sociopolitical and professional considerations exert great pressure
on the system. Minority groups, for example, because of their
overinclusion in the mentally retarded population, challenge the
validity of assessment instruments and the criteria by which retardation is currently defined. Some of their leaders assert that the
instruments employed to determine the level of tested intelligence
fail to reflect the true level of intellectual potential. Some of these
leaders would restrict the definition of mental retardation to persons having organic etiology.

Some educators, by contrast, would set the intellectual parameters even higher than set forth here in the firm belief that margi-
nally intelligent people have learning problems that require special
or remedial educational efforts. Medical and vocational rehabilitation professionals would stress still different definitional criteria.

These conflicting pressures graphically illustrate the impossibil-
ity of developing a classification system that is responsive to different ideologies and that at the same time applies objective standards for identifying persons in need by virtue of intellectual and
behavioral impairments. The 1983 classification system is based on
empirical and scientific evidence and reflects the state-of-the-art on
the relevant issues. Admittedly, knowledge is imperfect in several
critical dimensions. We do not know precisely the relationship
between intelligence and social competence, how much intelligence, as measured by tests, is needed in order for individuals to

adapt satisfactorily to societal demands, or the nature of intelligence and whether, in fact, it can be accurately assessed with existing instruments across diverse populations. Our ability to assess impaired behavior in a variety of cultural contexts and environmental settings is also limited, and clinical judgment depends heavily on the acumen and experience of clinicians. Similarly, the delineation of social–environmental variables most crucial to the developmental process awaits further refinement.

Despite these limitations, and others not noted here, an empirically based system is preferable to one dictated by the vagaries of litigation, political processes, and the pressure of special-interest groups. Every system of classification must be periodically upgraded to incorporate new discoveries and changing concepts. Conceivably, as we learn more about the adaptive capacities of individuals with limited intelligence, the parameters of our definition may require changes.

Among the many utilizations of classification systems for research, epidemiological studies are the most directly dependent, since they are concerned with the study of factors that influence the occurrence and distribution of various diseases and conditions. The distribution of any disease or defect clearly requires skilled clinical diagnosis to separate those who have the condition from those who do not. The lack of highly sensitive instruments for diagnosis and measurement and limited reliable methods for case-finding, although handicapping to accurate diagnosis, is more likely to operate at the individual case level than in population statistics. The descriptions of clinical syndromes and age-specific functional performance contained in this classification system are not only an aid in the identification of retardation but in specifying the classification and diagnosis to which individuals should be assigned.

We stress that classification systems deal with population groups (not individual cases), are fundamental to the study of any phenomenon, and form the basis for all scientific generalization. Clinicians deal with individual diagnoses that collectively provide *population* data; however, classification systems are concerned only with the latter. Population-based information provides the statistics on incidence, prevalence, and related conditions that are essential to program planning and service-delivery systems.

The 1983 classification system can be applied to a variety of functions, including research and evaluation of service programs, as discussed in Chapter 6. To be fully useful, classification systems must embrace the entire age span; be simple enough to encourage wide application by practitioners, planners, researchers, and diagnosticians; and be compatible with other systems in use.

Misuses of classification systems. Much of the current concern regarding intelligence testing and the potentially stigmatizing consequences of labeling individuals as mentally retarded has in some quarters generated an anticlassification movement. Proponents of this view have failed to distinguish between classification and labeling. Although labeling—or more precisely, diagnosis—is essential to classification, each has distinctive purposes and uses.

As noted earlier, classification systems are population-based and usually impersonal. Any effort to categorize the totality of any individual, even by multiaxial indices, is clearly not possible. Especially at the upper levels of mental retardation, where discrepancies between adaptive behavior and measured intelligence are common, the determination of deficient performance and who should be classified is often confounded by sociopolitical considerations and processes.

Labeling, in contrast to classification, may be highly personal. Although the process is usually regarded as a formal administrative procedure applied by personnel in schools, institutions, clinics, and other settings for purposes of placement, treatment, or establishing eligibility for financial benefits, it also takes place informally, through interpersonal encounter. Individuals may perceive themselves as others see them. People are more likely to react to their awareness of the incompetence of retarded persons than to the formal label. Thus, the stigmatizing effects commonly attributed to special-class placement or institutionalization may, in fact, occur long before the label is applied because retarded individuals have been exposed to attitudes and reactions that make them feel inferior. Most children in special education begin school in regular classes. Academic failure and disruptive behavior in the early years of schooling result in teacher rejection and peer ridicule. These encounters may very well result in self-labeling, a process that is later confirmed and reinforced by subsequent special-class placement.

Communication about individuals or categories of individuals is not possible without labels for the conditions they manifest. Unfortunately, when labels are assigned pejorative meanings by the public, they generate images and stereotypes of labeled persons, thus concealing their differences and individualities. Blindness, deafness, and delinquency are not meaningless terms, but they are immediately associated with "disability" or "badness," which describe but a single and sometimes less critical facet of the total personality. The concept of mental retardation in the public view tends to be associated with dependency and physical stigmata. In fact, the majority of persons who are mentally retarded are mildly retarded. The large majority of mildly retarded people have no physical stigmata and are capable of considerable independence in adulthood.

Clearly, labels are not a substitute for a complete diagnostic profile; however, used as a signal that children may require special help and as a stimulus to in-depth evaluation, potentially harmful effects can be avoided. In brief, labels are not inherently evil, although they can be disadvantageous.

The Assessment Process, Diagnosis, and the Need for Services

Identification of persons as mentally retarded implies that they are unable to perform many of the functions carried out by their age peers, and hence they may require special services and protections. An assessment that leads to the diagnosis of mental retardation enables arrangements to be made for special habilitation, education, and other services, perhaps a protective residential placement.

Such an assessment is typically arranged because the person's general development appears to be impaired. Perhaps slowness in the acquisition of speech and language was observed, together with a failure to make expected adaptations in everyday living. If the impairment is general, early, and severe, the assessment and diagnosis will come as early in life as infancy; however, children who have only mild mental impairment are typically not observed to be different from "normal" until school age, when academic failures are experienced. Early clinical assessment should be encouraged in order to minimize the child's experience of failure in school. A comprehensive assessment of children's functioning in various areas determines whether the problems may be described as mental retardation or attributed to other causes. If the presence of mental retardation is determined, the children are provided with the special services afforded to mentally retarded populations. If, however, the diagnosis of retardation is not made because the symptoms have some other etiology, then other treatment and services may be provided.

Problems in Identification of a Person as Mentally Retarded

As indicated in Chapter 5, mental retardation consists of two general categories. The first is associated with more or less specific biomedical signs and symptoms leading to specific diagnoses such as Down syndrome. In these so-called "clinical types," the existence of the mental retardation condition is generally obvious, for it is usually of a lower level: moderate, severe, or profound, although the level could be mild. Ambiguities in diagnosis typically do not occur with retardation of this type, although differential diagnosis of etiology may be difficult.

The second type of mental retardation is found among people who exhibit no particular biomedical sign or symptom associated with retardation or causative of it. Functioning that does not depend upon the use of intelligence tends to be near normal, as with the previously mentioned children whose impairments are not evident until school-age. For such people, the level of mental retardation is most often mild. Obviously, some ambiguities may occur when differentiating the highest level of mild retardation from borderline intelligence (not mentally retarded). Diagnosis therefore requires the careful clinical consideration of all available information, including test scores. It is necessary for clinicians who are making diagnoses in such instances to employ some specified highest level or *degree* of impairment of intelligence and adaptation to serve as the maximum level of inclusion.

Upper IQ Limit for Mental Retardation

The upper limit of IQ 70 has been arrived at by professional consensus, after consideration of the consequences of setting a higher or lower value. The maximum specified IQ is not to be taken as an exact value, but as a commonly accepted guideline. It is true that legislation, the courts, and service agencies often employ exact IQ values to determine eligibility for services, but the consistent point of view of AAMD and of professionals serving mentally retarded populations is that clinical assessment must be flexible. Therefore, the judgment of clinicians may determine that some individuals with IQs higher than 70 will be regarded as mentally retarded and others with lower IQs will not. For that reason, the recommended ceiling may be extended up through IQ 75, particularly in school settings where intellectual performance is a prerequisite for success and special educational assistance may be required.

It has become increasingly clear through research and experience that most individuals with IQs below 70 are so limited in their adaptive competence that they require special services and protections, particularly during the school years. Although this need is also evident for some people with IQs above 70, it is less critical and less frequent.

In previous AAMD manuals, an equivalent but slightly different upper limit IQ for such identification was recommended, namely, an IQ "under two standard deviations below the mean." This meant IQ 67 for the Stanford-Binet Intelligence Scale and other scales having a standard deviation of 16 and IQ 69 for the Wechsler Intelligence Scale for Children, the Wechsler Adult Intelligence Scale, and other scales having a standard deviation of 15. The IQ of 70 has been substituted for "under two standard deviations" for several reasons. The employment of the two specific numbers, 67 and 69, implied a degree of precision in IQ assessment that was not intended. The use of the statement "IQ approximately 70" avoids the implication of such precision.

The use of exact standard deviation sizes to determine the levels of retardation also led to problems. Many users tended to ignore differences in standard deviations of tests. Many schools employed their own classification systems. The level of 70 maintains a conceptual continuity with the previous "minus two standard deviations" and hence incurs no shift in the implied prevalence of mental retardation. Finally, the use of IQ 70 is consistent with the laws or regulations in the United States and with world-wide practice, as represented by the World Health Organization (ICD-9).

Setting the cut-off IQ at 70 appears to be the best solution for most of the problems encountered with the diagnosis of mental retardation of people who are in the "gray area" of retardation–average. Treating the IQ with some flexibility permits the inclusion of persons having higher IQs than 70 who truly need special education or other programs. It also permits exclusion of those with somewhat lower IQs than 70 if the complete clinical judgment is that they are not mentally retarded. Marginal persons who are determined not to be mentally retarded would, as a rule, not be entitled to services intended for the retarded group. Such people probably have problems that require attention, given that they had been brought into the clinical assessment process. Excluding these people from services for mentally retarded individuals should make them eligible for services intended for some other classification, but some gaps in provision of services to needy persons may exist.

The Obtained IQ and the Zone of Uncertainty

Any measurement is fallible. An obtained IQ should be used as one value within a probable band of IQs. It is customary to think of an obtained IQ as surrounded by a "standard error of measurement" of approximately 3 (Wechsler) or 4 (Stanford-Binet) points; in other words, if the test were repeated, the new IQ should be within 3 or 4 points of the initially obtained value two-thirds of the time and within about 6 to 8 points 95 times out of 100. Hence, an IQ of 70 is considered to represent a band or zone of about 66 to 74 (2/3 probability) or 62 to 78 (95/100 probability). Consider an 8-year-old student who is not coping adequately in his daily life and is experiencing failure in schoolwork. The intelligence test yields a professionally determined IQ of 73, at the boundary of borderline intelligence. A diagnosis of mental retardation will depend on the extent to which all other clinically derived information and the case history provide a picture of impaired behavior of mild degree or of a mentally slow but nonretarded person whose judgment and reasoning in daily life appear to be adequate, but whose behavioral problems have some principal etiology other than mental retardation.

The effect of raising the upper limit beyond 70 or lowering it below 70 should be considered also as raising or lowering the band of uncertainty. Increasing the upper limit to IQ 75 would make more people eligible for special education, job training, and other habilitation services; however, such an increase also adds to the number of false positives, that is, individuals who are not, in fact, retarded and for whom special-class placement and other services might be inappropriate. This risk of misidentification is small, but real. Similarly, to lower the recommended maximum to 65 would reduce the already small risk of misdiagnosis but would deny services to many who need them. The proposed ceiling appears to be the best compromise between over and under identification and most likely to ensure access to services for those who need them.

The Use of Adaptive Behavior Appraisal in Diagnosis

Our previous discussion has involved IQ and the problems attendant to its interpretation. We have assumed that the "full clinical study" stressed throughout our discussion of diagnosis includes the appraisal of the adaptive functioning of the individuals who are brought into the assessment process. Measurement of such functioning may involve observation or informal interview or the employment of a standardized scale of adaptive functioning, such as the AAMD Adaptive Behavior Scale. (These issues are explored further in Chapter 4.)

Currently, there has been less experience with the use of adaptive behavior scales than with intelligence tests. Furthermore, scales differ in the types of behavior measured and the scoring systems applied.

Expectations of adaptive behavior vary for different age groups; DEFICITS IN ADAPTIVE BEHAVIOR will vary at different ages. These may be reflected in the following areas:

During INFANCY AND EARLY CHILDHOOD in:
1. Sensorimotor Skills Development
2. Communication Skills (including speech and language)
3. Self-Help Skills
4. Socialization (development of ability to interact with others)

During CHILDHOOD AND EARLY ADOLESCENCE in Areas 1 through 4 and/or:
5. Application of Basic Academic Skills in Daily Life Activities
6. Application of Appropriate Reasoning and Judgment in Mastery of the Environment
7. Social Skills (participation in group activities and interpersonal relationships)

During LATE ADOLESCENCE AND ADULT LIFE in Areas 1 through 7 and/or:
8. Vocational and Social Responsibilities and Performance

During infancy and early childhood, sensorimotor, communication, self-help, and socialization skills ordinarily develop in a sequential pattern reflective of the maturation process. Delays in the acquisition of these skills represent potential deficiencies in adaptive behavior and become the criteria for mental retardation.

The skills required for adaptation during childhood and early adolescence involve complex learning processes. This involves the process by which knowledge is acquired and retained as a function of the experiences of the individual. Difficulties in learning are usually manifested in the academic situation, but in evaluation of adaptive behavior, attention should focus not only on the basic academic skills and their use, but also on skills essential in coping with the environment, including concepts of time and money, self-directed behavior, social responsiveness, and interactive skills.

In the adult years, vocational performance and social responsibilities assume prime importance as qualifying conditions of mental retardation. These are assessed in terms of the degree to which individuals are able to maintain themselves independently in the community and in gainful employment as well as by their ability to meet and conform to community standards.

It is these deficiencies in adaptive behavior that usually determine the individuals' needs for programs or services and/or legal action.

In infancy and early childhood, deficits in sensorimotor development, in acquisition of self-help and communication skills, and development of socialization skills point to the needs for medical services, early childhood education, or family guidance.

During childhood and early adolescence, deficits in learning and coping skills indicate needs for specialized educational, prevocational, and recreational programs.

In the late adolescent and adult years, deficits determine the needs for vocational training, placement, and a variety of supportive services.

Within the framework of the definition of mental retardation, an individual may meet the criteria of mental retardation at one time in life and not at some other time. He or she may change status as a result of changes or alterations in intellectual functioning, adaptive behavior, or societal expectations, or for other known and unknown reasons. The decision to classify an individual as mentally retarded at any given time should always be made in relation to behavioral standards and norms and in comparison to the individual's own chronological age group.

CHAPTER 4

ASSESSMENT OF INTELLIGENCE, ADAPTIVE BEHAVIOR, AND SOCIAL–ENVIRONMENTAL FACTORS

INTELLIGENCE

Intelligence refers to the ability that enables people to learn, remember information and use it appropriately, obtain insights, solve problems, acquire and employ language, exercise good judgment, find similarities and differences, use abstractions, and so forth. Intelligence refers, then, to the use of the "mind" or mental process in making adaptations. Intelligence is an inference made about people's adaptations; it can be known or measured only through observations of behavior. Intelligent behavior can be and often is exhibited by people who lack coordination in movement or who are blind or deaf. In order to appraise that behavior for the purpose of inferring intelligence, it is necessary to distinguish between performance limitations that are due to sensory or motor impediments and those that are due to impaired intelligence.

Intelligence develops as children grow. Individual differences occur in intelligence just as they occur in weight, stature, motor coordination, and other characteristics. Individual differences in intelligence tend to be stable, particularly after the preschool years. Differences in intelligence among people are due in unknown proportion to both genetic and environmental factors. Both physical and psychosocial factors can influence the development of intelligence. Examples of physical factors operating prenatally or postnatally to impair brain structure or function are drugs, infections, and injuries. Similarly, examples of psychosocial factors that adversely influence intelligence are either understimulating or overstimulating home environment, inappropriate instruction, and poor mental health or motivation.

27

The Assessment of Intelligence

Intelligence is manifested by success in academic and occupational life to the extent that success requires mental process and not personality or sensorimotor skills. It is exhibited in the precision and subtlety of language (although poverty of language as such may be due to disadvantage in background or to hearing impairment or other causes, not necessarily to poor intelligence). Thus, intelligence may be assessed by noting the degree of success a person has exhibited in adapting to requirements of school, business, or everyday life.

It is generally too expensive and inconvenient to observe people's daily behavior sufficiently in school and work to obtain a dependable measure of intelligence. One problem with observation is that it is all but impossible to standardize the conditions of everyday life to permit fair comparisons. Intelligence tests, however, do contain standardized series of tasks or work samples that provide for the efficient assessment of intelligence. Such intelligence tests or scales are administered under highly controlled conditions so that an individual's score may be appropriately compared with the norms secured for other people.

In the following discussion, some typical tasks or items in intelligence tests are described. This should provide some insight into what is meant by the term *intelligence* and, concomitantly, by *mental retardation*, the label that may be applied to people who fail the items intended for a given age or developmental level.

At the level of infancy formal tests are used, and evaluators also secure developmental information by asking questions about the infant's everyday competencies of manipulation, locomotion, and language. Standardized observations are made of the extent to which and the age at which infants orient to a sudden sound; remember where an object has been hidden and discover it; whether language is employed, receptively and expressively; and whether simple requests are heeded.

In preschool years the test items sample children's ability to discriminate colors and shapes and to match them, show ability to cope with size differences, and follow simple commands about taking, putting, or indicating. Pictures or objects with missing parts are shown, and children are asked to indicate what is gone. They are given a series of two or more unrelated words or numbers and told to repeat them without missing any or changing the order. Vocabulary is sampled. One might ask, "How are a cow and a horse different?"

In early elementary school years, similar tasks are administered, but they are more complex and require more abstraction, generalization, and reasoning. For example, children may be asked to indicate how some unlike items are alike; for example, butter, ham, and apples or planes, trains, cars, and buses. The memory test items contain more items than in previous tests. Drawing a complex model may be required, whereas at preschool age, a simple + or 0 might have been the model to draw. One might ask for absurdities to be explained (for example, the boss said to the new office boy, "Take no advice." What is peculiar about that?)

At older ages and into adolescence, "normal" performance is reflected in greater degree of abstraction and complexity of the tasks expected to be mastered. For example, the proverbs would be interpreted. Explanations would be made of natural phenomena such as why smoke rises or ice floats. Arithmetic reasoning would be required; for example, "A man received a raise of 20 percent, which gave him 5 dollars more a day. How much did he make before the raise?"

At all levels nonverbal or performance tasks that do not require the use of language are employed. These involve such activities as copying a geometric figure, indicating missing parts of a picture, arranging cartoon pictures into a sequence that makes a sensible story, making designs with blocks to match a pictured design, and assembling puzzles. Reliance is placed on tests with nonverbal items if children have severe language handicaps or are deaf.

It is possible to divide the tasks given in intelligence tests into groups based upon underlying factors of ability, and certain theorists propose that there are dozens of separate abilities; others propose both specific related abilities and a general ability factor. In the context of mental retardation, it is customary to assume a general nature of intelligence and to employ those scales that contain a variety of different tasks. Hence, scales that are generally employed to assess mentally retarded people tend to yield single scores and are interpreted to reflect a general picture of the person's intelligence.

Scores yielded by intelligence tests. The principal and universal score is the IQ (intelligence quotient). Before describing its salient properties, we must first explain the MA. Contemporary testing of intelligence began with Binet, who, besides developing test items still in use, also invented the concept of MA. His reasoning was this: a 5-year-old child has more intelligence than a 3-year-old, on the average, but is not so bright as an 8-year-old; therefore, mental test items are age-scaled according to the age levels at which most children succeed. This provides a convenient age-scale of intelligence. Items of the Stanford-Binet Intelligence Scale passed by the typical 4-year-old child indicate a 4-year-old MA; those passed by the typical 7-year-old child define an MA of 7, and so on. Mental growth continues as children grow, but the rate slows down in adulthood.

Thus, if test results indicate that a person scores like a typical 8-year-old but is 12, this means that he or she has less mental development than is typical for his or her age. If one divides the MA 8 by the chronological age (CA) of 12 and multiplies by 100 to remove the decimal, the IQ is 67: MA $8 \div$ CA $12 \times 100 = 67$. If this 12-year-old received an MA of 6, the resulting IQ would be 50. If, however, the child were only 6-years-old, then the IQ would be 133: MA $8 \div$ CA $6 \times 100 = 133$.

Standard score IQs.   For many years IQs were calculated by dividing MA by CA as shown. This was convenient and conceptually simple; however, several problems emerged. As indicated in our previous discussion, the Stanford-Binet type of mental growth was believed to slow down after about age 15. That meant that the CA divisor for IQ ceased to have value in the ratio of MA/CA, so compromises had to be made, for example, use of some maximum CA divisor such as 15 years.

Second, there were great variations in the spread or range of IQs found at different ages and between different tests. Since about 1940, Wechsler's lead in abandoning the ratio concept of IQ in favor of an arbitrary basis for the distribution of IQs was followed by publishers of other important scales. Wechsler adopted a standard deviation of 15 points (and a mean IQ of 100). Later the standard score IQ, with the mean at 100, was also adopted for the Stanford-Binet, but the standard deviation of 16 points was continued.

Interpreting IQs.   If minor differences among scales having standard deviations of 15 versus 16 points are ignored, some interpretations of IQs can be made. These are benchmarks to help one grasp the relative value of IQs of different magnitudes (see Figure 2).

1. An IQ of 100 is the mean, median, and mode of appropriately selected normative groups. Hence, a person receiving an IQ of 100 is precisely average.
2. About one-half of IQs are between 90 and 110. This is often said to indicate the range of "average" intelligence.
3. About two-thirds of IQs are between one standard deviation below the mean of 100 and one standard deviation above the mean. Hence, with a standard deviation of 15 points, two-thirds of IQs would lie between 85 and 115, one-sixth below 85, and one-sixth above 115. On the Stanford-Binet the cognate numbers are 84 and 116.
4. About 2.3 percent of IQs lie below 70 and 2.3 percent exceed 130. On the Stanford-Binet the cognate numbers are 68 and 132. Thus, to delimit the diagnosis of mental retardation to people with IQs of 70 or below is to suggest that about 2 percent of the tested population is mentally retarded, but elsewhere in

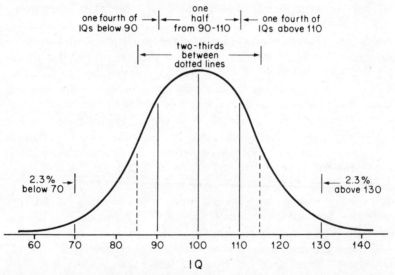

Figure 2. The "normal" distribution of IQs. This assumes a standard deviation of 15 points, characteristic of many scales. The Stanford-Binet has a standard deviation of 16 points; other scales have higher or lower values. By convention the mean IQ is always 100. The proportional values have been rounded.

this classification system, other factors affecting prevalence are
discussed and users are warned against assuming that low IQ
alone is sufficient for diagnosis.

In general, IQs are distributed on a so-called normal or Guassian
curve. Most cases, as indicated previously, are located around the
mean; fewer and fewer people obtain extremely high or low scores
(for example, 150 or 50); however, more persons are retarded than
would be predicted by calculations based on the normal curve (see
Figure 2). This excess is easily explained. The normal distribution
of IQs was empirically determined for people with normal bodies
and normal health. There is a disproportionate number of individuals with IQs below 50 because of biological etiology.

IQ levels in mental retardation.   Level of mental retardation has
customarily been expressed in IQ ranges. In the 1977 manual,
standard deviations were considered. For tests such as the Wechsler
scales that have a standard deviation of 15 points, these ranges
would be 55 to 69 for mild, 40 to 54 for moderate, 25 to 39 for
severe, and under 25 for profound mental retardation. Just as the
IQ of 70 as the upper limit of mental retardation is to be taken not
as an exact but as an approximate number, these numbers should
also be considered as approximate. These numbers would also vary
slightly with a scale having another standard deviation, for example, 16 on the Stanford-Binet or the McCarthy Scales of Children's
Abilities. Because of the variability among tests, overlaps in levels
exist, as shown in Table 1, p. 13). Later in this chapter descriptions
are provided of the characteristics of mentally retarded people
placed into the four levels, ranging from the rather complete
helplessness and dependency of profoundly retarded individuals
to the nearly normal status of mildly retarded people.

The meaning of mental retardation as expressed in MA. It is convenient to consider again the nature of intelligence as something that
grows as the individual grows. One may express levels of intelligence in terms of such growth. Consider a mentally retarded adolescent or adult who, by virtue of CA, has reached the limits of
maturation of intelligence. If, upon being tested, this person receives an MA of 3 years or less, results would suggest that he or she
has the mentality of a nonretarded infant of 3 years or less. This
person would likely be considered to be profoundly retarded. If
the MA is in the range of 3 to 5 years, the person's level of

retardation would be severe. If the MA is over 5.5 but under 8 years, the person may be compared to a nonretarded child in kindergarten or even up to second grade, and the retardation level would be moderate. The person would begin to display a command of concepts and thinking typical of nonretarded children of the age in question. If the MA is over 8, up to about 12 years, the person is mildly mentally retarded and, if adequately instructed, can be expected to achieve levels of occupational and educational attainment similar to those of nonretarded children up to age 12 (that is, third- to seventh-grade-level school work).

These comparisons should not lead to the conclusion that for a retarded person an MA of 3 years or 6 years or any other level constitutes the same kind of mentality as for a nonretarded child of the comparative CA. Actually, there are some interesting qualitative differences between mentally retarded people and nonretarded children having the same MA.

The comparison of MAs of retarded people with the characteristics of children whose CAs are of similar magnitude is insufficient for describing the course of mental development of retarded children who are still growing. It is possible to employ IQ as a bench mark in order to describe mental growth of people of different levels of intelligence. If one assumes that IQ has the historical value of being the ratio of MA/CA, then an IQ of .50 (with its decimal point restored, of course) means that the MA is half the CA. One may make the further assumption that this rate of growth, a half-year of MA for each year of CA, is a constant, and draw the curve shown in Figure 3. This figure contains several IQ parameters to illustrate the idea. Observe that with an IQ of 50, the MA at age 4 is 2, at age 10 is 5, etc. All the curves have been drawn to show deceleration in MA growth to the final plateau.

The preceding argument and the curves in the figure should not mislead readers, for rarely are such ideal curves obtained in longitudinal research. Rates of growth are not constant, and an error of measurement may also intrude. The figure presents the basic concept. Another interpretive caution is that the age at which mental growth terminates varies with individuals and with the type of mental function being examined. For example, mental growth represented in receptive vocabulary tends to increase until perhaps 30 years of age for people whose education continues. Results of longitudinal research suggest that, in fact, the lower the IQ during

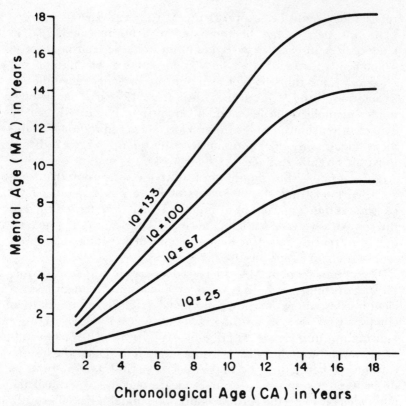

Figure 3. Hypothetical curve of mental age growth.

early life (for example, ages 3 to 7), the younger the age at which mental growth ceases. Thus, the mental growth curve of profoundly retarded persons begins to level off at about 10 to 12 years; for mildly retarded persons, it may not level off until about age 25.

Description of Mental Growth as a Cognitive–Developmental Sequence

Research in child development now permits a richer description of the nature of mental growth than is provided by the MA norms previously discussed. These norms do indeed have value when placed into a scale permitting comparison of groups and of ages on a quasiquantitative basis and as a means of expressing the state of an individual's development in the terms of the scale; however, a developmental–sequential description features the actual evolution of growing children's competence from one phase to the next. It constitutes a qualitative rather than a quantitative description and shows how early phases must come before and serve as foundations for the later phases. A baby developing locomotor skills will sit up before standing, will stand before walking, will walk before running, skipping, etc. Mental growth also develops sequentially. Cognitive–developmental theory demonstrates how children progress in mental competence from the primitive reflexes of the newborn up through intermediate stages to arrive in later childhood at the ability to think abstractly.

The most comprehensive description of the sequential mental growth of children is that of the Swiss psychologist Piaget. His description is expressed as a series of stages in each of which a child demonstrates increasing mental grasp over the environment and more independence of thought from the immediate contemporary surroundings. Mental retardation can be related to this model. In the following description of each stage is an accompanying brief summation of the relevant mental retardation level, based, in part, on the work of Inhelder, an associate of Piaget.

The age brackets provided with each stage are only approximations and are based on research evidence from different cultures. We assume that slow-developing children will take longer to reach stages and that precocious children will take less time. What is important is that the *sequence* is the same for all, except that mentally retarded children will not be expected to attain the higher levels. The sensorimotor level, birth to 2 years, can itself be differentiated into a half dozen substages, according to Piaget.

Sensorimotor stage: birth to 2 years. Newborn children have at their command only a few vital reflexes and otherwise have no competency to react to environmental stimuli. Progressively, however, in the first 2 years, infants acquire various sensorimotor competencies, such as defensive reactions; skill in grasping, manipulating, and exploring objects, determining what can be bitten and what should not be. Children comprehend the reality and the constancy of objects and their basic relations; what goes on top, behind, between other things; who the common people in their lives are and what their relations are to the child. Children also acquire a primitive level of language usage. Adults whose mental growth has not advanced beyond such a sensorimotor level would be profoundly retarded and probably understand few if any concepts. They would be helpless in the environment, having no command over it except as help is elicited through vocal or other signals of distress.

Preoperational-transductive level: 2 to 4 years.   Objects and people not only have developed reality and constancy, but now also have names so that most children can react to commands containing the words used to label objects or persons and can ask simple questions about them. Perceptions of likenesses and differences emerge, as do some basic ideas of unity versus multiplicity. Children at this level do not yet have knowledge of true concepts and reveal few generalizations. Adults whose competencies to adapt have reached but not advanced beyond this level would be considered to be severely mentally retarded. They would have only a simple communication about objects and persons, would lack the ability to generalize and form class concepts or useful categories of objects and persons, and could not impact the environment beyond the immediate place and time.

Preoperational-intuitive: 4 to 7 years.   There is no true "thinking" yet, but most children at this stage can show intuitive or prelogical reasoning based upon the appearance of objects and of phenomena. Hence, if children are to classify unlike objects, they do so on the basis of some surface appearance rather than underlying function. At this age children do acquire useful concepts. Colors are distinguished from objects that they color, and children understand that colors are attributes of objects, as are forms and sizes. Perceptions still dominate judgment. Adults whose mental development is delimited to the conceptual-intuitive level appear to fit the level of moderate mental retardation (trainable). They can use concepts and simple classes and can carry on some conversation, but they are unable to understand abstract concepts or solve problems other than by trial-and-error.

Concrete thinking operations: 7 to 11 years.   Children at this level can demonstrate actual problem-solving based upon logic. If required to make a prediction or a rearrangement of objects or materials, they can reason through to an outcome without having to have a physical demonstration. In Piaget's celebrated "fluid conservation" demonstrations, children can mentally anticipate that water from a wide jar poured into a narrow one must rise higher, and they can perform other simple mental transformations. In classifying unlike objects, they can now do so on a basis of fundamental rather than surface attributes, such as appropriately classifying as transportation various unlike modes of transportation.

Children with a mastery of concrete operativity do not yet think in purely abstract terms. (Not until they approach 11 or 12 years of age do they find the degree of command over abstract systems, such as advanced language, to permit them to employ such systems as thinking tools. "Advanced language" in this sense would mean language as used in logical propositions, such as algebra or finite mathematics.) Adults who have difficulty advancing beyond language as a simple communicative skill will be somewhat limited in the skills of reading comprehension, writing, and arithmetic problem-solving. This limitation would be characteristic of people identified as mildly mentally retarded. Although they may be taught the basics of reading and arithmetic, these individuals are not able to think on an abstract level and use language systems independently as tools for abstract thought.

Formal thinking operations: 11 through adulthood. The abstract employment of symbolic tools discussed in the previous stage marks the level of formal thinking operations, which nonretarded children attain at about the age of 11 or 12 (although people of this age and older do not necessarily employ the formal level in all aspects of their everyday life). Attainment of this level permits the study of formal rhetoric, algebra, etc. Gifted children might enter this stage earlier than 11 years. This level differs from concrete operativity. At the concrete level children may reason that if 3 plus 4 equals 7, then to take 3 away from 7 should leave 4, etc. At the level of formal operativity, however, the proposition would be universalized, as in the proposition given that $a + b = x$, followed by its derivatives. Thus, systems of axioms, "if–then" propositions, etc., facilitate formal operativity. Many nonretarded people are unable to think in formal operations, and surely all those identified as mentally retarded would not.

In terms of this Piagetian cognitive–developmental description, then, mentally retarded individuals of the various levels are seen as being limited in the maximum state attained. Mildly retarded people, as just noted, do not appear to enter into formal-thinking operativity and may have difficulty with concrete operativity. Profoundly retarded persons emerge little, if at all, from the sensorimotor level. In their final mental development, severely retarded persons appear to stop at the operational-transductive and moderately retarded persons, at the preoperational-intuitive stages.

Developmental Appraisal: Program Planning

Piaget's description of the sequential stages, or any similar developmental description, may be employed in the determination of individual habilitation or individual educational plans for mentally retarded individuals. A careful appraisal of where the person is in the sequential development of cognitive, language, social, and other skills constitutes a description of just where habilitative or educational plans must start. Hence, if a child is at a one-word stage in language communication, a language lesson based on whole sentences should not be selected. If a child is just learning to handle food with his or her fingers, it is too soon for instruction in table manners, but the next step, the use of the spoon, would be appropriate. Tests for use within a Piagetian perspective have been developed and may be commercially available in the future.

PSYCHOLOGICAL ASSESSMENT

In the context of service in mental retardation, *assessment* refers to the various procedures employed by professionally trained people to appraise learning, adjustment, and other qualities of retarded individuals and to secure estimates of their abilities and proficiencies. Some of the principal purposes of assessments are the diagnosis of individuals as mentally retarded, facilitation of appropriate placements on the basis of appraised characteristics, and provision of a foundation for individual habilitation or educational programs. The employment of standardized tests and of other inventories or scales is a component of the assessment process, as are interviews, direct observations, and information from previous reports and records.

Reasons for Utilization of Standardized Instruments

Some estimate of mental ability may be obtained by careful and systematic observation of behavior, for example, by a teacher who observes a learner's behavior daily. Such estimates, even at their best, however, are variable and insufficient for arriving at objective, precise, and stable measures of intelligence. For this reason standardized instruments are considered to be indispensable when making assessments, even if they are not sufficient in themselves for use in final diagnoses and planning. Standardized tests, inventories, or rating scales have been carefully developed. Various administrative formats and items have been tested, refined, and selectively retained, and scores obtained from the subjects' responses have been validated by carefully selected criteria. Reliability of the scores has been determined. As used here, reliability refers to the extent to which a second measurement made by another equally qualified examiner yields the same results and the extent of internal consistency. In addition, the final forms of standardized instruments have been administered to sufficient numbers of one or more reference groups to provide an experience table or norms. A fair comparison of a score obtained on a person who is being clinically evaluated with scores of specified norm groups is possible so that objective judgments may be made as to whether the person examined, by virtue of his or her score, does or does not resemble some particular group, such as moderately or severely retarded populations, in the characteristic that has been measured.

Measuring instruments are simply carefully designed observations that have been standardized in several respects. Thus, results are more stable and meaningful than would be expected from an ad hoc informal process. This statement is not meant to imply that tests and inventories are all ideal, nor does it mean they are always used and interpreted properly. Misuse is minimized if they are employed by well-qualified professionals. Furthermore, the claim of the superiority of standardized instruments does not deprecate the use of informal observations or interviews for determining other qualities of subjects, confirming the test results, or securing information not subjected to standardized measurement. The emphasis here is to recognize that securing *nonstandardized* information runs risks of interpersonal difference in emphasis, modes of procedure, dependence on subjects' moment-to-moment variations, and interpretations based only on observers' personal norms.

The Use of IQ in Clinical Practice and Establishing Eligibility for Services

State education agencies, school districts, and other service providers usually set IQ levels as criterion for eligibility to special services for mentally retarded people. The use of tests to secure

IQs may also be required to determine that individuals with problems are *not* mentally retarded, so that they may become eligible for programs designed for those with other diagnoses and corresponding needs. For example, admission to special programs for learning-disabled students generally requires that the problems experienced not be associated with mental retardation; and children whose language is different from that used in the schools can be assigned to a bilingual program.

The specification by various agencies of a qualifying IQ for program eligibility has led to some misunderstanding of the role of IQ in the diagnosis of mental retardation and has caused many people to believe that diagnosis is a simple matter of administering an intelligence test. In addition to these misunderstandings, this assumption has led to some unfortunate litigation. Indeed, IQ is an important component of the definition of mental retardation, and determination of IQ is a salient clinical step; but both the definition of mental retardation and diagnostic practice go beyond IQ. The posture of the American Association on Mental Deficiency has always been that diagnosis is made in a thorough clinical assessment of the person, which should include appraisal of adaptive behavior; review of information secured from informed people such as teachers, parents, and family physicians; and direct observation of behavior. All steps are to be conducted with due regard for the safeguard procedures listed in "Safeguarding the Assessment Process," which appears later in this chapter.

Intelligence Scales Commonly Utilized in Assessment

A list of scales commonly employed in clinical service with retarded populations follows. The scales are categorized by the CA or developmental age for which they were designed and normed, although competent clinicians may adapt their use to groups outside these limits. For example, in assessing clients of school or adult age who function at a very low level, useful information can be secured by employing certain scales designed for nonretarded infants and preschool-aged children. This list does not include all scales used with these populations.

For infant–preschool level
    Bayley Scales of Infant Development
    Cattell Infant Intelligence Scale

Gesell Developmental Schedules
McCarthy Scales of Children's Abilities
Stanford-Binet Intelligence Scale
Wechsler Preschool and Primary Scale of Intelligence

For older childhood levels
McCarthy Scales of Children's Abilities
Stanford-Binet Intelligence Scale
Wechsler Intelligence Scale for Children-Revised (WISC-R)

For adults
Stanford-Binet Intelligence Scale
Wechsler Adult Intelligence Scale
(Instruments intended for the infant-preschool level and the older childhood level may also be employed with adults whose functioning approximates that of nonretarded people of the ages in question.)

These scales should be administered only by appropriately prepared clinicians, under favorable circumstances, and on an individual basis. *Under no circumstances should group tests of intelligence, as listed in measurement textbooks, be employed for making clinical diagnosis of retardation.* Group scales are valuable for screening purposes, however. In addition to the listed scales, adaptations of some of them and specially designed scales are sometimes used with individuals who have sensory and/or motor disabilities. In general, such scales have lower predictive validity than do the Wechsler and Stanford-Binet scales, and should therefore be used only by expert clinicians. Examples of such scales are:

Perkins-Binet Intelligence Scale (for blind)
Columbia Mental Maturity Scale (for motor impaired and/or nonverbal)
Leiter International Performance Scale (for nonverbal or non-English speaking)
Hiskey-Nebraska Test of Learning Aptitude (for deaf)
Porteus Mazes (for nonverbal or non-English speaking; adapted for cerebral palsied)
Merrill-Palmer Scale of Mental Tests (adapted for deaf or nonverbal)

For most of these scales, moderate positive correlations between their scores and scores on the Stanford-Binet and Wechsler scales are reported. We strongly emphasize, therefore, that results must be interpreted by highly skilled psychologists who exercise caution in using them; nevertheless, in combination with other information, they can provide valuable adjuncts to diagnosis.

ADAPTIVE BEHAVIOR

Since 1959, the AAMD definition of mental retardation has included the consideration of adaptive proficiencies in addition to a measure of intelligence. *Adaptive behavior* refers to the quality of everyday performance in coping with environmental demands. The quality of general adaptation is mediated by level of intelligence; thus, the two concepts overlap in meaning. It is evident, however, from consideration of the definition of adaptive behavior, with its stress on everyday coping, that adaptive behavior refers to what people do to take care of themselves and to relate to others in daily living rather than the abstract potential implied by intelligence.

Informal Appraisal of Adaptive Behavior

Informal appraisals may be made by observation or by asking people who are in daily contact with the subject to note the extent to which self-care needs are met, determine whether the person can come and go in the home and neighborhood, and whether he or she displays basic social amenities, communicates needs, takes direction, etc. Those best qualified to describe adaptive behavior are people who are fully acquainted with the everyday life of the subject—teachers, parents, or other care providers.

Adaptive behavior appraisal is informally, if unintentionally, employed when authorities or parents request a clinical assessment to determine whether a child is mentally retarded. The behavioral development of that child has already been observed to be much slower than normal, and he or she has difficulty meeting simple requirements.

Standardized Adaptive Behavior Assessment

Other than the Vineland Social Maturity Scale developed by Doll, until recently there were few formalized and standardized measures of adaptive behavior. Many standardized scales are now available, such as the AAMD Adaptive Behavior Scale (ABS) and the forthcoming revision of the Vineland, that permit clinicians to make determinations that are far more objective than those based on unstructured interviews or limited observation. These scales, like measures of intelligence, are standardized in administrative procedure and scoring. Many have adequate norms, and most are accompanied by interpretive manuals.

Although adaptive behavior scales yield information that is sometimes closely correlated with IQ, especially for persons at very low-functioning levels, this close correlation is not always present. The two types of measurement differ in significant ways, including the following: (a) Most measurements of adaptive behavior were designed to determine a person's common and typical performance, whereas intelligence tests seek to determine the highest potential for performance. (b) Adaptive behavior items reflect everyday proficiencies of self-care in such areas as eating, dressing, toileting, communicating needs, and meeting ordinary social responsibilities; intelligence tests emphasize language, reasoning, and abstract abilities. (c) Adaptive behavior information is generally secured through interviews with informants, this being an efficient way to gather the information; intelligence tests are administered in a controlled clinical testing interview with the subject. (A very few adaptive behavior measures (for example, Balthazar's scales) employ testing or observation methodology; the vast majority do not.)

Scales of adaptive behavior. The current marketplace for scales of adaptive behavior is large. The new measures vary greatly, not only in quality and norming but also in intended application. Some have been intentionally delimited for use, for example, with profoundly and severely retarded people or to measure vocational readiness. Some are intended not to assist in the diagnosis of mental retardation and the establishment of level but rather to allow fine-grained appraisal of a person's competencies in order to set targets for training. As a consequence, clinicians must be careful to select those scales most suited to their particular needs. Furthermore, much more experience must be accumulated in the utilization of adaptive behavior scales and their scores for the same degree of confidence to be placed in them as is currently placed in the use of intelligence measures. Standardized measurement of adaptive behavior is here to stay, however, and the use of such scales will increase. A list of scales that have adequate norming for subjects for whom their use is intended follows:

Broad-ranged scales or scales with different levels
  AAMD Adaptive Behavior Scales[a]
  AAMD Adaptive Behavior Scales—Public School Version[a]

Adaptive Functioning Index
BMT Instrument
Camelot Behavioral Systems Checklist
Client Centered Evaluation Model[a]
Minnesota Developmental Programming System
Progress Assessment Chart
Vineland Social Maturity Scale

Scales with limited functioning level or limited content
Adaptive Behavior Inventory for Children
Balthazar Scales of Adaptive Behavior[a,b]
Cain-Levine Social Competency Scale
California Preschool Social Competency Scale
Camelot Behavioral Systems Checklist
Competitive Employment Screening Test and Remediation Manual
Fairview Development Scale
Fairview Social Skills Scale for the Mildly and Moderately Retarded
San Francisco Vocational Competency Scale
Social and Prevocational Information Battery[c]

Scales followed by the superscript[a] also contain subscales measuring maladaptive behavior. No attempt was made here to list scales assessing only maladaptive behavior. The use of the superscript[b] refers to scales administered partly by testing and observation. They are intended for use with profoundly and severely retarded subjects only. The superscript[c] means that the scale is a test battery.

As with intelligence tests, only trained professionals should interpret results of adaptive behavior measures. In most instances, they are administered by recording information obtained in an interview with a person sufficiently informed about the subject to answer detailed questions about that person's self-help skills. Instruments may be completed without the interview process by direct-service personnel who are well acquainted with the subjects.

Special concerns in the utilization of adaptive behavior scales. The scaling of adaptive behavior is more recent than the scaling of intelligence, resulting in less experience both in the evaluation of scales and in the interpretation of results. Furthermore, there has been some history of less than careful use of such scales. Some specific problems that have been reported are: Personnel who are insufficiently acquainted with the subject are expected to provide information or complete the form and may resort to guessing. This may happen, for example, with a day-shift technician in a residential center who has not observed supper-time and going-to-bed behavior. Completion of forms has often been an added tedious task for personnel. Additionally, a given individual may perform with varied proficiency in different settings. For these and other reasons, more uncertainty has attended the use of adaptive behavior scales than of intelligence scales.

Single and multiple scores in adaptive behavior measurement. The Vineland Social Maturity Scale was designed to yield a single score, thereby reflecting a level of general social competence. Some of the new scales also yield single scores, especially those that delimit the scope to a narrow area, such as self-care in dressing, use of language, or vocational readiness. Most of the new scales, such as the AAMD ABS, yield multiple scores, one for each "domain" or content area. Thus, the ABS provides 10 scores for different aspects of adaptation in Part One and 14 scores for different aspects of maladaptation in Part Two.

Presently, there is no movement to consolidate all the ABS information into a single quotient or age-type score. There are reasons for this reluctance. First, so many different facets of a person's proficiencies are sampled that to use a single score would tend to omit a description of the proficiencies in everyday life terms. Second, there is more within-subject variation in adaptive behavior than in intellectual behavior, and, hence, there is a need to report component scores. Third, users like to have a profile of scores for programming purposes. Such a profile has significance for those responsible for making appropriate plans for clients, including selective placement into programs and residences and planning for habilitation and education, for example, release into the community and entry into special job training. Because ABS items consist of specific proficiencies, it is possible to set priorities for the most needed training and utilize clients' strengths. Some of the adaptive behavior scales have been constructed specifically for the purpose of establishing training targets and of measuring progress before and after treatment. The use of information on maladaptive behavior is particularly relevant to the special kinds of residential care that may be required. Tendencies to run away, be aggressive, or express undesirable sexual behavior are factors considered by community residence operators in the selection of residents.

Still another use of adaptive behavior information is to report on client characteristics to government and other agencies and to delineate population statistics for the purpose of governmental or agency planning. Establishing the number of people who are ambulatory, who can or cannot communicate needs, who have impaired vision, or can be trusted in the community without daytime supervision provides essential information for program development and budgeting.

Illustrations of Adaptive Behavior Levels by Age

Although there is some variability in level of competence on different dimensions of adaptive behavior, patterns of skills tend to develop or be performed with a fairly high degree of consistency. Some illustrations of patterns are presented in Appendix A, with the approximate level of adaptive behavior deficit for selected age levels indicated above the pattern.

In each case, the highest degree of performance routinely found for a particular dimension (or sequence of skills) is described for a given level at a specified age. Descriptions begin with a pattern of behavior that indicates PROFOUND deficit in adaptive behavior for all individuals over 3 years of age. Next is a pattern found in many 3-year-olds with SEVERE deficit and many older persons with PROFOUND deficit.

By selecting the pattern that most closely resembles the *highest* level of routine functioning for a given individual, one can check by age and determine the approximate level of deficit. It seems impractical at this time to suggest fine gradations that can be achieved with accuracy, and, in the final analysis, clinical judgment is needed to arrive at an estimate of adaptive behavior level.

If one keeps in mind that these examples represent the highest degree of competence to be expected from individuals of given ages at the levels indicated, the information given in this appendix may help to increase reliability of estimates of adaptive behavior levels. Study of the appendix may also assist in indicating the probable course of development of adaptive behavior and thus provide useful information for program planning for individuals of various levels.

This appendix is intended to illustrate the kinds of behavior expected and measured by some of the scales. Standardized scales, supplemented by clinical judgments wherever possible, should be applied in making diagnoses.

SOCIAL–ENVIRONMENTAL MEASURES OF THE FAMILY

In most societies, the nuclear family serves as the primary socializing agent. It is in this setting, or substitute thereof, that children develop a sense of identity, learn right from wrong and the values of their culture, and acquire the tools and skills for mastery over the environment. Here, too, personality is formed, early language and communication abilities are learned, and the foundations for social behavior are established.

Although child-rearing is a complicated task and crises arise periodically in the normal course of development to tax parental skills further, most families discharge this responsibility reasonably well; however, when the child, because of biological insult or for other reasons, falls far below parental and societal expectations, the coping strategies of the family to maintain its stability, integrity, and life style are sorely taxed. Few problems are potentially more disruptive to family life than those posed by the retarded child.

Families vary considerably in their reaction to retardation in one of their members. Where the intellectual disparity between parents and child is great, as is often the case with severely damaged children, there may be intense feelings of disappointment, disillusionment, and despair that threaten parental self-esteem and family unity. For most, they represent a form of acute crisis that is eventually resolved without undue disturbance or self-sacrifice; for others, the guilt and anxiety generated are a pervasive source of chronic stress.

In families where both parents and children are similarly deficient in intellectual and coping skills, the child's "difference," as viewed by the larger society, may be neither acknowledged nor recognized. These families are more likely to be preoccupied with the struggle for daily survival. Mental retardation per se becomes a problem only when the family is confronted with the child's failure in school or problem behavior that brings the child into conflict with law enforcement or social agencies.

The impact of retardation on parental child-rearing behavior, family relationships, and coping strategies has been extensively described in the literature. The phenomenon bears mention in this book primarily because of the well-known reciprocal relationship among family-interaction patterns, stress, and child development. Unfortunately, the application of this concept to studies in mental retardation has been very limited, perhaps because of the widely held view that brain damage imposes severe constraints on the developmental process. Nevertheless, it has become increasingly clear through implementation of innovative training technologies that even the most severely retarded individuals have capacities for some growth.

The inhibitory effect on the developmental process of adverse environmental experiences, especially within the context of the family, has long been recognized in classification schemata of mental retardation. Earlier manuals included the term *cultural-familial retardation*. That term has been supplanted by *retardation associated with sociocultural or psychosocial disadvantage*. Each of these designations assign increasing emphasis to the role of life experience in the nature–nurture equation.

The denial of basic family goals and aspirations and the disruption of family stability sometimes occasioned by a retarded child can seriously distort parent–child relationships and limit the child's growth potential. The impact of these factors may be manifested in emotional disorders, personality aberrations, and, most significantly for a classification system in mental retardation, in cognitive performance.

An essential ingredient in the development of cognitive structures and elaboration of cognitive processes is the mediation of children's learning experiences. This is accomplished primarily through significant adults who interpret the meaning of objects, events, and relationships in the child's social surroundings, thereby also transmitting cultural values and beliefs and providing a sense of cultural identity. Various family members, but especially the mother, participate in this process.

It is important to note that whatever the etiology of the child's condition, the severity of his or her handicap, or the socioeconomic status of the family, cognitive performance may be influenced by the frequency and quality of mediated learning. Individual performance on tests of measured intelligence and adaptive behavior provide useful information on *current* levels of functioning only and dictate the classification to be applied; understanding *why* requires an assessment of the social environment. The multiaxial coding of such factors, by emphasis on variables known to affect cognitive processes, may provide clues to the individual's learning *potential* and the focus and nature of treatment efforts.

The proposal for a multiaxial coding of social–environmental factors is not intended to alter the classification of a specific child. Although adverse life experiences are generally inimical to optimal growth, their impact may be variously manifested both in degree and kind in personality disorders, behavioral problems, intellectual deficit, or any combination of these. Physical health, functional impairment, and temperament are important determinants. Conversely, many children draw character strength from adversity and rise above the growth-inhibiting effects of their surroundings. Since apparently similar individuals may respond and be affected differently by similar life experiences, the presumption that moderately retarded children who live in a depriving home would perform in the mild range under better social–psychological conditions lacks scientific validity. By the same token, children from disadvantaged homes performing in the mild range of retardation *cannot* be assigned additional IQ points on intelligence tests because their family, social, and learning experiences are deemed inadequate. Although it may be possible to categorize environments on a social–psychological–economic continuum, interactional effects can be determined only when conditions are changed over a reasonable period of time.

For these reasons, only measures of intelligence and adaptive behavior, supplemented and reinforced by clinical judgment, should be applied in classification. Profiles of the family and environment can prove invaluable in social diagnoses and prescribing treatment, but in the absence of appropriate services or significant change in experiences, the children's status may remain unaltered.

These concepts highlight the dynamic nature of mental retardation, its modifiability and potential reversibility in some instances. Disregard of individuals' current level of functioning in the belief that they are "potentially normal" and, therefore, not in need of special attention could prove a great disservice.

Environmental characteristics to be included in classification schemes are distinct from those in traditional reporting systems. The former set of items have etiological implications. They describe those elements in the social domain that presumably contribute to intellectual and behavioral performance. The latter are far more comprehensive in scope, but not pathologically oriented. They include a wide range of demographic and identifying data on individuals and their families, medical history, physical status, and functional abilities.

Variables affecting intellectual performance and behavior can be categorized as either *proximal* or *distal*. As these terms imply, proximal attributes of the environment are likely to have more immediate and direct impact on development than do distal attributes. These attributes, however, are inter- and intrarelated over time. Thus, race (a distal factor) may dictate negative societal reactions (proximal), which hamper skill development and lead to reading deficiency (proximal) and school failure (distal). Also, social class may prescribe parental teaching modes, leading to a belief system that promotes aggressiveness and delinquency.

Clearly, being black or Mexican-American and of lower social class can predispose children to proximal environmental events detrimental to their development; however, individual differences *within* ethnic groups or social classes are likely to be as great or greater than *between* such groups. Variations in child-rearing practices, affectional relationships, parental expectations, discipline-control practices, mental stimulation, and other factors bearing on the quality of life are critical determinants.

By the same token, individual differences in constitutional endowment, personality, and temperament influence how people respond to stimuli in their environment and the responses they evoke in return. For these reasons, it is not possible to predict with any degree or confidence what level of intellectual proficiency or social competence individuals might have attained had they been reared in a qualitatively different environment. Although it is possible, and even desirable, to be able to categorize social settings on some continuum of adequacy for promoting development and behavior, adjustment of IQ based on such considerations is a highly questionable process. Readers should be reminded that retardation is *defined in terms of current functioning;* adding some number of points to an individual's measured intelligence because of depriving living conditions presumes predictive capabilities we cannot legitimately claim. Classifying the environment introduces the notion of social diagnoses to our understanding of etiological and contributory agents on performance and can provide a basis for prescriptive treatment. Until and unless the environment is modified, however, alterations in behavior are not likely to occur. Potential that remains unrealized has little meaning for social adaptation. Disregard of an individual's current status on the assumption that he or she would certainly perform better under more favorable conditions is unwarranted. Given the importance of social–environmental conditions in development, this assumption could prove valid when applied to mentally retarded populations. It cannot, however, be applied to individuals whose assessment becomes the basis for classification systems.

The emphasis on current functioning in the definition of mental retardation underscores the dynamic nature of the condition and offers an additional rationale for extending the multiaxial classification system to social dimensions bearing on developmental processes. The identification of pathological factors in the environment for an individual performing within the retarded range should alert clinicians to the need for periodic reevaluation. Meaningful modification of the environment, depending on age and nature of severity of the condition, could change the individual's classification level or his or her designation as retarded.

Among the variables that may impede development and impair adaptive behavior, the following are illustrative: (a) parental absence, apathy, rejection, neglect, abuse, or lack of controls and limits; (b) lack of appropriate mental, sensory, and verbal stimulation; (c) family disorganization and conflict; (d) inadequate role models, socialization, and teaching approaches; (e) limited opportunity for positive interpersonal relationships with peers, teachers, and other socializing agents; (f) limited access to social and vocational opportunity structures; and (g) cultural conflict within families.

Assessment of the Quality of a Family and Other Residential Environments

Various methods are available for appraising a family as a growth-enhancing environment for children and other dependents. Most of these have been produced in the study of general child development. They consist of interview formats, self-administering inventories, or observation schedules. Some have been especially valuable for the study of natural and foster homes of mentally retarded children.

Two are self-administering inventories. The Moos Family Environment Scale yields scores on 10 characteristics of the caregiving respondent (for example, the mother or father or both). Some scores have been shown to characterize families whose de-institutionalized mentally retarded members are returned to them or those who become foster families. Others have been shown to be valid indicators of family harmony and adjustment. The Henderson Environmental Learning Process Scale secures information on the practices of the family as they relate to facilitating academic learning and push for achievement and is therefore appropriate for use with homes having mildly retarded educable and learning-disabled school children.

Three instruments require a visit with observation. Caldwell's Home Observation for the Measurement of the Environment (HOME) requires that the child be present so that some adult–child interaction may be observed. One form is appropriate when the target child has a developmental level under 3 years. The form for ages 3 to 6 years is suitable for use with families having mentally retarded children of moderate or lower level up to about the age of 15. It is not appropriate for mildly retarded (EMR) children beyond the age of 10 nor for adults. Some of its subscales have been shown to be predictive of growth and adjustment of mentally retarded children. The Fels Parent Behavior Rating Scale is used to appraise a child's home environment. The rater visits in the home to observe the parent–child relationship. The resulting 30 parent behavior variables are scored. These ratings are used as a basis for the interpretation of the dynamics of the child's environment and for the description of that environment. Clusters of variables indicate clarity of policy, interference, and acceptance of the child. Another instrument requiring observation of the residential premises is the Wolfensberger-Glenn Program Analysis of Service Systems (PASS-3). The highly detailed appraisals required to complete this instrument are based on the authors' philosophy of "normalization"; therefore, unless results are interpreted consistent with this philosophy, they may be misleading.

Various instruments have been employed to determine parental attitudes about rearing mentally retarded children. Other instruments have been developed for appraising the qualities of the environment in group or institutional settings and can be used, with some reservations, in the study of home life. These are the Jackson Characteristics of the Treatment Environment and the King, Raynes, and Tizard Child Management Survey; a revision of King et al.'s scale is also available.

These scales are objectively administered and have reasonably good measurement characteristics in terms of reliability of score and ease of administration, and they have some validity for predicting welfare and progress of mentally retarded people of selected categories. Professionals have also used semistructured interview procedures in which information about various aspects of the home environment is sought. It is possible to inquire about how a mentally retarded family member (or foster family resident) impacts the household in such significant areas as sleeping, eating, shopping, and vacationing; alteration of educational, professional, and residential plans; effects on relatives and neighbors; awareness of the person's disability; apparent confidence in coping; need for respite care. Some parents are willing to keep diaries in which they record not only routine but critical events in the retarded person's adjustment. This information, when collated, is helpful in parent and family counseling and causes parents to become more objective in their observations of their child. As is the case with other rating scales and self-report instruments, however, caution must be used in their employment.

Cautions in Interpreting the Quality of the Family Environment and Other Residential Environments

The determination of the characteristics of the home or of any other residence is performed for various purposes. Among these are providing assistance in child-rearing of difficult-to-manage mentally retarded dependents, planning for the future when the careproviders may be unable to cope because of age, providing emotional support, and arriving at decisions with respect to change of residential placement, utilizing services, and securing respite care.

Great care is required in interpreting information about the family or residence. It is important to take into account any subcultural norms of family living and child treatment. There are many differences between subgroups in such practices as the use of physical punishment, the strong expression of love or anger, and the demand for achievement. These subgroup norms must be considered before making a judgment that remediation is needed or before advocating a change in residence.

SAFEGUARDING THE ASSESSMENT PROCESS

The utilization of clinical assessment procedures often results in rather significant consequences for the persons being assessed.

These persons are brought into assessment because of presenting problems, such as severe school failure. Causes need to be distinguished, diagnoses arrived at, and decisions made about treatment, training, and change of placement. The best professional safeguards can*not* be taken for granted.

Because of the concern by some professionals that tests may be inappropriately employed in diagnosis and placement into treatment, certain safeguards have been enacted into law by both state and federal governments. These laws now codify what have always been the best practices. Enactment of PL 94-142, The Education for All Handicapped Children Act of 1975, included provisions for so-called protections in evaluative procedures, or PEP. Although enacted with respect to educational programming of school-age children, they apply rather generally to clinical appraisal with mentally retarded people. Some of the principal safeguards are:

1. In general, assessments are to be initiated only for sufficient cause. For example, referrals from teachers or doctors, etc., should be scrutinized to determine that there is adequate cause for bringing the person into the formal evaluation process.
2. The parent or guardian of a school child must give consent to the making of an assessment and has the right to participate in and to appeal the determinations made and the placement and program decisions that follow and under some circumstances can request an external assessment.
3. Assessments are to be undertaken only by fully qualified and licensed professionals under laws and regulations that govern their specialties.
4. Assessment procedures are adjusted to account for specific deficits in hearing, seeing, health, or movement and modified to accommodate those whose background, culture, or language differs from the general population.
5. Those conducting assessments will refer to appropriate specialists any person suspected of having hearing, health, or other problems.
6. Conclusions and recommendations are made on the basis of all information, including that determined from interviews with people acquainted with the subject and from observations of the subject's behavior. Diagnosis or placement is not to be based upon a single determiner (such as an IQ or interview).

7. Periodic reassessments are to be made, not only to confirm or correct previous judgments but also because changes in growth rate do occur and programming changes may be in order.

Emphasis on Sound Clinical Practice

The mandate for such formally stated protections in assessments testifies to the fact that to identify someone as mentally retarded who has no biomedical syndrome must be a judgmental process. As discussed earlier, some level of mental impairment must be adopted by consensus that is a reasonable IQ cut-off applicable in most cases and that provides a boundary between (a) needing special programming or care because of mental impairment and (b) not requiring special care or not requiring it for that reason. Second, the obtained information must be interpreted for the individual case, without absolute observance of the numerical cut-off. Some problems of agreement and consistency are to be anticipated, but the periodic mandatory reassessments are particularly helpful in working with mildly retarded individuals. Diagnostic judgment should include consideration of the daily living adaptations of the person, observed or reported competencies or deficiencies, health and developmental history, and the evidence secured from specialists, such as communication-disorder professionals.

Limitations on Assessment Technology

All measurement, including physical measurement, is fallible, although scores secured with standardized measurement tend to have smaller rates of error than do data secured from informal observation and interview. Appropriate assessment is conducted with a knowledge of potential error in the securing of test scores or other indicators and with regard for changes in scores over time and between conditions. Of vital concern in the diagnosis of mental retardation and the determination of level for purposes of programming are the mental tests leading to such scores as IQ and MA and to the measurement of adaptive behavior.

Temporal variation in IQ. Changes in IQ may occur over time for various reasons. That is a reason for use of multiple sources of information and clinical judgment and for periodic reassessment.

One source of variation is change of children's mental growth rate or change in adult's mental status. Changes have often been reported in the longitudinal investigations of nonretarded children; sometimes progressive gain or decline of IQ is associated with characteristics of the living or educational environment. The possibility of change of mental competence due to drugs, injury, or physical deterioration is evident. Temporal variations tend to be smaller for mentally retarded individuals, particularly those at the lower levels, than for people of higher intelligence; however, as a safe rule, one should never conclude that an IQ of any given person is fixed, despite data that show that it tends to be stable for most people.

Error of measurement of IQ. In addition to the possibility of temporal change, an obtained IQ must also be considered in terms of its fallibility as a measurement. All measurement has some potential for error. For example, presume that several measurements have been secured in a short time by different examiners and that there are no examinee practice or fatigue effects. Obtained scores may show a range of several points. Such variations around a hypothetical "true score" are due to minor variations in subjects' performance and between examiners and to other, often unknown, factors. Fluctuations in scores secured in a short time period do not represent actual changes in the person's status. They are unavoidable; their presence and magnitude must be recognized in the appropriate employment and interpretations of the results obtained with measuring instruments. This is interpreted to mean that if a retest is promptly given with the same instrument, discounting any practice effect, the second IQ would be within 1 standard error of measurement of the first IQ about two thirds of the time. For greater confidence, one should determine the .05 probability (or perhaps the .01 probability) limits of the score.

Other sources of IQ variations. A principal source of IQ variation lies in the difference in test content between different scales and between different levels of the same scale. For example, perusal of the Stanford-Binet content shows a progressive increase of verbal-type items as one goes from early to later ages. The IQs determined on verbal tests, such as the Verbal IQ of the Wechsler scales, can differ from those obtained on nonverbal tests, such as the Wechsler Performance scale. Variations also may be attributed to differences in the standardization norms of different instruments and to changes between different editions of the same scale. For example, investigators find some difference between the WISC and its revision, the WISC-R, and between the 1960 and 1972 editions of the Stanford-Binet, although the differences for either scale have been minor with regard to mental retardation.

These interscale and interedition differences tend to provide greater variations in IQ than those that are due to error fluctuations in the use of one scale. Hence, a difference between performance and verbal IQ of 8 or 10 points for a mildly retarded subject is not unusual. As with error of measurement, such variations must be interpreted by appropriately prepared clinicians to avoid literal and absolute use of any obtained score.

Despite all of the problems mentioned, IQs are more reliable than most other scores and tend to remain fairly constant for most people over long time periods. Although constancy of obtained IQ must never be taken for granted, stability may be presumed to occur for most subjects, especially if no critical change in psychological, social, or medical condition has occurred.

rdation to adaptive behavior is less precise; some individuals
IQs in the moderate range can achieve some degree of self-
iciency with proper training and supervision.

atal and Perinatal Factors

pproximately 9 out of 10 cases of biologically based mental
rdation are prenatal in origin and manifested at birth or early
nfancy. It is not surprising that disturbances in fetal growth
etimes cause central nervous system deficits, for this is a period
apid brain development. The *mature* brain can survive the
cts of infections, radiation, trauma, and other noxious agents,
they can be devasting to the *developing* organism. Any factor
ing maternal ill-health—physical or, in some instances, even
tional—or an adverse uterine environment can affect the un-
child.

fectious disease. The role of maternal infection in the etiology
ental retardation is fairly well defined. Although not a major
e of mental retardation, infectious diseases are, nevertheless,
ortant; furthermore, they can be prevented in many situations.
achievement of this goal in diseases such as syphillis and
lla, for example, has been made possible by a better under-
ding of the pathogenesis of the infectious process and knowl-
of the characteristics of the microorganisms involved and
r transmission. Treatment with antibiotics has proved effective
yphillis, and vaccines and mass immunization techniques have
ented rubella and associated tragic fetal outcomes.
he nature and extensiveness of damage occurring from infec-
depends, in part, on whether it is congenital or acquired.
genital toxoplasmosis, for example, in both its "neurological"
"generalized" forms, has widespread symptomatology, includ-
characteristic abnormal spinal fluid, anemia, and convulsions.
prognosis for such children is extremely poor. Of those who
ive, 85 percent are mentally retarded, and most have associ-
convulsive disorders, spasticity, or impairments in vision.
ut 1 in 10 are normal at 4 years of age. By contrast, acquired
s of toxoplasmosis may result in encephalitis or other symp-
, but with far less severe consequences. When rubella and
negalovirus inclusion disease occur during pregnancy, they
uce congenital malformations as well as mental retardation.

CHAPTER 5
TYPOLOGY OF MENTAL RE

RETARDATION OF BIOLOGIC

Mental retardation of biologic origin, othe
tors, accounts for only approximately one-fc
population but an overwhelming percentag
agents. These agents, which are generally mar
brain maldevelopment or dysfunction, embra
of factors. They include genetic and chrom
fectious processes, toxins and chemical agents
of metabolism, gestational disorders, compli
and delivery, and gross brain disease, many
gin. They occur in families in all strata of s

The number of newly recognized causes
creasing rapidly because of significant ad
methodology, sophisticated instrumentation
trometry, and increased interest of clinic
researchers. With the discovery of new specif
teratogens, and biochemical abnormalities, th
has become increasingly difficult. What app
disease may be one part of another syndror
dent on the existence of some co-factor. Th
most of the conditions in the 1983 classificati
both clinically and scientifically validated; l
certain that no book can keep pace with the p
edge from biological research.

Organic retardation is far less frequent tha
vantage," as defined here. Yet, in some respe
problem. Individuals in this category are, as
disabled, have associated physical handicaps
pendent on adults in their environment fo
Although not perfect, the correlation betw
and biologic retardation is very high. The r

59

Embryonic tissues are particularly susceptible to damage from disease since the human fetus appears to show no detectable immunological response early in gestation. The capacity to produce antibody increases significantly for infants from 6 to 12 months of age.

The frequency of infections during pregnancy is influenced by many factors, including geographic location, seasonal variations, maternal age, and the occurrence of epidemics. Socioeconomic conditions, such as nutrition, hygiene, housing density, availability of medical care, exposure, and contact with animals, also affect vulnerability to disease.

Genetic disease. Genetic disease constitutes an appreciable fraction of pediatric practice. About 20 percent of patients sick enough to require hospitalization in children's facilities have gene-related diseases. One in 10 institutionalized retarded persons has a genetically based condition. The incidence of such conditions is especially high for more severely handicapped children and includes several degenerative disorders, such as Tay-Sachs disease, that result in early death.

In recent years investigators have significantly advanced our understanding of cell structure and function and how genetic materials are transmitted. Most noteworthy is the regular discovery of new inborn errors of metabolism—single gene defects—that may lead to structural abnormalities. The transmission of enzyme deficiencies follows the usual pattern of Mendelian laws of heredity for recessive or dominant traits. Many such defects can now be identified prenatally in cases where a previously affected child has been born to the mother. Population screening for heterozygous carriers is also possible for some diseases concentrated in specific groups, for example, Tay-Sachs in Ashkenazi Jews of Eastern European descent.

Other well-known enzyme deficits include phenylketonuria, galactosemia, maple syrup urine disease, familial cretinism, and several forms of glycogen storage disease. The rarity of these conditions is due, in part, to the fact that affected individuals do not ordinarily reproduce, and their genes are thereby lost from the population. As is true in most cases of recessive inheritance, however, consanguineous matings increase the risk of defective offspring. For first-cousin matings, the risk is five times greater than in matings between unrelated persons.

Down syndrome, the most common form of genetic aberration, results from a variation in the number of chromosomes present. Trisomy, which is an aberration occurring among the autosomes, is a consequence of nondysjunction, an error in cell division. In the human species there are 23 pairs of chromosomes in the cells of the body, thus 46 in all. In Down syndrome there are 47 rather than the normal 46 chromosomes. Other syndromes result from alteration of particular chromosomes, but the cause(s) of nondysjunction are as yet unknown.

The development of techniques for prenatal diagnosis has greatly increased the value of genetic counseling and preventive measures. Metabolic errors and chromosome anomalies can now be accurately detected through a culturing of fetal cells obtained from amniotic fluid. This technology has value, too, for identifying X-chromosome-linked disorders and extending our knowledge of genetic linkages. The well-known relationship between Down syndrome and advanced maternal age further highlights the significance of prenatal diagnostic capabilities.

Prematurity and low birthweight. Numerous prenatal factors are associated with low birthweight, including adequacy of prenatal care, maternal nutrition, toxemias, previous premature births, illegitimacy, smoking, infections, and parity. The relative contribution of these factors, the role of hormonal disturbances, and other complications of pregnancy and the mechanisms underlying the onset of labor, however, remain obscure.

The more immediate sources of low birthweight or prematurity of infants are many and varied. Some infants are born at term to mothers of small stature, due perhaps to genetic influences. They have relatively low morbidity rates. Other full-term infants may be malnourished *in utero* because of placental insufficiency or effects of noxious agents. These "small for date" babies tend to show retarded fetal growth and later neurological sequelae distinct from those of low gestational age. Those who are truly preterm, born after a shortened gestational age, are especially vulnerable to neurological damage if very premature or of very low birthweight (below 1,500 grams).

Much progress has been made during the past two decades in developing facilities and treatment for the intensive care of such high-risk infants. Biochemical abnormalities such as hypoglycemia and hypoxia can now be readily diagnosed and effectively treated.

Respiratory distress and anoxia, once major causes of brain damage, are now also subject to treatment without consequent morbidity in most cases. Overall, there is preliminary evidence that although low birthweight per se has not declined significantly, the proportion of those showing evidence of mental retardation has dropped considerably.

Low birthweight and prematurity are probably most accurately perceived as factors associated with but not sufficient causes of mental retardation. Except for infants at the low end of the gestational age and birthweight continuum who frequently evidence demonstrable central nervous system abnormalities, learning disabilities seem to be confined primarily to infants in lower social class families. This phenomenon strongly supports the view that although biological determinants may dictate birthweight and gestational age, the psychosocial experiences of children bear heavily on their mental status and capabilities. For the large majority of such children, therefore, and for selected other conditions as well, the interaction of biological and social factors, before and after birth, offer the most viable explanation for retardation.

Other biomedical causes. Although the vast majority of pregnancies are uneventful, there are, nevertheless, a host of agents in the physical prenatal environment capable of disturbing normal fetal growth and causing or contributing to mental retardation. Among these are chemical agents, irradiation, nutrition, and birth trauma.

The impact of toxic substances such as lead and mercury are generally manifested in childhood but can also affect the fetus from asymptomatic mothers. Pregnant women who drink lead-contaminated water and breathe similarly contaminated air can accumulate these toxins in their blood and transmit them across the placenta. Sperm damage has also been noted in men working in factories manufacturing batteries and in other industries. Mercurial pollutants in food and drinking water resulting from waste products and pesticides have caused severe brain damage, cerebral palsy, and mental retardation in infants born to mothers ingesting these elements.

Chemical agents involving various additive drugs, alcohol, pharmaceutical substances, and smoking are of special concern because of the very large number of people implicated. In today's drug culture, many pregnant women addicted to heroin are giving birth to infants who show marked physiological withdrawal symptoms. The effect on the nervous system is unknown, but suspect. Drugs such as LSD have been noted to induce meiotic chromosome damage and damage to human leukocytes, and chromosomal abnormalities underly some types of mental retardation. Even therapeutic drugs taken during pregnancy and childbirth have been linked to respiratory delay after birth.

Particularly alarming is the fairly recent finding that chronic alcoholism and "binge" drinking are associated with a range of congenital malformations and mental retardation. The resulting physical and intellectual anomalies have given rise to a new condition—the fetal alcohol syndrome.

The role of smoking as a contributory cause to mental retardation may be indirect and mediated through reduction in birthweight. Animal studies, however, suggest that the chemicals in cigarette smoke can directly retard fetal growth or cause stillbirths.

Irradiation in large doses during pregnancy, as in the nuclear holocaust at Hiroshima, has been shown to cause mental retardation, microcephaly, and leukemia. The most critical age for sensitivity to radiation appeared to be between 7 and 15 weeks of gestation. The cumulative dosage effects of diagnostic, fluoroscopic, and therapeutic radiation, although not fully substantiated, is of increasing concern to medical practitioners.

The independent role of maternal malnutrition in human mental retardation is difficult to isolate from the conditions of social–environmental deprivation in which the offspring of such pregnancies are reared. Animal research, however, indicates that malnourishment *in utero* during critical periods of brain growth results in offspring with permanent deficits in cell size and number, reduction in protein synthesis, and severe neurochemical (RNA–DNA), electrical, and morphological changes in the brain. Reactions of apathy, lassitude, appetite loss, and other kinds of deficient behavior are common in these animals. Most significant, the effect on physical and brain development persists across generations, even when the offspring of a malnourished mother are in turn well fed. Other animal studies suggest that inadequate protein consumption during the early postnatal stages leads to impaired performance.

Field studies with human populations are more difficult to interpret. In human beings, and in other species as well, there is little relationship between brain size (as measured by head circumference) and intelligence. An additional complicating fact is that although brain growth stops when children are still young, intellectual development continues through adolescence and later. Mental ability of human beings is a function of experience as well as brain structure. Nevertheless, malnutrition of pregnant women may result in low birthweight and prematurity and, in famine conditions, in a high incidence of stillbirths, infant mortality, and morbidity. Thus, although the role of maternal malnutrition in mental retardation is difficult to document and quantify, there is strong evidence to suggest that in conjunction with other physical and social–psychological factors, it is a significant etiological agent.

Other prenatal factors associated with a higher risk of abnormality in infants include toxemia, hypoglycemia, hypoxia, maternal diabetes, and complications of labor. Birth injury, in terms of intracranial hemorrhage and compression, anoxia or edema, when resulting in convulsions, impaired respiration, or other indices of infant distress, are further causes. Some of these conditions, as with low birthweight and prematurity, become manifested in mental retardation, primarily in interaction with psychosocially disadvantaged living conditions.

Factors of Postnatal Origin

Some of the same etiological agents underlying reproductive casualty may also originate during infancy or childhood. These include various infectious diseases, physical trauma, toxic substances, and nutritional disorders. Some conditions of biologically based mental retardation, especially the heredodegenerative diseases, are prenatal in origin, although the symptomatology does not appear until later in life, even into adulthood.

Some infectious agents devastate the fetus but have little impact on maternal health because they do not affect the mature central nervous system. Rubella and toxoplasmosis are cases in point. The increasing capacity of the growing organism to develop antibodies to viral and bacterial agents, however, is no guarantee to immunity. Fortunately, most common childhood diseases such as measles, chickenpox, diptheria, and scarlet fever rarely involve the brain; yet various forms of encephalitis do occur, and although they do not account for a large number of postnatally based causes of retardation individually, collectively they are important. This is especially true in underdeveloped countries where medical care is unavailable or inadequate and high body temperatures consequent to infection may continue unchecked for long periods of time.

Accidents during childhood are a major source of physically handicapping conditions and, to a lesser extent, of mental retardation. The relative softness of the skull in early infancy, a period of rapid brain growth, offers little protection from injury, accidental or otherwise. In older children, skull fractures sustained in auto collisions, falls, and athletic pursuits can result in loss of consciousness, convulsive disorders, neurological sequelae, and serious brain damage. Perceptual and learning disorders short of mental retardation per se are more common outcomes. Much depends on the extent of damage, the particular segments of the brain affected, and the age at which the insult occurs.

In recent years, much public attention has been focused on child abuse, but largely outside the domain of professionals in the mental retardation field. Attempts have been made to characterize the parents of battered children as being of lower intelligence (a concomitant of psychosocial disadvantage forms of retardation), aggressive, impulsive, immature, and self-centered. Not all such parents abuse their children, and those that do seem more likely to direct their behavior to children who tax their limited resources and coping skills. Premature or seriously ill infants, who are often separated from their mothers during the newborn period, with possible impairment of affectional ties, are particularly vulnerable to abuse. Thus, children who are biologically vulnerable to retardation by virtue of prematurity may be further jeopardized by the psychological burden their status evokes.

Lead encephalopathy, once an important cause of brain damage of slum-raised children, is less significant today. This is partly due to greater public awareness of the hazards posed to children from ingesting the paint from crumbling walls, stricter regulations for the construction of public housing, and the general societal concern with environmental pollutants. Yet, although the role of lead at *toxic* levels is firmly established as a cause of mental retardation and efforts at prevention have been initiated, the importance of low lead exposure is a matter of increasing concern. Several sources of lead contamination have been identified: exhaust emissions from automobiles, fumes from certain industries, and the ambient air in delapidated dwellings. The significance of these generally pervasive sources of pollution is that most of the population is at risk for exposure. The findings from recent research that low lead levels in children are associated with subtle disorders in learning and behavior merit continuing attention.

It is estimated that more than 300 million children throughout the world suffer from varying degrees of malnutrition. Because of the great difficulty in carrying out long-term dietary surveys in human populations, height and weight are used as crude indicators of past nutrition. In poorly fed communities, diets are adequate during the first 6 months of life when infants are breast fed but become increasingly deficient, especially in protein, through the third year of life. Under these conditions, clinical malnutrition (Kwashiorkor) is common. If breast feeding is terminated early or not used at all, severe malnutrition and growth failure may occur in young infants.

The effects of clinical malnutrition on intellectual development are extremely difficult to isolate from the very deprived social–environmental conditions in which they inevitably occur. It is clear from animal research, however, and in human autopsy material as well, that brain structures are permanently affected and likely to produce functional, though perhaps not formally measurable, consequences. Malnourished children, however, also suffer from many other disadvantages affecting intellectual development. They are likely to lack vitality, motivation, social responsiveness, and attentiveness and are subject to frequent illnesses that reduce their opportunities for learning.

Malnutrition and sociocultural factors are best viewed as acting synergistically to depress both physical and mental growth and development. The relative contribution of each is difficult to assess precisely; however, several large-scale studies indicate that the microenvironment—the degree of stimulation in the home—accounts for about the same level of variance in IQs as does the nutritional insult.

In the human condition, undernourishment is generally chronic rather than acute. From an ecological perspective, the mothers of undernourished children were probably similarly deprived and were at greater biological risk for the reproduction of children. They tend to bear children at an early age and have too many too rapidly. Children born under these conditions are likely to be smaller at birth, frequently ill, and lacking medical supervision.

Failure in school leads to failure in adult life and apathy and poverty in succeeding generations.

Biosocial factors. Most investigators concerned with mental retardation, learning disabilities, and related disorders have looked to the period of pregnancy for causal explanations. The concept of a "continuum of reproductive casualty" that has emerged from this biomedical orientation has been useful in defining the relationship of predisposing events to later deficits, especially for conditions at the more severe end of the continuum. For many of the complications of pregnancy, however, insult to the organism becomes manifested in behavioral deficiencies only in the context of an adverse social-psychological environment. In these instances, reproductive casualty is a necessary, but not sufficient cause of the condition. Examples of these biosocially determined causal agents are anoxia, prematurity, and prenatal stress. The biosocial nature of malnutrition and psychosocial retardation has been presented in other sections. In contrast to anoxia, etc., which occurs in all social classes, thereby allowing for an assessment of interactional effects, the latter are limited to severely disadvantaged populations only. Thus, the contribution of genetics to mild retardation can only be studied by experimentally manipulating the environment or examining the effect of naturally occurring, but drastic, changes in a child's life experiences through foster home placement or adoption.

Animal studies indicate that cerebral oxygen deprivation during the perinatal period produces brain damage and later deficits in learning. Longitudinal studies on children are less definitive. Although anoxic infants appear impaired during the first days of life on measures of maturation, visual responsiveness, irritability, muscle tension, and pain threshold and continue to show some adverse cognitive and neurological effects at 3 years of age, by age 7 they perform as well as nonanoxic control children.

The nature of the postnatal environment is an important determinant in the learning status of these children at school age. Parental attitudes and caretaking approaches are not likely to be distorted in these families, because in many instances the parents may be unaware of any asphyxia in the infant and prolonged hospitalization is seldom prescribed. The correlates of low social class, however, tend to be operative, so that children of disadvantaged homes are more likely to show long-term cognitive deficits than are similar children in middle-class homes.

The biosocial components relating prematurity to mental retardation provide a classical example of the interactional effects of perinatal hazards in the subsequent quality of life experiences. The causes of prematurity are varied and complex, and outcomes vary according to whether the infant is small for gestational age or full term of low birthweight. Infants born very prematurely (under 28 weeks) or of very low birthweight (under 1,500 grams) have a high incidence of neurological sequelae. In these cases biological factors alone can account for later deficiencies.

The overwhelming majority of premature infants, however, are delivered later in gestation and range in weight from 1,500 to 2,500 grams. Epidemiological studies consistently show a strong social-class relationship among children in this category who demonstrate mental retardation or learning disabilities. A stimulating environment can apparently compensate for the early deficits of the immature organism; for disadvantaged children, the impact of biological and social factors are additive.

The observed relationship of demographic variables and prematurity to mental retardation should not obscure variations in the microenvironment within social classes. The extended period of hospital stay, the enforced separation of mother and infant and its effect on attachment behavior and maternal anxiety, and possibly guilt regarding the infant's precarious status are all sources of potential distortions in the mother–child relationship. If these are not appropriately resolved, the resulting social climate may prove noncompensatory.

Social-status variables play an important role in modulating the effects of other complications of pregnancy as well. Aberrations in newborn behavior, associated with less severe symptoms of neurological disorder, have very limited utility in predicting later problems in adaptation. Infants at high risk for later academic problems are likely to come from economically depressed environments in which there is poor health care; the prevalence is greater in minority families, particularly those in which maternal IQ is within the retarded range. Conversely, infants who suffer perinatal complications generally show little, if any, later effects if they are members of advantaged families. Thus, the hypothesized relationship between early trauma and late deviancy must be modified by a careful consideration of intervening experiential factors. The quality of caretaking in these cases has a stronger influence on the causes of development than does perinatal history.

The proper classification of some forms of mental retardation requires, therefore, a biosocial perspective to improve diagnoses and to establish a sounder basis for prescriptive treatment. The multiaxial classification system described in this classification system and the introduction of criteria for assessing the social milieu of retarded persons are efforts to accomplish this goal.

SOCIAL–ENVIRONMENTAL FACTORS

Etiological Agents

The specific etiology of mental retardation classified as *psychosocial disadvantage* is still somewhat obscure. Unlike many forms of biological defect in which a single causitive agent can be identified, this form of mental retardation appears to involve several sets of interactive factors, none sufficient in themselves to account for the intellectual and behavioral deficits manifested. The involved individuals come from environments that are psychologically, socially, and economically impoverished. Housing and hygiene are poor, nutrition and medical care inadequate, and infectious diseases common. One or more of the parents and other children in the family evidence mentally subaverage performance.

Among the several sets of factors identified for their possible etiological significance, genetic factors have been historically assigned a crucial role and at one point generated a widespread sense of eugenic alarm. The polygenic model of inheritance, put forth to explain the concentration of retarded persons in the lower classes and among minority groups, enjoys less currency today. Largely, this stems from our growing awareness of the effects of early stimulation and strategies of environmental enrichment. Nevertheless, individuals vary genetically on intellectual as well as physical traits, and it is highly probable that some disadvantaged people owe their retardation in large measure to genetic factors. This view gains some credence from the empirical observation that retardation due to social–environmental influences is not randomly distributed among the poverty stricken who share common vicissitudes of living, but is most often encountered in families in which there is low maternal intelligence. Such observed relationships between maternal and child IQ are only suggestive, however, for an alternative hypothesis is that retarded mothers have difficulties in providing suitable learning climates for the development of their children.

Somatic factors that are nonheritable and may cause subclinical defects that cannot be measured by existing technology may also contribute to social environmentally induced retardation. Such children are frequently born to teenage mothers, to women who are undernourished or malnourished, and to those who receive inadequate prenatal and postnatal care. These women are particularly vulnerable to noxious agents such as infections, trauma, and intoxications, and their children have a high incidence of prematurity and low birthweight, all of which can affect children's intellectual and physical growth. In the absence of clinical manifestations, the impact of these somatic factors as independent agents is problematic; however, considered in combination with other depressing psychological and social forces, the cumulative adverse effect on intelligence is probably significant.

The last set of factors contributing etiologically to mild retardation relate generally to the quality of living experiences and, more specifically, to the nature of family relationships, especially with the mother, and to child-rearing practices. The lack of childhood stimulation in its most extreme form (severe social isolation) can cause serious retardation; in lesser form it can prevent children from realizing their innate potential.

Disadvantaged children, sometimes because of large family size and closely spaced births, overwhelm parental capacities for attention, affection, and mental stimulation. In some instances, parental preoccupation with social survival leads to child abuse and neglect, but more commonly the limited parent lacks the communication skills to stimulate the child's acquisition of language and cognitive development. Speech and thought are essential to problem-solving and the regulation and integration of social behavior. Communication deficits weaken the process of early cognitive development and the later stages that build upon it. The restrictive speech patterns characteristic of the lower social classes and their reliance on nonanalytical, concrete verbalizations in contrast to the "elaborated" explanatory speech mode of the middle class, places them at a distinct disadvantage in educational settings employing formal language and concepts.

The family environment of psychosocially disadvantaged children carries other risks to development as well. Often, such children are the products of unwanted and unplanned pregnancies or are the victims of marital disharmony and pathological family re-

lationships. Their infancy and early childhood are not devoid of
sensory stimulation, but the input is often chaotic and disorganized, exploratory behavior is discouraged, and positive behavior is
seldom reinforced. Under these conditions, behavior tends to assume maladaptive forms, for as the children grow older they have
few worthwhile adult models to emulate and are brought into
continual conflict with social norms and expectations for which
they have been poorly prepared.

The relative importance of these sets of factors in the etiology of
mild mental retardation of psychosocial origin cannot be fully
substantiated at this point in time. Genetic factors may not be as
critical as previously thought; however, there is little doubt that
innate potential and a stimulating environment are *completely necessary* determinants of intellectual growth. Heredity or environment, whichever is lower, sets the ceiling for intellectual development. The genetic potential of these individuals is at best suspect;
the environment, on the other hand, is clearly lacking in nurturing
qualities. It is reasonable to assume, therefore, that improved living
experiences would enable many of these individuals to function at a
level beyond the retarded range.

The extended multiaxial classification system describing individuals' social milieu is an attempt to specify in more precise terms the
correlates of psychosocial disadvantage and provide clues for more
effective environmental manipulation and social planning.

Prevention and Treatment

Any effort to reduce the incidence or prevalence of retardation
significantly rests heavily on society's ability and willingness to
improve markedly the quality of life for the most deprived segments of the population. The many opportunities for the primary
prevention of mild retardation is implied in the previous description of etiological factors.

The disproportionate contribution of unwed teenage mothers
and mothers of low intelligence to retardation highlights the importance of family planning as a major preventive technique. Very
young mothers frequently have low birthweight babies, are members of impoverished minority groups, and lack the parenting skills
to promote optimal growth of their children. Mentally limited
mothers share in these deficiencies and are often further overbur-

dened by large, unplanned families. The observed inverse relationship between family size and verbal intelligence, regardless of social class, relates to the dilution of parental care and assumes even greater significance for already marginal mothers.

These women generally have access to voluntary family-planning activities. They are often clients of public welfare agencies and other social institutions and are likely to deliver their babies in municipal hospitals. Providing these women with birth-control information and contraceptive devices could meaningfully reduce the number of potentially retarded children. Freed of excessive demands for child care, these women might be better mothers to their children.

Realistically, many parents are unwilling to control the size of their families, and children are born who are potential casualties of their environment. Physiologically well-born children tend to progress within normal developmental limits during the first few years of life and do not manifest retarded performance until school age. Whether retardation is acquired as a consequence of cumulative deprivation or escapes detection at an earlier age because of fewer environmental demands or problems in intellectual assessment, it appears that skilled intervention can modify the developmental outcome.

Intervention strategies can be child-focused or parent-focused but are likely to be most effective when both are involved. Preschool nursery and day-care programs directed toward sensory and language stimulation, achievement motivation, problem-solving skills, and interpersonal relations can do much to counteract the growth inhibiting atmosphere of the disadvantaged home. These benefits, however, will be at least partially dissipated if discontinuities between the preschool center and home are allowed to persist. Improvement in parental homemaking skills and child-rearing practices may help to ensure carry-over. Home-intervention programs, designed to train parents to assume active teaching roles with their children, particularly with respect to language, have also demonstrated promising results with lower class families.

Malnutrition and undernutrition during pregnancy and early childhood represent additional social–environmental factors contributing to low mental performance. These factors almost never appear in isolation from other adverse experiences; therefore, it is difficult to assess their comparative role in etiology. Evidence from animal research, however, as noted earlier, indicates that animals malnourished during critical periods of brain growth showed a range of permanent deficits and behavioral manifestations.

Information on human beings is less complete but largely correspondent with these findings in general. There appears to be a period in human development extending from early pregnancy through the second year of life when the brain experiences its maximum and perhaps only opportunity to grow properly. The supplemental feeding of prospective mothers and infants during these critical periods, especially if provided in conjunction with other strategies for intellectual enrichment, can be an effective measure in the prevention of mild retardation.

Although the foregoing discussion has emphasized early intervention, programs aimed at amelioration, even to the level of nonretarded functioning, can be effective later in life as well. This may occur through environmental manipulation or social engineering, education, vocational training, or changes in the economy and technology. In many cases of mild retardation, this happens naturally by virtue of lesser demands for intellectual prowess during adulthood. The two-dimensional criteria of mental retardation—low intelligence and impaired behavior—account in large measure for this phenomenon, for both are amenable to change, and improvement in either one has functional consequences for individuals.

Numerous epidemiological studies indicate a marked drop in the prevalence of mild retardation beginning at age 15. Mortality rates play little part in this phenomenon, which is best explained by: (a) retarded persons' ability to succeed in work in contrast to their failure in school, (b) slow, but progressive social maturation in learning to cope with societal demands, and (c) delayed intellectual maturation. Increments in IQ during late adolescence and early adulthood, often quite substantial, have been reported among the most disadvantaged individuals.

Long-term social follow-up of children attending special classes after World War I indicated far better adjustment than would have been predicted from their childhood histories. Although the adjustment levels achieved may be considered marginal by middle-class standards and are in some cases dependent on the presence of "benevolent benefactors," most successes were realized without special help, except for the school experience. We assume that planned intervention would result in more rapid and complete improvement in socially adaptive behavior. The success of vocational training and placement programs, experimental programs of foster-home group care, and the guided use of the peer group as a major socializing agent supports the validity of the assumption.

Based on research data, social–environmental retardation must be viewed as dynamic in nature and subject to change through individual, family, or community modification. Early testing has questionable predictive value for adult performance of social–environmentally retarded persons. In some cases, change may occur spontaneously; in others, particularly in situations involving severely adverse living conditions that are prolonged, intervention is essential if retardation of a permanent nature is to be avoided.

INCIDENCE AND PREVALENCE

The incidence and prevalence of mental retardation are closely tied to the social, economic, and health conditions in society and the resources it provides for the education, development, and habilitation of its children and adults. Thus, in underdeveloped countries lacking mass immunization programs, proper nutrition, hygiene and sanitation, prenatal care for pregnant women, and other public health services, the incidence of mental retardation and other disorders is high. Under these conditions, whereas *incidence* may be high, prevalence may be comparatively lower because of excessive infant mortality. In more developed countries, the opposite may be true; that is, there may be fewer casualties of reproduction, but advances in medical practice and ancillary services may greatly increase survival rates and life expectancy.

Given the functional nature of the definition of mental retardation and the role of adaptive behavior, it is clear that social–environmental variations among countries could also affect prevalence. For example, literacy and intelligence may have less adaptive value than strength and manual dexterity in an economy dependent on farming and fishing skills. In these settings, most mildly retarded individuals could meet the natural demands of their environment. Only as they moved to more complex environments would behavioral deficiencies likely become manifest. Although there are no data on the subject, it is reasonable to assume from our

knowledge of etiologies that in underdeveloped countries the incidence of biologically based retardation would be relatively high
(compared to industrialized societies) and the prevalence of mild
retardation comparatively low. These assumptions are predicated
on the bidimensional definition of retardation. The application of a
single criterion of IQ would markedly inflate the prevalence of
mild retardation.

The incidence of mental retardation in the United States is
generally estimated at about 125,000 births per year. There is less
consensus about prevalence data, however. The most widely
quoted figure is 3 percent of the general population, or somewhat
in excess of 6 million persons. This national estimate, although
corroborated by a number of state- or county-wide epidemiological
studies, is based on IQ criteria alone. The data are consistent with
the normal distribution of intelligence, according to which almost
3 percent of the population would fall two standard deviations
below the norm.

Because of the imperfect correlation of intelligence and adaptive
behavior, especially at the upper ends of the intellectual range of
retardation, some authorities have computed the "true" prevalence
of retardation in the United States to be considerably below this
widely cited estimate. Unfortunately, there are no reliable studies
on community-based populations to either refute or confirm this
observation. There can be little question that many individuals with
IQs below 70 who are regarded as retarded during school age lose
this diagnosis in adulthood. The proportion who fall into this
category is unknown. Some may improve in their adaptive capacities with age and maturity; but for others, the change may lie in
the reduced expectations and demands of the environment for the
kinds of intellectual skills needed to master school work.

Age-specific data on prevalence support these notions, doubling
in magnitude from age 0 to 5 years to the 10- to 14-year peak. The
latter age group represents the period of schooling when higher
level mental functions and more complicated abstract thought processes are required for learning. Following this age category, there
is a marked drop in *identifiable* prevalence and possibly true prevalence as well. In estimating adult prevalence, however, we note
that, whereas an unknown percentage of persons with IQs below
70 are not behaviorally impaired, others with IQs above this level

are impaired. A determination cannot be made at this time as to whether these two groups are comparable in size.

The issue of whether 1 percent or 3 percent, or some figure in between, of the general population is mentally retarded has obvious implications for national planning and allocation of needed resources. At the operational level of service delivery, however, such estimates have limited application. For example, anywhere from 10 to 30 percent of the school-age populations of poor rural communities and urban ghettoes are reported to be functioning in the retarded range. By contrast, in affluent communities most retardation is of biological origin, with a far lower prevalence rate. Such marked variations in prevalence between communities highlight the inadequacy of national estimates in determining the extent of the problem at local levels, distributions by age and severity of handicap, and the nature of services required.

In sum, knowledge of incidence and prevalence is still uncertain. The occurrence of mental retardation is influenced significantly by changes in definition, the use of single or dual criteria, variations in environmental conditions, and the inability, in many cases, to identify the cause of retardation or age of onset. Until such issues are resolved or better specified, the magnitude of the problem can be defined only in the grossest terms.

CHAPTER 6

APPLICATION OF THIS CLASSIFICATION SYSTEM TO THE DELIVERY OF SERVICES AND RESEARCH

The classification system that we have presented has many applications, primarily with regard to:

1. The study of the history of mental retardation and the efficacy of preventive measures by analysis of changes in incidence and prevalence in the symptoms over time in general and specific syndromes in particular.
2. Determination of the extent and nature of the problem in specific communities or geographic regions and the associated conditions and factors peculiar to it.
3. Evaluation of the efficacy of service-delivery systems as reflected in intellectual and behavioral change of clients and in the prevention of conditions and disease states related to mental retardation. Such information can provide a realistic base for projecting future service needs and fiscal and resource planning.
4. The study of the onset and progression of various disease states in order to describe their natural history and identify populations at risk.
5. The search for causes of mental retardation by studying the incidence in different groups as defined by demographic, heritability, and experiential factors; behavior; and environment.

SERVICE-SYSTEM MANAGEMENT

Effective management of a service system is dependent on the coordination of classifications and terminologies that are used throughout the system. The primary objective of a delivery system is, of course, the direct provision of services to clients. To a great extent, the quantity and quality of services provided are dependent

79

on the appropriateness and integration of services within a total plan, hence, the concept of case management. Recent trends in case management have been toward the use of interdisciplinary teams for client needs assessment, program planning, and evaluation of outcomes. This approach cannot succeed without common terminology and shared classification systems. For example, using the proposed classification system, the physician on an assessment team would contribute information on etiology of the condition and associated medical problems; the psychologist would provide an estimate of intellectual and adaptive behavior functioning; and the social worker might apply social and environmental information, including the quality of the family and other residential environments. Each team member's contributing information must be meaningful and useful to the rest of the team in order to develop a cohesive plan.

Decisions regarding client placement outside of and within a service system should be based on objective criteria, incorporating such items as age, sex, health status, behavior, and skills development. Subsequent evaluations of placement decisions are most meaningful if the same criteria are taken into consideration. Adaptive behavior data, for instance, have been used to predict successful placement in group homes, to assist in educational placements, and to assess stress factors related to the interinstitutional relocation of clients.

The management of a service system obviously requires a great deal of record-keeping and decision-making that is indirectly related to the actual provision of services. For example, objective data are required to determine client eligibility for various types of financial assistance, such as Supplemental Security Income (SSI) and Medicaid, and to complete utilization reviews to justify the appropriateness and need for services. In another application, service facilities are periodically required to provide data for licensing and accreditation procedures. Service systems must also maintain comprehensive records on services provided, and, to be most effective, they should be compatible with other classification systems, such as cost accounting and client-identifying information. Interagency coordination of activities is greatly facilitated by common classification schemes. A case in point is the use of the AAMD etiology codes; as clients move from one service agency to another, the diagnoses they carry with them communicate valuable information to new agencies with little risk of misinterpretation. Good service-system management relies on parsimonious use of data and maximizing information to assure internal efficiency and enhance communication efforts outside the system.

PLANNING

An analysis of longitudinal movement data (admissions, transfers, caseload totals, average length of service) and information abstracted from the multidimensional factors outlined in this classification system can be instrumental in long-range program planning. A prediction of future population make-up and client flow allows service-system personnel to anticipate needs and plan accordingly. Epidemiological studies on the incidence and prevalence of mental retardation can be especially useful for this purpose. Recent emphasis on deinstitutionalization, for example, has resulted in some large residential facilities caring for more severely disabled clients and community agencies serving greater proportions of mildly disabled people. These changes have affected demands for certain types of programs within the service systems.

New educational legislation (PL 94–142) emphasizes the right to an appropriate education for all handicapped children, including mentally retarded children, and maximum integration with nonhandicapped peers. Educational classifications, handicapping conditions, behavior, age, and school records are data elements critical to effective planning of school programs, facilities, and student–teacher ratios.

The balance between effective service delivery and efficient use of funds is a delicate one. In every service system the ratio of staff to clients served must be considered in planning decisions. Community service agencies have assessed client–staff ratios over a period of time to plan for social worker and casemanager needs and to estimate caseload sizes. Also, recent emphasis on affirmative action has caused service agencies to consider ethnic distribution of clients in staff-hiring procedures.

Historically, residential facilities have used information on behavior, health, etiology, and other client information to assist in grouping residents by programs and in the initial development of program concepts. Similar data have been used in planning for new buildings and allocation of existing space in facilities.

The Developmental Disabilities (DD) State Plan requirement in PL 95–602 calls for a description of the needs and distribution of the state's services resources. Implementation plans for DD service network objectives must be based on a detailed base of information. The guidelines recommend that the population be described by type and degree of disability within specified age groups and geographic divisions and that direct and support service needs be quantified. States with access to an accurate data base can extract the necessary information with relative ease. Compatible classification systems across states are particularly important during this process.

The implications and value of a comprehensive data system for budget planning and justification are obvious. Every aspect of planning is tied closely to resources and priorities, and plans must be quantifiable in terms of numbers and characteristics of persons to benefit from services.

EVALUATION OF SERVICES

A natural extension of the use of a classification system in addition to service-system management and planning is evaluation. Evaluation is often defined as a process by which relevant data are collected and transformed into information for decision-making purposes. The multidimensional factors considered in this classification system can be applied to several aspects of the evaluation of services for retarded populations. Standardized information from the assessment of intelligence, adaptive behavior etiology, associated medical conditions, and the social environment can have particular relevance to the evaluation of the efficacy of service-delivery systems as reflected in intellectual and behavioral change of clients and in the prevention of conditions and disease states related to mental retardation. Such information can provide a realistic base for projecting future service needs and fiscal and resource planning. Evaluation is also considered to go beyond usual research objectives and to extend into judgments of benefit and the politics of program survival. For this and other reasons concerning a very fragmented area representing many political and scientific fields, heated controversies abound in evaluation methods. Listing some general problems common to evaluative efforts should be instructive with regard to the complexity of the process.

1. Evaluators who believe that the introduction of evaluation facts and findings will make an argument more rational and less political are dangerously deluded. There are usually several audiences waiting to use the data in their own way as tactics in a continuing political struggle. Hence, data are frequently being fed into an adversary process.

2. Interventions and programs rarely remain stable over time. Furthermore, clients involved in these programs continually change. Such realities make it extremely difficult to employ traditional methodologies and designs in conducting evaluation studies.

3. An example of tradeoffs involved in evaluation is the conflict between "truth" or scientific validity and immediate relevance or "utilization." The rigor demanded by scientists has frequently led to the charge by program administrators that findings from such efforts are trivial to program staff and lack practical utility. Persons with program concerns usually are interested mainly in enhancing immediate and often idiosyncratic benefits to their clients that fail to generalize to other situations or similar populations. This condition makes their work high on immediate utility but low on external validity. Such conflicts can be reduced if evaluation considerations are worked out prior to the initiation of programs.

4. Many other facets of controversy in the field could be enumerated; however, most of these larger issues surrounding evaluation are beyond the scope of this book and will not be presented. Rather, a narrower approach to evaluation is offered in the context of a classification system. Hence, clinical approaches to evaluation, including scaling, theory, cost-benefit models, client satisfaction, and peer review models, are not discussed.

In the context of this classification system, evaluation refers to the association of services delivered with circumscribed measurable benefits to individual clients. Ideally, an evaluation system should in turn benefit service delivery in the following ways: (a) more effective treatment programs, (b) improved administrative practices, (c) better legislative and public understanding of necessary services, (d) more efficient professional training, and (e) elimination or revision of interventions found to be ineffective.

In general, an evaluation system is based upon a number of stages and related collection forms. Basic to any system is client identification and background information usually obtained on intake. Included are such items as name, address, birthdate, sex, and race. In addition, items on the family make-up, family income, and client problems are used to judge eligibility for service as well as to gain an understanding of factors influencing past development. A second important stage involves diagnosis and evaluation, which should include a psychological and medical evaluation specifying degree of intellectual and adaptive impairment as well as a medical classification based on etiology. This information is important for determining clients' needs and treatment objectives for meeting these needs. Finally, residential placement or living plan and associated services are commonly recorded in order to monitor client movement from one living plan and/or service to another.

Although the preceding information is considered to be important by the majority of states that have implemented evaluation and reporting systems or are planning to, it is of interest that some of the data are frequently unavailable. For example, it is not unusual to find IQs unavailable for as many as one-half of the clients in certain situations who are receiving services under the category of *developmentally disabled*. Mental retardation level is also unreported for perhaps 25 percent of the clients; etiology of mental retardation is estimated to be available for a far higher proportion of persons in institutions than those residing in the community. Some of this missing information is the result of staff time needed for assessments as well as uncooperative clients who are so profoundly handicapped that they are reported to be untestable with standardized instruments.

A conceptual framework for characterizing the service process is suggested that is central to any evaluation model based on client data. The following five stages should be valuable in distinguishing the various modules needed for an evaluation of services provided.

1. A needs assessment based on client-intake information, psychological and medical evaluations, behavior profiling, and case conferencing is necessary. The purpose of this step is to identify individual needs, specify current developmental levels, and set future goals.

2. A program plan that includes individual habilitation or pro-

gram plans, problem-oriented records, and master planning guides is currently in use in many states. The objective of this step is to specify the goals and objectives set for individual clients in a very detailed manner, using either a checklist or written record. Identification of priorities is usually included, and barriers to service delivery are considered.

3. Services provided, including housing plan, are a primary cost consideration and represent a central part of most statewide accounting systems; however, there are currently no standardized service categories in use. Each agency has its own coding system. Under even the most ideal situations service categories must be very complex, including specification of who provides the service, how often, and for what duration. Some work has been done on conceptualizing a master coding system wherein idiosyncratic labels used by any agency could be recoded into a standard service category. Still, usable standardized service categories appear to be only a remote possibility at this time.

4. Client outcome includes the developmental and health status of the individual as monitored by the responsible agency. For obvious reasons, death or communicable diseases have historically been reported by law. Only since the late 1950s has any consideration been given to a more detailed account of retarded persons' health and developmental status. Although health evaluations can be found in the records of most agencies, standardized accounts are usually unavailable. In contrast, developmental records, including adaptive behavior level and educational and vocational status, are becoming very popular. The purpose of this step is to monitor the overall status of retarded individuals on at least an annual basis. It has been common practice to record the developmental progress of nonretarded children through the schools by report cards and standardization examinations. No such tradition exists for retarded individuals. Although there is still resistance by some providers to take this step, it is long overdue and is included in the evaluation component of the new DD Law, PL 95-602. It is equally important to distinguish overall evaluation of developmental progress from selected elements of an individual habilitation plan or problem-oriented record. These latter reports are important clinical tools for documenting the problems that staff members deem important and treatable and for assessing the efficiency of treatment modalities. Such records do not summarize the

overall growth of an individual on a set of prespecified general criteria or domains.

5. The last stage is a review process in which outcome data are interpreted and programmatic changes can be considered. Presumably, the review process can lead to modifications in the previous four stages. Under ideal circumstances all four stages would be computerized and the output used for the review process. Currently, this is not possible for most agencies, particularly in connection with standardized habilitation plans or services. Although some attempts have been made to objectify these components, their measurement needs much more work.

The conceptualization presented here is only one of many such efforts to characterize the service process in terms of an evaluation reporting system. A number of states have computer software and data-collection forms that can be borrowed or modified by other states or agencies interested in a statistical reporting system.

All of these systems use some form of a case number based on a name code for purposes of confidentiality. Since the issue of privacy is currently very important, the AAMD Ad Hoc Committee on Data Banks issued a special report on "Data Bases and the Privacy Rights of Mentally Retarded Persons." They acknowledged that there is a tradeoff between the right to know and privacy that affects retarded people in different ways than it does the population at large in terms of beneficial interventions. Nevertheless, they concluded that personal identification and information should be entered into automated systems only upon legislative mandate or the informed consent of individuals or their legal guardians. In addition, access to specific items of information should be strictly limited to professionals' genuine "right to know," for example, when such information would be of direct personal benefit to the retarded individual.

As mentioned earlier in this section, there are no easily prescribed ways in which evaluations should be done or irrefutable methods to conduct data analyses. We can only discuss briefly the manner in which such data have traditionally been treated with currently available methodologies. In this context the quasi-experimental design has become a popular approach for conducting evaluation in natural settings where data-collection procedures are well scheduled but there can be no control over the clients' exposure to experimental stimuli or treatment program, which makes a true experiment possible. In such situations various statistical procedures and designs are employed to appraise some facet of client outcome (for example, survival or gain in adaptive behavior) relative to the clients' previous status, selection into the program, and other factors not under the investigator's control.

Good experimental designs and appropriate statistical procedures cannot compensate for bad data; hence, consideration must be given to essentials of good measurement, particularly with regard to tests, questionnaires, and rating instruments. In general, well-standardized existing instruments are far superior to makeshift attempts to provide a seemingly more suitable local instrument of unknown reliability, validity, homogeneity or factor purity, or norms. Buros' *Mental Measurements Yearbooks* provide very helpful reviews of instruments for assessment and evaluation.

With the assumption that the measurement process is adequate, a good experimental design would depend on an evaluation of some outcome measure after random assignment of individuals to specified experimental and control groups representing procedures to be evaluated. Because it is usually impossible to accomplish such random assignment in actual practice, statistical procedures may compensate. Accomplishing this task usually depends on a combination of multivariate methods using repeated measurements, such as analysis of covariance and covariance structures, multiple partial and partial correlations with and without corrections for attenuation, stepwise regression, and discriminant functions.

Of particular interest in this context, structural equation modeling of latent variables shows considerable promise through the use of LISREL. This modeling is based on a combination of confirmatory factor analysis and path analysis. Hence, investigators can postulate what variables combine to make a latent variable or factor as well as specify which latent variables are dependent on other such variables. For example, it might be of interest to examine what type of client (characterized by latent factors) benefit from designated environmental factors in terms of positive changes or adaptive behavior factors. Using LISREL, it is possible to hypothesize such relationships and, based on the covariance structure among the observed variables, to test statistically whether the proposed model well fits, or well represents, the observed data.

Other specialized techniques, such as path analysis, cross-legged panel analysis, Markov chains, and quasi-Markov simplex models, are also available. Finally, a hybrid of techniques based on small segments of longitudinal measures over the entire age range of a sample and using a repeated measures analysis of variance has been employed successfully in research on aging for evaluating the shape of growth curves for specified groups of individuals in terms of their environment or treatment experiences. In other words, because it is impractical to study the development of mentally retarded persons over their entire life span, a combination of longitudinal and cross-sectional approaches are required and can be used to estimate a life-span growth curve for particular samples of individuals. Although all of these approaches may appear formidable, explanations and examples of their use can be found in the literature (for example, *American Journal of Mental Deficiency*, *Annual Review of Psychology*).

When used in typical situations where random assignment to programs, environments, or treatments is impossible, findings from these types of procedures are open to other rival explanations that could be used to explain away an effect and hence to question whether a genuine effect of the treatment had been demonstrated. Such rival explanations are due to "threats to validity" and have been discussed extensively in the evaluation literature. Currently, some writers are proposing methods of internal replication to reduce the magnitude of this problem. In addition, because some of these statistical procedures can mask shortcomings regarding the validity of the results reported, it may be advantageous in certain situations to use simple, more descriptive procedures such as interrupted time series designs or the regression discontinuity design. Moreover, giving immediate feedback to the agency providing the data used in the evaluation study could also be a useful check on the validity of the result.

Despite the problems involved with evaluation efforts, most professionals in mental retardation and related fields believe that some attempt to evaluate our services is better than none. In addition, accountability is being demanded by recent legislation on the licensing of facilities and the education of their residents. We must also realize that competent evaluation studies require a relatively comprehensive data-reporting system, which includes individual identification and background information, living plans, and some specification of services received as well as longitudinal data on achievements, health status, and changes in services and placement. This would be facilitated if more service agencies would become involved in this important area.

RESEARCH

One of the most obvious applications of a classification system is to provide a common terminology for research. In mental retardation, standardized definitions of the problem, including specific diagnoses, are essential to studies on causation and prevention, epidemiology and natural history, treatment, and family implications and counseling. If we are to learn more about the organic and behavioral deficits with which we deal and about our modalities of treatment, a standardized classification system must become an integral part of our operations. The need for a greater understanding of the causes of mental retardation in over 75 percent of the individuals so identified is still critical, as is the discovery of more effective treatment and child-rearing programs for all these people.

The mentally retarded population comprises a very heterogeneous group of individuals in terms of behavior and etiology. Planning services, specifying possible causes, and identifying opportunities for prevention require uniform specification of clinical patterns found to exist in individuals labeled retarded. There are five factors, coded for research purposes, currently being proposed in this classification that should be considered in the clinical evaluation of the clients: (a) severity of intellectual impairment, (b) assessment of adaptive behavior functioning, (c) etiology of the condition, (d) associated medical and behavioral problems, and (e) evaluation of the social environment.

Research on causes of mental retardation has historically relied on case findings of individuals diagnosed with a specific disorder. The first step in this process consists of identifying cases in a broad etiological classification in order to select further the subset of individuals of specific interest. Without a uniform method of classifying different subtypes of dysfunctions, the task of casefinding would be impossible. Moreover, it is important to search for cases of mental retardation by studying the incidence in different groups as defined by demographic, heritability and experiential factors, behavior, and environment.

Epidemiological research in the area of mental retardation depends upon a useful classification system. In order to plan services that are adequate to meet the needs of retarded persons, it is necessary to know the numbers of individuals who will make use of them; however, published estimates of prevalence and incidence of retardation demonstrate considerable disagreement. The primary reason for the variability of these estimates lies in the different definitions and procedures used in counting individuals as retarded. Nevertheless, fairly accurate estimates of prevalence of severe mental retardation can be made. The variability is found mainly in the borderline and mildly retarded groups.

Determining the efficacy of preventive measures (for example, rubella vaccinations) by analyzing changes in incidence and prevalence over time requires a classification system. For example, such investigations would include studying the onset and progression of various disease states, describing their natural history, and identifying populations at risk. Other examples include determining the extent and nature of the mental retardation in specific communities or geographic regions and the associated conditions and factors peculiar to it.

We also need research on the effects of a wide variety of intervention strategies, for example, living settings and methods and materials used in education and habilitation. To evaluate such effects, we need uniform, meaningful data. All too often such data are unavailable. Basic data are needed for most applied research regarding natural history, treatment, and family implications. For example, data on the needs and placement of community residents, their subsequent movement, their adaptive behavior and demographic characteristics, and their survival and health status are needed for larger program evaluation and natural history studies. Furthermore, these data serve as baseline information against which to test the efficacy of clinical programs.

Despite recent great achievements in research, there is still much to be learned about the complex phenomena of mental retardation. It continues to be important that more professionals—both clinicians and research scientists—become involved in collaborative research efforts in community and institutional settings. Clients' needs could be better met with concerted well-planned studies. The classification system has been in the past and can continue to be in the future the basic foundation on which to carry out this necessary effort.

CHAPTER 7
CLINICAL APPLICATIONS

MEDICAL MANAGEMENT[1]

Mental retardation is a syndrome, that is, a constellation of clinical manifestations with many etiological factors. This clearly has varying implications from the viewpoint of management and clinical practice.

Diagnosis

Adequate medical diagnosis is a very important aspect of management because it clearly delineates (a) the many medical management problems that may exist, which, if not identified, may not be properly dealt with; and (b) etiological factors as they relate to treatment and perhaps more importantly, prevention. Some causes of mental retardation, such as phenylketonuria and congenital hypothyroidism, if appropriately identified early in life, may be treated and retardation prevented. In other cases even though specific intervention may not result in prevention of mental retardation, there may be implications for medical management to ameliorate the problem. Finally, the delineation of etiology has major implications in long-range planning for prevention, for example, the successful introduction of mass screening programs, immunizations, and identification of genetic disorders that can be prevented by appropriate genetic counseling. Mental retardation is often associated with other handicapping conditions and, of course, the basic state of health of the individuals affected. In general, the more severe the level of retardation, the greater the likelihood of other types of handicapping conditions. Retarded

---

[1] This section is focused mainly on the special medical needs of retarded children. We are aware that retarded adults also have special medical needs, particularly those who have reached an advanced age.

individuals often have a variety of other difficulties. For example, sensory problems are important not only because they occur in a considerable number of retarded persons but also because of the total number of persons in the general population who are afflicted. Sometimes after individuals are identified as being retarded, their evaluation ends, which has caused considerable difficulty in planning for other types of necessary services.

A careful medical history and a physical examination, including appropriate neurological appraisal, is important in assessing retarded individuals and delineating their health status and concomitant medical problems. Laboratory studies can often be of great value but should not be done routinely; X-rays of the skull, for example, generally contribute little but are indicated for specific problems such as microcephaly. More recently, newer techniques such as x-rays using the computerized axial tomographic technique have strengthened our ability to discover abnormal states of brain structure. As valuable as this procedure is, it, too, must be used wisely and, in general, only after careful neurological examination has indicated the possibility of some localized or structural brain deficit. Routine bone x-rays to determine bone age are generally of little value, but in the case of severely retarded children, particularly those with cerebral palsy, delayed bone age may occur. Little correlation has been found between delayed bone age and diminished thyroid function. Similarly, routine studies of thyroid function are generally not indicated. As noted earlier, screening programs for newborn infants can identify the problem of congenital hypothyroidism. This problem, which occurs more frequently than phenylketonuria, can be specifically treated, thus preventing another cause of mental retardation.

The routine use of electroencephalography (EEG) in the diagnosis and assessment of retarded individuals is not indicated. There may be some abnormal findings, but except in the case of epilepsy, it seldom clarifies the clinical problem. The diagnosis of epilepsy is based on clinical findings and cannot be determined only on the basis of an abnormal EEG. There are no specific correlations of an abnormal EEG in any learning or behavioral disorder.

Many severely and profoundly retarded persons have epilepsy. Their resulting problems are often very severe as well as complex, reflecting considerable disturbance of brain function. The management of these seizure difficulties is often much more difficult than are typical seizure problems of nonretarded individuals. Often, more than one medication has to be used, with side effects of drowsiness and poor coordination. Further complications from these medications reflect basic disturbances of biologic function. The management of complex seizure disorders in such people is very difficult, frequently resulting in trying to straddle the fine line where one can have effective management of seizures without undesirable side effects from the medication. The goal of freedom from all seizures is sometimes impossible with individuals having serious disturbance of brain function. People with these complex problems must be carefully evaluated and monitored with regard to the management of seizures, the use of anticonvulsant medications, and ways in which these problems relate to their overall condition and adaptation. Careful medical and often neurologic supervision are crucial.

There have been major advances in the development of laboratory techniques to delineate chromosomal abnormalities. This field of cytogenetics has acquired much new knowledge that has great value in the assessment of some retarded individuals; however, it is unnecessary to do routine studies of chromosomes. Certain clinical manifestations suggest a greater likelihood and indication for these studies. Multiple organ system involvement with maldevelopment of the face, ears, and distal extremities, low birthweight at term, dermatoglyphic peculiarities, and a maternal history of fetal loss are examples that offer reliable clues for selection of children with possible chromosomal abnormalities. The identification of translocation carriers and the tendency for recurrence of the same or other chromosomal aberrations in a family are other indications for chromosome investigation. The hereditary type of Down syndrome resulting from a "normal" parent carrier of a translocated G chromosome is relatively rare; however, young mothers of Down syndrome children should have chromosomal studies since the risk factor for recurrence is at least one to three when the parent is a carrier.

In the past decade much information has been revealed on disorders of metabolism that impair function of the central nervous system and cause mental retardation and/or deterioration. It is impossible to discuss and identify here all of these disorders. Generally, the clinical manifestations are nonspecific, such as failure-to-thrive, and, in many instances, it is extremely difficult if not impossible to establish a specific diagnosis during life. Most of the disturbances of amino acid metabolism can be detected almost immediately after birth when infants are placed on a diet containing sufficient amounts of protein and naturally occurring amino acids. Generally, when a disturbance of amino acid metabolism is present, infants fail to thrive and often have developmental difficulties, which suggests the need for more detailed investigation of possible metabolic errors. On the other hand, routine investigations of metabolic factors are generally not necessary in uncomplicated problems of mental retardation, particularly mild retardation or when other clearly defined causes are present. Certainly, a family history of similar disorders in addition to failure-to-thrive suggests the need for further and careful evaluation for underlying metabolic disorders. More recently, we have initiated the screening of newborns for such potential problems as phenylketonuria, cretinism, or congenital hypothyroidism as well as other metabolic difficulties. These efforts have been very fruitful in identifying and appropriately treating affected individuals, thus preventing mental retardation. The treatment of unusual metabolic disorders is generally performed best in a very specialized central facility identified as having the competence and capacity to deal with these difficulties.

The basic diagnosis and assessment requires careful investigation of biological, psychological, and sociological factors. Because of the high percentage of neuromuscular and communication problems seen in association with mental retardation, these functions must be carefully evaluated. Evaluation by physical and occupational therapists is clear in those cases with evidence of neuromuscular involvement. Because of the difficulty in distinguishing between mental retardation and the still vague area of central communication disorders, careful evaluation by speech and hearing specialists is often indicated. Certain population groups such as Down syndrome are at greater risk for otitis media (infection of the middle ear) and associated deficits in hearing. For this reason such youngsters deserve careful scrutiny for this possible complication.

General Health Supervision

Mentally retarded children require the same, and in many instances more, general health care and supervision as do nonretarded children. Immunizations for the prevention of infectious disease must be given and special needs determined. Diet is important. Some children, particularly those with more severe or complex problems, require frequent routine examinations. These children are often irritable, and increased irritability may be caused by a hidden infection, such as otitis media, abscess of a tooth, or urinary tract infections. Poor dietary and hygienic habits increase the chances for nutritional anemia or intestinal parasitic disease. These factors (plus a possible immunologic deficit as seen in Down syndrome) may lower their resistance to disease and lead to frequent, repeated infections.

Dental care and hygiene is a frequently neglected facet of general health care, particularly for retarded individuals, especially those with Down syndrome, who have a high rate of dental abnormalities. Serious dental decay in such children may be the result of failure to initiate appropriate dental hygiene measures, including proper tooth-brushing skills and the indulgent giving of candy and soft drinks containing sugar.

Physical activity and fitness is beneficial to the general physical health of retarded persons and can add to their socialization, particularly retarded children with associated physical handicaps.

Special Medical Needs

The prevalence of associated physical and sensory handicaps is much greater for moderately, severely, and profoundly retarded individuals and for those in the lower levels of mild retardation.

Physical handicaps. The prevention, amelioration, or correction of physical defects is imperative. Because of their more limited ability to compensate, retarded children are more negatively affected by physical defects than are nonretarded children. Failure to obtain help for such defects will greatly increase the parents' despair arising from the lack of a treatment for the intellectual deficits.

Physical therapy and occupational therapy should be initiated when there is any evidence of neuromuscular imbalance. Evidence has suggested that early application of newer neurodevelopmental techniques, particularly for very young infants, may prevent some of the abnormal muscle tone, incoordination, and deformity associated with cerebral palsy. Parents should be taught proper handling and positioning of their child in order to facilitate more normal motor patterns and reduce the development of deformity; this will also involve them directly in their child's treatment program. These children should spend little time on their back since this usually increases extensor tone and permits less movement. Both prone and side-lying will generally result in improved tone and facilitate the use of upper and lower extremities.

Feeding children with severe cerebral palsy can present a major problem. Since control of the tongue and pharynx is essential to eventual speech production, teaching children to drink and chew has important implications beyond nutrition. In addition, prolonged struggles with frequent choking, gagging, and vomiting can cause serious emotional tension and needlessly prolong the feeding time. Furthermore, without resolution, there is an increased risk for aspiration with resultant lung complications. Relatively simple techniques can greatly facilitate feeding and drinking. The feeding position should be one that breaks up the asymmetric tonic reflex or total hyperextension or hyperflexion of the body. Children with severe sucking and swallowing problems and with functional retrusion of the mandible should be put in the prone position for feeding in order to reduce extensor tone and achieve better position and coordination of the mandible, lips, and tongue.

Surgery plays an important role in some cases. For example, plastic surgery can be used to correct cosmetic deformities. Improving children's appearance can also improve their self-confidence and chances for peer acceptance. Orthopaedic treatment may be necessary for the correction of deformities by either conservative or surgical means. Neurosurgical procedures now make it possible to aid many children with meningomyelocele or progressive hydrocephalus who were formerly considered inoperable.

Communication problems.   Communication problems are common to all mentally retarded persons. Hearing deficiencies should be identified and corrected as early as possible. Newer techniques, including the use of brainstem evoked potentials, can identify such deficiencies early in infancy. The early years are equally critical for language development of retarded and nonretarded children. When appropriate, retarded children can be taught to wear and will benefit from properly fitted hearing aids. Expert evaluation and guidance on the need for speech or language therapy should be obtained during the preschool and early school years since retarded children have a high incidence of articulatory defects, among other aspects of defective speech production. The need for language training devoted to improvements of their cognitive development and social interaction must also be stressed. Speech stimulation within a social setting is often an effective means of improving language and social interaction.

The prevention of obesity of retarded children is often overlooked. Obesity probably results from several factors, ranging from diet to a lack of physical activity. A major factor often is the indulgence and overprotectiveness of parents and individuals who may resort to the giving of food as a sign of their affection. It is even more difficult for parents to place their retarded adolescent on a strict reducing diet. Counseling parents during the infant or toddler stage regarding adequate nutrition may often serve as a very effective measure to prevent obesity. Physical activity is most important in the prevention and management of obesity.

Sleeping. Retarded individuals may have sleeping problems that can result in parental tension and fatigue. Children who rock the bed or bang their head at night present a most difficult management problem. Sedatives and tranquilizers rarely provide long-term solutions for these difficulties. Occasionally, the use of increased physical activity during the day may ameliorate or prevent some sleep difficulties.

Genetic counseling. Genetic counseling has become increasingly important in the area of mental retardation, particularly for those disorders in which the genetic components of the disease that has caused the problem have been clearly identified. In recent years many genetic factors associated with or causing mental retardation have been classified. Counseling has particular implications for the prevention and sometimes the treatment of genetic disorders. In general, risk factors are relatively accurate for disorders associated with known patterns of Mendelian inheritance and less accurate for the chromosomal abnormalities. For mental retardation of unknown origin, additional information is necessary to define risks better. For some disorders, such as Tay-Sachs disease, laboratory tests can identify carrier states in certain individuals, namely, Jews from Central Europe, where the risk is greater for this disorder. Genetic counseling clearly has implications for family planning and therapeutic abortion. Additional information may be obtained from amniocentesis, biochemical screening, and other procedures.

EMOTIONAL–BEHAVIORAL DISORDERS

Description of Disorders

Mentally retarded individuals, particularly those who are severely and profoundly retarded, are known to be at significant risk for the development of emotional and behavioral disorders. In addition, they have high prevalence rates for various types of maladaptive behavior. Epidemiological studies of total populations have shown that many retarded individuals demonstrate high rates of maladaptive behavior as recorded by their parents, and even more demonstrate high rates in the classroom. Parental-rated deviance is three times that of the general population. The teacher-rated behavioral abnormalities are four times that of the general population. In some studies overt psychiatric disorders have been reported in 50 percent of the severely retarded population.

Short attention span is one of the most frequent types of problem behavior of retarded people, but aggression, dysphoria, and poor peer relationships, among others, are also common. This association of problem behavior with low intellectual functioning applies across the whole IQ range, although it is most common at the lower levels. Problem behavior is more frequent in children of low normal intellectual functioning in comparison to children of superior intelligence, just as it is more frequent for severely retarded children than for nonretarded children.

Although both individual types of deviant behavior and overt psychiatric disorders are considerably more common among retarded people than they are among the general population, it is important to recognize that there is *no unique* psychiatric syndrome associated with retardation. Epidemiological studies have shown that the distribution of psychiatric disorders among retarded individuals is about the same as it is for nonretarded people, at least, within the mild range of retardation. Thus, rates of emotional, conduct, personality, and developmental disorders are all higher for retarded individuals than for the general population. Studies that have been conducted in clinic and hospital populations have also shown that psychiatric disorders of retarded persons are just as heterogeneous as they are for persons of average IQs.

There are certain psychiatric syndromes and certain types of deviant behavior that are more common among retarded than nonretarded populations. In general, these tend to be rare conditions and can be considered to be *fairly* prevalent for retarded people (even though they are not characteristic) because of their rarity in the general population. The most important of these is the DSM-III diagnosis of attentional deficit disorder with hyperactivity (also frequently known as the hyperactive child syndrome, the hyperkinetic syndrome, or minimal brain dysfunction). This disorder occurs in about 5 percent of school-age boys and is somewhat more common for retarded children. It is characterized by a short-attention span, gross overactivity inappropriate to the age of the individual, and impulsive behavior. The syndrome is much more common in boys, begins early in life, and, although the activity level manifestations may diminish in adolescence, the syndrome, if untreated, is associated with the development of social and psychiatric pathology in later life. Although it is important to recognize that there is a strong association between this syndrome and mental retardation, one must also recognize that the majority of the children with this syndrome are not mentally retarded. Although the syndrome has been found to be associated with incidents that could have caused brain damage and with overt brain damage, such as cerebral palsy and epilepsy, the majority of the children with the syndrome have no evidence of brain damage.

Two psychotic disorders of childhood—infantile autism and disintegrative psychosis—are also far more common in the retarded population. Infantile autism is characterized by a failure to develop interpersonal relationships, a receptive and expressive language abnormality, cognitive deficits, and ritualistic and compulsive behavior, beginning before the age of about 30 months. The syndrome is rare in the general population. Most children diagnosed as having infantile autism have IQs below 50, but some, perhaps 25 to 30 percent, have IQs as high as 70. Autistic children also show an extreme variability in intellectual functioning, with poor performance on verbal tasks but sometimes good or even superior performance in motor abilities. Infantile autism is also more common among boys. It is one of the few disorders that tends to have an increased prevalence rate in children whose parents are of middle and upper social class status.

It is also important to recognize that the IQ of autistic children does not increase to any great extent with improvement in the autistic child's clinical state. Indeed, IQs of very young autistic children have been shown to be stable and good predictors of intellectual functioning in adolescence and early adult life. In this disorder, the IQ level is also the single best predictor of prognosis for overall adaptive capacity later in life.

Disintegrative psychosis is an even rarer disorder than infantile autism. It is differentiated from autism by a normal period of development up to the age of 2 to 4. At this time, there is a profound regression, often following a period of vague, undefined illness. The regression is characterized by a loss of social skills and speech, a decline in intelligence, and the development of over-activity and stereotyped behavior. There may be clinical signs of neurological impairment. Prognosis is extremely poor.

In addition to these three disorders, which have a strong associa-tion with retardation, there are two behavioral problems that also do—stereotyped repetitive movements and pica. Stereotyped body movements of trunk and hands and self-injurious behavior, such as rocking, are more commonly practiced by severely and profoundly retarded individuals, particularly those in unstimulating envi-ronments. Retarded individuals with added handicaps, such as blindness and lack of ambulatory movement, are more likely to demonstrate stereotyped repetitive movements. Pica is the inges-tion of inedible substances, such as paint or dirt, and is known to occur in young children of all intellectual levels; it is more fre-quently practiced by lower level retarded persons at all ages.

Thus, psychiatric disorders of retarded people may take the form of diverse clinical pictures. The etiology of such disorders among retarded individuals is likely to be related to multiple in-teracting factors; very rarely does a single mechanism account for psychiatric disorder in a retarded individual. For treatment plan-ning, it is important to consider possible mechanisms. Psychiatric disorders of persons with IQs below 50 are likely to be associated with organic brain dysfunction of one type or another. Even for nonretarded children, organic brain dysfunction, particularly in-volving disorders above the level of the brainstem, is highly associ-ated with development of psychiatric disorders. Since a substantial proportion of persons with IQs below 50 have demonstrable or-ganic brain dysfunction, such dysfunction is likely to be the major contributing factor for severely retarded individuals. It is not the only factor responsible for the high rate of psychiatric disorders of retarded persons, however, since this high rate is present among retarded people who have no demonstrable evidence of organic brain dysfunction.

Certain temperamental personality features, such as poor adaptability to new situations, marked irregularity of physiological functioning, high intensity of emotional response, and markedly negative mood have been shown to be important in the genesis of behavioral disorders of nonretarded children. Some of these temperamental characteristics are more common among retarded people and probably play some part in the causation of their psychiatric disorders. Thus, deviant and temperamental characteristics and the presence of organic brain dysfunction are probably the two most important factors associated with psychiatric disorder of severely retarded children. In the case of retarded individuals with organic brain dysfunction, malfunction of the brain is more important than loss of function.

Adverse social consequences, educational failure, general physiological immaturity, social rejection, and language delays may play a more important role in the genesis of emotional-behavioral disorders of mildly retarded persons. Delayed and limited language are very frequent accompaniments of mild retardation. Epidemiological studies indicate that children with speech and language delays have a rate of psychiatric disorders far above that for the general population, and among language-delayed children, a low verbal IQ is frequently associated with the presence of an emotional or behavioral disorder. Since the use of language increases peer interaction, young children and school-age children with poor language may be handicapped in their social and emotional development.

Educational failure from whatever cause is highly associated with the development of psychiatric disorders of all types, particularly conduct disorders. Educational failure may lead to dissatisfaction and status at school, with emotional and behavioral disorders resulting from the lack of status and satisfaction. Although retarded people are certainly not immune to family pathology or family discord that leads to psychiatric disorders in nonretarded people, relatively speaking they are probably affected less by impaired familial functioning.

Finally, certain forms of drug treatment may aggravate preexisting behavioral problems or play a role in the genesis of new behavioral problems for retarded individuals. Likewise, poor quality of care can adversely affect psychological, emotional, and behavioral development of retarded as well as nonretarded persons.

In summary, psychiatric disorders and deviant behavior are more common for retarded than for nonretarded populations. There is no specific type of psychiatric disorder that characterizes retarded individuals; they are just as likely to have neurotic, conduct, or personality disorders. There are, however, certain rare psychiatric disorders, such as infantile autism, that have a strong association with retardation. The mechanisms of the development of retarded people's psychiatric disorders are associated with multiple factors, and an assessment of the relative importance of these factors is needed for proper treatment planning. The assessment and treatment of psychiatric disorders of retarded individuals probably require more skill than they do for treatment of nonretarded people.

Psychopharmacological Management

There are many solid reasons that psychopharmacologic agents should be considered as treatment modalities for certain retarded individuals. As just discussed, retarded individuals are at high risk for the development of psychiatric and behavioral disorders of all types. Many nonretarded people who exhibit such disorders have been shown to respond to certain psychoactive agents. For example, manic episodes may respond very dramatically to lithium; depressive episodes, to tricyclic anti-depressants; and schizophrenic episodes, to major tranquilizers, such as phenothiazines. Moreover, although there are currently no psychoactive agents that *cure* mental retardation, there are many agents that may make some retarded individuals more amenable to *other* forms of treatment. Behavior modification, vocational, and educational rehabilitation programs are difficult to implement for retarded individuals who are grossly hyperactive, distractible, and inattentive. The use of a proper psychoactive agent to alleviate some of this symptomatology may make the primary therapeutic modalities more effective than they would otherwise be.

There are also valid reasons why psychopharmacologic agents should be used judiciously with retarded people. Psychoactive drugs, as do all medications, may have unpleasant side effects and idiosyncratic effects, and like any other effective form of therapy, psychopharmacologic agents may be misused in an attempt to substitute for insufficient or inadequate staff members or the absence of other therapeutic modalities.

The fact that an agent can be misused, however, is not an argument for not using the agents at all. The control of negative aspects of a retarded individual's behavior and other serious symptomatology by psychoactive agents is not different from the control desired in any other therapeutic endeavor of medicine, whether it be vaccination, surgery, or some other type of intervention.

The decision to use psychoactive agents with retarded individuals should be based on the severity of the condition, what is known about the untreated outcome, and the clinical efficacy and safety of the medication. In essence, clinicians must answer the questions: Is there a psychopharmacologic agent that is clinically effective for any of the retarded individual's symptoms? Is this drug not only effective but safe? Among the choices of drugs, which might be used for the current set of symptoms, that is, what is the best drug? What other therapeutic modalities will be necessary in this individual case in addition to the use of some psychoactive agent?

General principles of psychopharmacology. No drug should be instituted without a comprehensive diagnostic evaluation, which should include observations and information from as many sources in the retarded individual's life as possible, including parents, ward staff, school personnel, and the patients themselves. Evaluation should include a physical and neurological examination and appropriate laboratory studies, as well as psychological evaluation. In the physical examination, at least a screening of all body systems should be done, with particular emphasis on the central nervous system.

Prior to starting any medication, a proper baseline assessment should be made of *all* the target functions that are likely to be affected by the use of the medication. It is almost imperative to have some measure of learning as a way of assessing the effects of any medication; there is some evidence that certain psychoactive medications may be effective in controlling behavior but have *adverse* effects on school performance.

The primary factor in the selection of a psychopharmacologic agent should be solid clinical evidence in the literature of its safety and efficacy for the clinical symptomatology to be treated. Unless there is a great deal of experimental evidence for the superiority of a new drug, a familiar and tested drug should be used as a first choice. Except in cases of severe acute symptomatology, which may require initial loading doses, the initial dosage of the medication should probably be the smallest available dosage. A knowledge of the duration of action of any medication is necessary. In general clinical use a medication will probably have to be carefully titrated until a clinical improvement is noted or until side effects occur that necessitate discontinuation or a decrease in dosage.

In general, there are few laboratory measures by which medication can be titrated. Clinical judgment must be relied on, based on information obtained from individuals in the retarded patients' environments and based upon direct observation of the patients. The same ratings of behavior (for example, attention span, perceptual speed) that were taken initially at baseline should be made at regular intervals. All other appropriate assessments, such as measurements of learning, height, weight, and neurological functioning, should also be carried out on a regular basis.

In general, there are only rough guidelines that one can use for optimal dosage of individual drugs on a milligram per kilogram of body weight basis for retarded persons; however, each case must be treated individually since there are large individual differences in blood level for comparable dosages of the same drug in people of the same body weight. Except for unusual circumstances, retarded individuals on chronic psychoactive medication should be given a drug-free trial at some time during the course of treatment. No psychoactive medication should be used any longer than is necessary to control the clinical symptomatology.

Finally, if psychoactive medications are being administered and are effective in ameliorating clinical symptomatology, clinicians still have the responsibility of identifying and eliminating possible causes of the emotional or behavioral disorder that is being treated by the psychoactive medication.

Effects of psychotropic agents. All drugs have multiple clinical effects and affect multiple bodily systems, all of which must be taken into account when a particular agent is used. The most important effects are on physiological systems of the body, activity level, cognitive functioning and performance, academic achievement, behavior, personality, and mood.

There are various ways to measure each one of these parameters, including physical examination, observations, and various types of electrical and mechanical instruments. Different measures of the same parameter may not yield the same results.

Psychotropic agents can be classified as follows:

Therapeutic Classification	Chemical Classification	Representative Trade Names
Stimulants	Sympathominetic Amines	Dexedrine Ritalin
	Xanthines	Cylert
	Acetylcholine Analogues	Deaner
Antipsychotics	Phenothiazines	Thorazine Mellaril Prolixin
	Butyrophenones	Haldol
	Thioxanthenes	Taractan Navane
Antidepressants	Tricyclics	Tofranil Elavil Sinequan
	Monoamine oxidase Inhibitors	Marplan Parnate Nardil
Sedative & antianxiety agents	Barbiturates	Phenobarbital
	Benzodiazepines	Valium Librium Tranxene
	Propanediols	Miltown Equanil
	Antihistamines	Benadryl Atarax Vistaril
Anticonvulsants	Phenytoin	Dilantin
	Phenobarbital	Phenobarbital
	Primidone	Mysoline
	Carbamazeprine	Tegretol
	Valproic Acid	Depakene
	Ethosuximide	Zarontin
	Acetazolamide	Diamox
	Clonazepam	Clonopin
	Benzodiazepines	Valium

Stimulants. Common stimulant drugs include the ampheta-
mines, methylphenidate (Ritalin) and magnesium pemoline
(Cylert). Deanol (Deaner) has been used much less extensively. As a
group these stimulants have a wide variety of indications for psychiatric usage for nonretarded children. A definite indication is
attention-deficit disorder with hyperactivity. Other possible indications include conduct disorders and specific learning disorders that
are due to major problems with attention.

There is a large body of research supporting the use of this class
of drugs with nonretarded individuals. Stimulants have not·been
widely used with retarded people, although theoretically they
might be expected to improve the same types of behavioral problems (hyperactivity, short attention span, and impulsivity) for retarded people as they do for some nonretarded individuals. What
little research there is with this class of drug, however, does not
support this proposition. In the great majority of studies with
retarded subjects using stimulants of various types, investigators
have reported largely negative results. Some have actually found a
decrease in rate of learning of retarded people secondary to the use
of stimulants.

There is only speculation as to why the effects of drug usage may
be very different for retarded and nonretarded individuals; however, there is some suggestion that retarded individuals may have a
narrower field of attention and that the effect of the stimulants
would be to narrow this even further, resulting in no change while
on the drug or worsening in certain cases. It is possible that specific
subgroups of retarded people with certain symptoms might benefit
from the stimulants, but at present this is only conjecture.

Antipsychotics. The antipsychotics are often called major
tranquilizers or neuroleptics. Those most commonly used with
retarded individuals include the phenothiazines, namely, chlorpromazine (Thorazine) and thioridazine (Mellaril). The
butyrophenones, particularly haloperidol (Haldol) are now also
more commonly used with retarded people.

Antipsychotics are useful in the treatment of the major psychoses
of nonretarded people. The ones that respond most dramatically
are those meeting the clinical criteria of classical schizophrenia:
formal thought disorder, hallucinations, or delusions. Individuals
with manic episodes also respond positively to antipsychotics. The

"psychoses" common to retarded individuals, however, namely, early infantile autism and disintegrative psychosis, do not necessarily respond as well as do those clear-cut psychoses of nonretarded people.

The phenothiazines are among the most commonly used drugs with retarded populations and also the most extensively researched. A good deal of this research lacks methodological rigor, however, and conclusions are thus very tenuous. Although uncontrolled studies suggest that problem behavior of retarded people, such as hyperactivity, aggression, stereotyped movements, self-injury, and destruction, may be controlled with the use of antipsychotic agents, the conclusions must be tempered by the fact that much of the research is methodologically flawed. There is better evidence to suggest that thioridazine is more useful in altering these types of maladaptive behavior of retarded individuals; however, with both chlorpromazine and thioridazine, there may be impairment of cognitive function. Thus, clinical judgment is imperative in the use of these antipsychotic agents for these nonpsychotic types of behavior.

The limited evidence published to date from controlled studies does suggest that haloperidol may be better than either of the phenothiazines in treating retarded persons, again for those nonspecific kinds of behavior such as hyperactivity, aggressiveness, and stereotypes; however, the effect of the drug for this type of individual is clearly not antipsychotic. The action of these agents on retarded persons is only to make certain individuals with maladaptive behavior more manageable and more amenable to other forms of therapy, such as educational or behavior-modification programs.

Antidepressants and antimanic agents. The antidepressants are among the most widely researched drugs in adult and child psychiatry. The established clinical indications for the use of tricyclic antidepressants with nonretarded individuals include a major affective disorder (namely, unipolar and bipolar depression), enuresis, and attention deficit disorder with hyperactivity. Possible indications include separation anxiety, conduct disorders, and specific learning disabilities. There is, however, essentially no research with regard to behavioral and cognitive effects of these drugs on retarded persons. Such individuals may lack the communicative

ability to report major affective disorder, and indeed the symptoms
of major affective disorder may be somewhat different for retarded than for nonretarded people.

Lithium is unique in psychopharmacologic usage in that it is the
first drug to be commonly monitored by blood levels, and it seems
to be effective for not only the active phase of an illness but has
some preventive effect as well. The established clinical indications
for the use of lithium with nonretarded people are the manic phase
of bipolar affective disorder and as a preventive for both manic and
depressive episodes of individuals with bipolar affective disorder.
Possible indications include a depressive episode of individuals who
have bipolar affective disorder and of aggressive individuals who
have no evidence of affective disorder.

There are a limited number of uncontrolled and controlled
studies suggesting that depressive symptomatology and hyperactive aggressive behavior of retarded persons may be positively
influenced by lithium carbonate; however, as with many other
drugs, much more research is needed.

Sedatives and antianxiety agents. The sedatives include the barbitu-
rates, discussed with the anticonvulsants, and the commonly used
antianxiety agents, including the benzodiazepines, the propanediols, and the antihistamines. These drugs are effective for the
anxiety disorders of nonretarded adults and have some usefulness
in treating insomnia, nightmares, terrors, and somnambulism.

Some studies of the benzodiazepines, especially those that are
well controlled and well designed, suggest that they may actually
increase undesirable behavior of retarded people. Likewise, there
is little evidence to suggest that the propanediols are effective with
retarded individuals, and the research with hydroxyzine is very
inconsistent. There are no well-controlled studies establishing the
effectiveness of the antihistamines, such as diphenhydramine
(Benadryl) with retarded individuals. Clearly, all of these drugs require much more research before their use with retarded individuals can be recommended with any confidence.

Anticonvulsants. Anticonvulsants are not psychotropic drugs per
se; however, they are included in this discussion because they are
used to treat a substantial number of retarded individuals who have
seizure disorders. Also, there is a school of thought that suggests
that nonretarded individuals who have certain types of behavior
and learning problems may in fact respond positively to an-

tiepileptic agents, even in the absence of clinical seizures. The evidence for this type of treatment of behavior and learning problems for nonretarded individuals is almost nonexistent, however. The studies have been done primarily with phenobarbital and phenytoin. It is possible that more modern drugs such as carbamazepine and ethosuximide may have more positive effects. There is some literature, again with nonretarded individuals, that those with definite seizure disorders treated with anticonvulsants may either have an improvement or a decline in mental functioning after treatment with anticonvulsant drugs. The interpretation of either an increase or a decline is made very difficult, however, because of multiple possibilities of either of these occurrences. Studies with phenytoin and phenobarbital do suggest that there may be a deterioration of mental function of nonretarded epileptic individuals, but it is not clear whether the deterioration in mental functioning is due to the drug effect, worsening of seizure activity, a degenerative process, or some other unknown possibility.

Some investigators have reported improvement in certain mental functions during use of carbamazepine and ethosuximide, but again the improvement may be due to the drugs' effect on seizure activity rather than any direct effect on mental functioning. Because anticonvulsants are used so frequently with retarded persons, much more research is needed with regard to their behavioral and cognitive effects on retarded individuals with seizure disorders.

In summary, results of several surveys suggest that somewhere between 40 to 50 percent of retarded residents of large facilities are on some type of psychoactive medication and between 25 and 35 percent of them receive anticonvulsant medication. Much less is known about the employment of these agents with retarded individuals who live in smaller settings; however, one study suggests that about 20 percent of them are either on a psychoactive agent or an anticonvulsant. In view of such common employment, one would expect a large amount of evidence to support such usage; however, although open studies indeed suggest that certain psychoactive drugs are effective for specific symptoms in certain retarded individuals, solid methodological evidence for their efficacy is lacking.

As has been noted previously, the methodology is flawed in much of the drug research with retarded subjects. Retarded individuals have been treated as heterogeneous groups, with no attention paid to subgroups based on behavioral, biochemical, biological, or other parameters. Thus, we know little about diagnostic indicators as to which retarded individuals might respond positively to which drug. Also, the long-term positive and negative effects of these drugs for retarded persons have not been extensively studied. Follow-up investigations of consistently treated individuals with and without psychotropic medication are lacking. Long-term studies with nonretarded individuals on certain psychotropic medications, such as major tranquilizers, suggest that there is a physiological risk with continued usage. These risks are not likely to be any less for retarded people, and in view of the fact that the established benefit of these drugs has not been conclusively proved for retarded people, clinical judgment must be on the conservative side for the use of these drugs to treat retarded people who exhibit maladaptive behavior.

Two of the most glaring omissions in psychopharmacological research with retarded persons are lack of measures relating to learning and how it is affected by psychoactive agents and the comparison of psychoactive agents alone and in combination with other treatment modalities used commonly with retarded people, most of whom are in special education programs and many of whom are in behavior-modification programs.

LIVING ARRANGEMENTS

In the past it was not unusual for clinicians to make drastic life-long decisions affecting the lives of people who were labeled as mentally retarded simply on the basis of that diagnosis. This obviously is not possible to do quickly with any degree of accuracy. These "life-affecting" decisions must be made in progressive stages.

Clinicians, working with retarded persons and/or their families, must be prepared to handle the practical details of advisory guidance—the details of everyday care of management in the natural home and the community—and, if necessary, be prepared to assist in guiding retarded people into living arrangements outside the natural home. In order to be successful in assisting these people in choosing the most appropriate residence, clinicians must have intimate knowledge not only of the resources of these individuals and their families, but also the community, state, and private resources. Clinicians must know the quality, variety, and availability of the resources. Arrangements must be flexible in order to meet the changing needs of retarded individuals.

The diagnosis of mental retardation, or the current functional level of mental retardation as determined by standardized tests, is not necessarily an accurate predictor of what would be the most appropriate residence. Strengths and weaknesses of the natural family setting and age, behavior, and social skills of the clients all must be carefully assessed.

Specific and particular needs of clients must be carefully determined. Although mental retardation may be the presenting complaint, associated handicaps, such as visual and auditory defects, neuromuscular disorders, orthopedic defects, and emotional disorders, must be considered. Mental retardation itself may not be the most disabling condition of the person under consideration.

It is true that the decision to place retarded individuals in residences other than their natural homes is often determined by factors other than their particular needs. The emotional stability and attitudes of the family, presence of other children in the family, age of the parents, economic status of the family, local and state customs, attitudes, policies, and laws all impinge on placement decisions. Appropriate living arrangements must be planned only after evaluation of a number of environmental and individual characteristics. Adaptive behavior assessments, when thoroughly and accurately done, are especially useful. The most practical assessments in making decisions for living arrangements would probably be one or more of the so-called "personal distress" or "family distress" scales, coupled with a determination of the individual needs of clients.

BEHAVIORAL AND EDUCATIONAL MANAGEMENT

The primary educational purpose of a classification system in mental retardation is not the development of a detailed program blueprint for a specific individual; however, information about a person's current level of intellectual functioning is useful in curriculum and program planning. For example, much of the evidence about learning characteristics of mildly retarded children suggests that they learn new skills in the same general sequence as do nonretarded children. Whether children of lower levels of mental retardation go through the same sequences is less clear, but evidence suggests that the highest stage in the sequence that can be predicted for severely retarded children will be well below that of nonretarded children. Such knowledge is useful in long-range planning and thus aids in selection of long-range goals and the specific objectives derived from such goals.

In areas such as speech development and correction and in motor-skills development, the classification system can provide guidelines for decision-making about the age at which corrective intervention might be most effective; for example, there is little reason to believe that speech therapy for articulation disorders of moderately retarded children will be effective during the early school-age years, but such therapy may be helpful to such children during adolescence. On the other hand, *language* training for young moderately retarded children may be effective.

Since many of the skill areas in which behavioral and educational interventions are used are also skill areas measured with adaptive behavior scales, knowledge of classification of a child is directly related to planning for service delivery. Thus, the understanding generated by use of a classification system may be helpful as one aid in planning for educational, habilitation/rehabilitation, behavioral adaptation, vocational training, and living arrangements for individuals as well as for groups.

Human learners are complex. Specialists who provide services designed to meet specific objectives recognize the interrelationships among objectives for the same person. Moreover, specialists from different disciplines have used similar methodologies; for example, both speech therapists and educators are concerned with language development, and both behavior managers and vocational teachers are interested in task analysis. Recognizing the overlapping of responsibility, specialists may select specific targets for primary emphasis and may continue to support the development of other skills at the same time.

Education

A spectrum of educational services is available today, some dating back many years. Until the second half of the 20th century, formal educational provisions for retarded students consisted of essentially three options, all still available. Early provisions included:

1. *Residential placement in a community for retarded persons, with educational training part of a 24-hour-a-day program.* In most of these placements, instruction of a formal nature took place in a variety of settings—in school buildings near dormitories, dormitories, or recreational buildings, and during field trips to various places. In some large residential settings, however, educational opportunities were reported to be quite limited. Most state-supported facilities (for example, large state schools, hospitals, colonies) maintained a separate school building in which educational instruction was provided for school-age residents and sometimes for those beyond the legal school age specified by the state. Such residential placements were available in almost all states, but less than 10 percent of retarded persons in the population were admitted at any time during life to residential state facilities.

2. *Separate special classes for mildly retarded students were provided in many public schools.* In EMR classes for mildly retarded students (called educationally handicapped in some states), which were usually for groups of 12 to 15 students, the acquisition of basic academic skills was emphasized. Where possible, methods featured actual experiences and "learning by doing" as a part of the instruction. Thus, projects such as field trips to various sites in the larger community might include visits to manufacturing plants, post office, or city hall as a way of increasing the meaningfulness of concepts being taught. At no time in the history of special education provisions in this country were more than 60 percent of educable-level students in the nation so served. Those EMR students who were not in special separate classes usually stayed in regular classes without organized special instruction until they reached the upper age limit for compulsory schooling; they then left the school system and attempted to find work in the competitive market place. A few states prior to 1975 provided special classes for moderately retarded students, usually called TMR (TMH, trainable). Until the implementation of PL 94-142, however, only a small proportion of school-age children who were moderately, severely, or profoundly mentally retarded received any public school education. The TMR population that was not served by public schools had the option of staying at home or being admitted to a state residential community.

3. *No systematic provisions by the systems for educational instruction.* Many retarded children stayed in their own homes (or in

some cases private residential facilities) and received what was for
the most part informal instruction in daily living activities, some
understanding of the world around them, and perhaps relatively
unstructured or uncoordinated instruction in basic academic skills.
For slow learners and mildly retarded children, it was not uncommon to have an apprentice-like educational program in which
students learned by observing, modeling, and practicing.

Several states enacted sweeping revision of their special education laws in the late 1960s and early 1970s; these were followed in
1975 by Congressional passage of PL 94-142, Education for All
Handicapped Children Act. Both the revised state laws and the
new federal law mandated education for all school-age children, no
matter how severely impaired. Every child became entitled to a free
and appropriate education at no cost to the family, to include not
only special education but other necessary services, such as
transportation and speech and physical and occupational therapy.
Each child was entitled to receive an individual educational plan
(IEP) suited to his or her needs and characteristics.

Schools were given the mandate to develop new or expanded
programs for severely and multiply handicapped students. The
system of educational programming is in many respects consistent
with the classification system discussed in Chapter 4; that is, educational provisions are related to chronological age and level of retardation. The development of a wide spectrum of educational
services and the relationship between certain types of service and
level of retardation was not mere professional whim, but represents
the application of results of hundreds of investigations and obser-
vational efforts to determine program effectiveness.

Thus, the spectrum of services available today includes all three
of the older types of provisions and several newer ones. The important point is that the classification of an individual as mentally
retarded and the specification of the level of retardation provide
guidelines for selection from the spectrum of services and give
some clues to the type of educational service appropriate for a
particular person at a given time.

The most common educational provisions to be found nation-
wide in the 1980s are described briefly in the following discussion;
social policy emphasizes using the least restrictive alternative. Provisions are listed in order of what is assumed by many professional
educators to range from the least to more restrictive alternatives.

We must recognize, however, that one provision may be more or less restrictive, depending on the way in which that provision is administered or implemented and the nature of the student's disability, so the hierarchy should be seen as only roughly indicating degree of restriction. These administrative arrangements that place retarded children with regular class pupils and teachers for a considerable portion of the school week are popularly referred to as "mainstreaming." In general, the types of provisions used today are:

1. *Public-school-supported educational services to and through regular classroom teachers who provide some type of special and systematic help within a regular classroom setting.* This special help might include the purchase of specific equipment or materials, the provision of teacher aides, or other assistance for educating retarded children in integrated classrooms of the educational system.

2. *Provision of special education resource personnel in public schools.* Such resource personnel work with retarded children in small groups or individually and for limited periods of time, usually daily, in settings outside the regular classroom into which retarded students are integrated for the major portion of the school day.

3. *Programs in which retarded students are provided education in public schools in settings in which a major portion of the school day is spent in a separate classroom.* Although classrooms are substantially separate, integration is used in those aspects of the school program in which retarded children are not at a major disadvantage. Curriculum emphasis is on learning functional skills, including basic academics for students who can master them.

4. *Programs in which retarded students are taught in a substantially separate setting (for example, classroom) within the public school or in a private school that provides the service on contract from a public school.* Students in such programs are those for whom the competition of a regular classroom or regular school is probably disadvantageous. Most students in such programs are seriously retarded. Moderately retarded and some severely retarded students would probably be in one type of separate class program whereas other severely and profoundly retarded students whose physical impairments are not prohibitive would receive most of their educational services in another group. Sheltered workshops are used for such young adults.

5. *Programs in special day schools for retarded individuals who have some additional handicapping condition(s).* Some retarded individuals have need for physical, occupational, or medical therapy or other specialty services. In small communities, and even in some urban communities where travel facilities are adequate, special schools may be developed for provision of services to students whose cognitive problems are complicated by difficulties in motor coordination. Such special schools are relatively rare, but they represent one step in a continuum of educational services. Their existence exemplifies the interrelationship between educational and other habilitative needs. Students in such programs are, like most retarded children, able to live with their own families and have the benefits of family life as well as a variety of needed services in a habilitative setting.

6. *Provision for instruction at home or in a hospital setting.* This provision may be the treatment of choice for direct educational service for seriously handicapped children for whom transportation may be hazardous, those who have multiple problems, retarded children identified at an early age for whom preschool home activity is planned, and children who are hospitalized for medical treatments.

7. *Programs in residential settings in which educational and other habilitative services are provided in a single setting away from family or natural home.* Such 24-hour care settings may be small units located in ordinary neighborhoods or larger facilities (usually subdivided into units) located on several acres of land. Although they may not be a part of the school system, and thus supported by some governmental agency other than the educational system, they are supported by tax funds. In some states, the local educational agency (LEA) is responsible for financial support even though the facility is managed by a mental health or state mental retardation agency. A small proportion of the retarded population is in private residential schools and may be supported by either tax funds through a contract or by the family.

The residential living setting has been considered by many professionals as the most restrictive of the alternatives. Therefore, other alternatives for provision of services are usually given first consideration. In making decisions, specialists must recognize the variability of programs within each type of provision and decide on an individual basis. As a general rule, the less handicapped the child, the less restrictive is the educational alternative.

Special Skill Training

Communication skills. A substantial proportion of the retarded population has additional disabilities. Speech and language handicaps are particularly prevalent, especially for moderately to profoundly retarded persons. The degree of speech and language delay or disability is related to the degree of retardation.

Most severely retarded and all profoundly retarded persons demonstrate severe language delay and will develop only minimal communication skills of any type, even as adults and with intensive training. One approach in recent years that has led to improvement in the development of communication for such persons was the design of techniques to teach some system of sign language or meaningful gestures. Efforts to improve spoken language of severely and profoundly retarded people had been minimally effective; the recent development of various alternative forms of communication has resulted in considerable improvement in adaptation through communication with careproviders and peers.

One such approach is the use of communication boards. These may be very simple homemade devices or quite complex, expensive ones. In one such system, Bliss symbols, pictorial representations of words are used; for example, a valentine heart represents emotion and additional symbols indicate the type of emotion. Other systems may be boards with many pictures representing objects or events of daily life, and nonverbal individuals can point to the pictures to facilitate communication with others and thus increase their range of interpersonal contacts. Staff members in educational and institutional settings have been highly inventive in devising boards that depict relevant aspects of life, and a large number of the communication boards in use are made to meet the needs of particular individuals, especially those with serious motor handicaps. Some boards are available commercially.

Other communication facilitators include electronic devices or modified typewriters and computers that can be manipulated with minimal use of muscles. Some severely retarded individuals have been taught to use small toy-like objects to communicate; these are usually designed for specific persons and may include such items as a cup, a spoon, or other object that represents needs.

In contrast to severely and profoundly retarded individuals, moderately to mildly retarded people are likely to be able to develop useful communication skills, including spoken language. The communication level ultimately reached by retarded individuals, however, may be somewhat limited. Language training by speech and language specialists or teachers having access to language consultants may be provided for a large proportion of the moderately retarded population; for mildly retarded people the development of language skills is likely to be the responsibility of parents and regular or special education teachers.

Speech or language disability combined with mental retardation is the most common of all the dual disabilities, according to federal reports. Identification of the level of retardation provides guidelines for decision-making about the type of services most likely to be effective, determination of age at which progress may be expected, and reasonable long-term goals. The development of improved language skills may make other changes in level of functioning possible so that individuals may move from a more severe to a less severe level of functioning. Some individuals with mild retardation may use newly developed language skills to increase other skills and thus may lose the designation of mental retardation.

Motor skills.   Special services in the area of motor-skills training and remediation are commonly needed by mentally retarded students, particularly those who are more seriously retarded. Although not as frequently required as speech and language help, such service is of considerable importance for retarded persons whose gross- and fine-motor skills are inadequate. Unlike deficient language, motor disabilities are not necessarily concomitant with retardation. Many of the same kinds of treatment and training are needed for nonretarded and retarded persons to develop gross-motor skills, often under the supervision of or by physical therapists, and fine-motor skills, taught by or under the supervision of occupational therapists. The degree of retardation provides indications about approaches to use or complexity of instructions; verbal instructions suitable for nonretarded students may need modifications or supplementation, for example, demonstrations.

Provisions for practice may need to include ensuring that assistants are present to help with the exercises.

Social and leisure skills. Development of mentally retarded persons' recreational and social skills may be quite beneficial. Although educational and physical educational programs have included some recreational activities and social skills training in past years, specific focus on this area by specially trained staff and systematic programs are relatively recent developments. Almost all residential facilities, many community programs, and some other programs feature recreation specialists, adaptive physical educators, and programs in training in interpersonal skills and group social activities.

Most instruction in social and leisure skills takes place within groups. For some individuals at some times, however, it may be necessary to develop individualized training schedules to help in acquisition or maintenance of certain basic social skills or to decrease inappropriate social behavior.

Programs designed to aid retarded persons to live as independently as possible will help them develop and maintain social skills that can be used in a variety of social settings. Helping retarded persons learn skills will facilitate self-initiated recreational activities during times when work and other required activities are completed. Although one cannot always tell whether an activity is work or play, particularly if the work carries no remuneration, using one's time constructively can be beneficial in many ways, particularly in development of a sense of self-worth.

Retarded persons, when they are in groups that include non-retarded persons, will probably have to deal with discrimination. Those who are able to minimize their "difference" in behavior and appearance are likely to suffer less discrimination than are those whose behavior or appearance varies markedly. Specialists who can assist in development of acceptable social skills and interpersonal behavior may make good adjustment to the environment possible for many retarded persons. Specialists engaging in such training represent several disciplines, for example, teachers who emphasize social activities as part of daily activities in classes, psychologists who design social skill training programs and/or understanding of group dynamics, and psychiatrists who work with families of retarded individuals in psychodynamic therapeutic settings. For spe-

cific training aimed at eliminating problem behavior, knowledge of
an individual's classification as retarded and of the level of retardation can aid in planning. For example, behavior-modification techniques appear to be especially appropriate for severely retarded
nonverbal children and adults and for behavior that can be precisely specified. Applied behavioral analysis is much more difficult
to implement with mildly retarded adolescents and adults who have
learned to engage in asocial or antisocial activity.

In the preceding discussion the use of some of the specialty
disciplines was intended to be illustrative. Numerous other examples would have been cited if space permitted, including training
and therapy, religious instruction, arts and crafts, and music instruction and therapy. Workers from any of these or many other
disciplines can find illustrations of applicability.

Work

In the United States the term *work* is defined by some agencies of
the federal government and some career-development education
specialists as inclusive of both paid and unpaid constructive activity.
It is a general goal of our society and of the educational system to
prepare students for assumption of an effective place in society.

When America was young and this country was agrarian, there
was little problem in helping young persons similar to those now
considered to be mildly retarded engage in productive employment when those persons reached the appropriate age. Many jobs
were simple enough to be learned through demonstrations, ap-
prenticeship activities, or relatively informal instructions. As in-
dustrialization and technology became prevalent in American society, opportunities for easy training and employment of handicapped persons of all types became somewhat more limited. Today
it is necessary to do a very careful evaluation of the employment
market as well as of disabled persons' skills if they are to be provided with opportunities to maximize work potential.

Opportunities that appear to hold the most promise for employment of mildly retarded persons include some of the service
occupations and semi-skilled work. The complexity of the work
that can be performed satisfactorily by retarded persons is directly
related to the degree of retardation. Survey data from recent
studies indicate that about 75 percent of the youth who are iden-

tified as mildly retarded during secondary school years will probably engage in competitive employment and handle their own financial affairs (sometimes with the help of family, friends, or advocates). Many obtain jobs as assistants to skilled craftsmen (for example, bricklayers, carpenters, bakers). Others work in industrial settings at tasks that may require decision-making without highly complex reasoning. Retarded persons who have learned good work habits are likely to be excellent and valued employees; like non-retarded persons, they are likely to lose their jobs if they have poor interpersonal skills or work habits.

Since the majority of retarded persons are mildly retarded and since most of that group are employed competitively, we can say that most retarded adults in the population are employed. The picture for moderately, severely, and profoundly retarded persons, however, is less bright. With preparation, and within a sheltered workshop, a large proportion of those who are in the moderately retarded range and some in the severely retarded range can engage in simple but useful work activity. Such employment, however, should not be expected to produce sufficient wages to provide financial independence. The type of work that moderately retarded adults can do includes supervised assembly of parts, packaging of materials, sorting, and other tasks that do not demand a high level of discrimination or problem-solving. All such tasks must be performed under careful supervision. Usually, in sheltered workshops employees are paid at the proportion of the hourly wages of nonretarded workers, depending on the amount of work that they can do compared to nonretarded workers.

Some professionals concerned with mental retardation have strongly advocated training moderately retarded persons and some severely retarded ones to perform household tasks such as cleaning and sorting clothing, as there is evidence to indicate that many housework activities are within their capabilities. In home settings, there is likely to be a parent or other adult who can supervise and monitor as well as encourage the worker. While living in their own homes, retarded people can be productive family participants and may feel more worthwhile if they can perform useful household duties. Therefore, whether moderately and severely retarded persons are able to develop skills that make them employable, training for care of their own living space and for doing some routine household chores is recommended by most educators. Such training is often provided after basic self-help skills are learned and along with higher level self-help skills. For at least some moderately retarded persons, it may be possible to use household skills in appropriate settings, for example, working under direct supervision in hotels or motels.

The very small proportion of the retarded population who are profoundly retarded and many of the severely retarded group (who together make up a small percentage of the retarded population) will be unlikely to develop sufficient occupational skills to maintain employment, especially if the job is competitive. Despite evidence from research laboratories that profoundly retarded adults can be taught, with careful task analysis and sequence of instruction, to do such tasks as simple assemblies, there is little evidence to suggest that profoundly retarded persons and most severely retarded ones will be able to work in any competitive setting or to transfer their knowledge from one skill of assembly to another. It is therefore especially important to help them develop skills in leisure-time activities and to provide work training when and if possible without assuming that a long-term job, even in a sheltered workshop, is a realistic goal. This may also be true for a proportion of the moderately retarded group, particularly those with additional limitations in motor activity and communication skills. Moderately retarded people constitute about 12 percent of the retarded population, but it is not clear what proportion of the moderate group is capable of learning skills necessary for paid employment.

The dignity of work has been a basic tenet of American life since colonial days when work was crucial to survival of the group as well as the individual. The work ethic is still prominent in America, but today there is much free time for all employees. For retarded persons who cannot engage in remunerative activity, as well as for other workers with much free time, serious consideration should be given to the dignity of leisure. Training for appropriate use of free time, then, should be an important goal for those whose disabilities prohibit meaningful or remunerative work activity.

CHAPTER 8

MEDICAL ETIOLOGICAL CLASSIFICATION

Since the 1977 edition of the American Association on Mental Deficiency's Manual on Terminology and Classification was published, both the World Health Organization's (WHO) International Classification on Diseases (ICD-9)[1] system and the American Psychiatric Association's (APA's) Diagnostic and Statistical Manual (DSM-III)[2] have been published. Insofar as possible, the ICD-9 and DSM-III material concerning mental retardation was developed to be compatible with the AAMD medical classification system; however, because the three systems were designed for somewhat different purposes, the other two manuals are not identical with the AAMD system, which was designed primarily for use by physicians whose primary interest is in mental retardation.

After the ICD-9 and DSM-III were published, extensive work was done to try to make the AAMD medical classification system completely compatible with those two systems. This was not possible for many reasons. The ICD-9 was designed for world-wide use and use with the entire gamut of medical diseases and syndromes. The DSM-III was designed primarily for use by psychiatrists. In each case, mental retardation represents only a part of the total scope of interest of physicians using the manuals for a broad range of medical disorders. In contrast, those who use the AAMD system are primarily interested in mental retardation and the various medical syndromes and diseases associated with retardation; therefore, parts of the AAMD medical classification system have greater specificity, particularly with reference to etiology, than will be found in the other two manuals. For use in the area of mental retardation, the AAMD system has served well for a number of

---

[1] *ICD-9, International Classification of Diseases,* Ninth Revision, World Health Organization, 1978.

[2] *DSM-III, Diagnostic and Statistical Manual of Mental Disorders,* Third Edition, American Psychiatric Association, Washington, DC, 1980.

years. It is employed and well understood by many of the physicians whose responsibility it is to make the medical diagnoses of disorders associated with mental retardation.

As a part of the extensive work of attempting to ensure compatibility across the three systems, it became apparent that the AAMD system provides useful specificity with reference to certain etiologies. The ICD-9 system differs somewhat from the AAMD system in that it does not classify etiology. The classification system of the American Psychiatric Association (DSM-III) provides for the diagnosis and the coding of mental retardation by levels, but not for the many etiological classes of the AAMD system.

The slight differences in the medical classification systems posed a problem for the AAMD committee; therefore, much discussion was devoted to it. In addition, the opinions of many of the physicians who work in mental retardation were sought. In general, those who have used the AAMD system were in agreement that the etiological system of AAMD was valuable. It does aid in planning and in research and is helpful for general communication purposes.

The decision was finally made to retain the etiological system of AAMD, updating with ICD-9 categories, which appear in parentheses, where appropriate. The DSM-III system is almost identical to the AAMD one for the primary diagnosis of mental retardation, although the definitions of mental retardation differ slightly. In the psychiatric manual, mental retardation is discussed in the following way:

Mental Retardation. The essential features are: (1) significantly subaverage general intellectual functioning, (2) concurrent deficits or impairments in adaptive behavior, (3) with onset before the age of 18. The diagnosis is made regardless of whether or not there is a coexisting mental or physical disorder.

The psychiatric manual uses "deficits or impairments in adaptive behavior" whereas the AAMD definition uses only the phrase "deficits in adaptive behavior." After much discussion, the AAMD committee decided not to include the word *impairments* because by definition it indicates that functioning has at one time been at a higher level and has worsened; this is not the case with most retarded persons. In any event, the definitions are almost identical for practical purposes, and the footnote in the DSM-III manual indicates that the definition was intended to be compatible with that proposed by AAMD in earlier manuals.

The DSM-III classification system is described as "multiaxial" in that it is designed to ensure that one can record several types of information that may be of value in planning treatment and predicting outcomes for individuals. There are five axes. Axes I and II "include all the mental disorders." Two classes of disorders, Personality Disorders and Specific Developmental Disorders (excluding mental retardation), are assigned to Axis II and all other mental disorders are assigned to Axis I. Axis III is used for Physical Disorders and Conditions, Axis IV for an indication of the Severity of Psychosocial Stressors, and Axis V for the Highest Level of Adaptive Functioning Past Year. Thus, principal diagnoses are made on Axes I and II and useful supplementary information is recorded on the other axes.

A primary diagnosis of mental retardation under the DSM-III classification system would be made in Axis I and would indicate the level of retardation and use IQ levels as guides for four subtypes, as follows:

DSM-III Coding and Subtypes of Mental Retardation		*IQ Levels*
317.0(x)	Mild Mental Retardation	50–70
318.0(x)	Moderate Mental Retardation	35–49
318.1(x)	Severe Mental Retardation	20–34
318.2(x)	Profound Mental Retardation	Below 20
319.0(x)	Unspecified Mental Retardation	—

Descriptions of the categories are essentially the same as those used in the AAMD system, with mild being roughly equivalent to the education term *educable,* moderate being equated with the education term *trainable,* and descriptions of behavior and prognosis for the other two groups comparable to those of AAMD. A major difference between the DSM-III and the AAMD criteria for determining level of retardation is the use of what appear to be sharp "cut-off" points between levels in the DSM-III system. Throughout the 1983 AAMD classification system, as well as in the 1973 and 1977 manuals, strong emphasis has been given to the importance of recognizing that there is some error of measurement in all tests, that tests differ somewhat in standard deviations and thus meaning of the obtained IQ, and the importance of using very sound clinical judgment in deciding on level of retardation. The recommendation for professional practitioners made by the AAMD committee thus provides relatively narrow bands at the borderlines of levels as a guide for determining the level of retardation. In addition, under the AAMD system, clinicians are encouraged to first determine that deficits in adaptive behavior do exist before considering whether an individual is retarded or the level of retardation.

The ICD-9 classification system is designed primarily for medical settings, where personnel will be concerned with a variety of disorders; thus, those disorders that are considered as etiological in the area of mental retardation are classified under different classes of disorders. In general, however, the section "Nervous System and Sense Organs" covers a large proportion of the disorders and conditions associated with retardation.

It is our belief that some of the changes made in the classification systems of the World Health Organization and of the American Psychiatric Association are improvements over older systems used by those organizations and by AAMD. Certain modifications of the AAMD system have therefore been made in order to improve this system and to be as consistent as practical with the other two systems.

REVISED AAMD MEDICAL CLASSIFICATION SYSTEM

In revision, the AAMD system provides for making a diagnosis of mental retardation by level, a diagnosis by etiology, and a diagnosis of concurrent problems of the individual who is diagnosed as retarded. The coding system of AAMD has been modified to make it consistent with the system of the American Psychiatric Association (DSM-III) insofar as level of retardation is concerned. As shown elsewhere in this book (see Table 1, p. 13), the AAMD classification of mental retardation is as follows:

317.0(x)   Mild Mental Retardation   IQ from 50–55 to
                                           approx. 70
318.0(x)   Moderate Mental Retardation IQ from 35–40 to 50–55
318.1(x)   Severe Mental Retardation   IQ from 20–25 to 35–40
318.2(x)   Profound Mental Retardation   IQ below 20 or 25
319.0(x)   Unspecified Mental Retardation

The Unspecified Mental Retardation category should be used when retardation is present, but there is great uncertainty about level. The descriptors of mild, moderate, severe, and profound are discussed in detail in Chapter 4 of this book; they indicate essentially the same functioning as has been described in the 1973 and 1977 manuals of AAMD.

For coding purposes, the major change will be use of four digits (including the decimal digit) to indicate level of retardation (see additional suggestions later in this chapter). Following the diagnosis and coding of mental retardation with level, a second diagnosis indicating association with known medical disorders should be made. This second, etiological, diagnosis should be made under a separate axis. Third, a diagnosis indicating concurrent medical or physical problems should be made. For this purpose, the ICD-9 diagnostic system may be used. Physicians who work in facilities in which the preference is for maintaining the 1977 AAMD coding system may use the AAMD codes. In general, however, the ICD-9 system may have wider application and therefore change to the etiological coding system of ICD-9 is encouraged. For convenience of diagnosticians who choose to continue use of the AAMD coding numbers, they are provided in this chapter. Illustrations of some of the code numbers used in the ICD-9 system are provided in parentheses after the diagnostic term used in the AAMD system.

To illustrate, the diagnoses and system for coding might be:

	Diagnostic Code		
Axis 1. Diagnosis of Mental Retardation and Level			
Mild Mental Retardation	317.0		
Axis 2. Etiology (associated disorder)			
Lead poisoning		035 (784, ICD-9)	
Axis 3. Concurrent Problems			
Sensorineural Hearing Loss, unspecified	389.10 (Old 43)		
Axis 4. Psychosocial stressor			
Death of parent			4

Note. The first column under diagnosis uses major numbers from either the AAMD, DSM-III, or ICD-9 systems. The second column is for etiology.

Note that "Concurrent Medical Problems," the section of the
AAMD manual formerly called "Additional Medical Information
Categories" has been supplanted by using the more comprehensive
classification of associated medical problems of the ICD-9 system.
For all of the conditions under "Concurrent Medical Problems"
(formerly "Additional Medical Information"), the coding system of
ICD-9 is shown in this book, and these codes should be used in
place of the more general ones used in the 1977 manual. For new
cases, and in reviewing of old cases, the new system for diagnosis
and coding of concurrent problems should be used.

Some diagnosticians may wish to record and code additional
information during the diagnostic process. Obvious examples are
level of adaptive behavior and level of measured intelligence; coding for these two variables are provided at the beginning of the
coding section of this chapter. There may be other information
that clinical diagnostic teams may wish to record for data banks.
The AAMD 1977 manual provided an extensive section on statistical recording. Because in many states such information must be
provided and coded in a format specified by state agencies or
departments, the statistical coding section of the 1977 AAMD
manual has not been provided in this book; the 1977 statistical
coding system may be useful to some teams who must provide data
for record-keeping purposes.

Another area of concern for some diagnostic teams is illustrated
by the DSM-III Axis IV "Severity of Psychosocial Stressors." That
axis of the psychiatric classification system seems to reflect recent
emphasis on taking aspects of the environment into consideration
when planning for treatments and also reflects to some extent
recent emphasis on ecological evaluation. For the benefit of those
who wish to provide an estimate of the "psychosocial stressors" of
an individual in diagnostic evaluation, the example of DSM-III
may be helpful; however, that system was devised for use with
persons of all levels of intellectual functioning, particularly those
who have average or higher intelligence. An example of coding of
stressors modeled after DSM-III is therefore provided here with
emphasis on stressors that are likely to be associated with retardation, particularly mild retardation.

Code	Term	Example
1	Mild	Change in teacher, vacation in new place, week-long visitors in home, parental illness of week or two.

Code	Term	Example
2	Moderate	Change to new school, chronic parental arguments, birth of sibling, illness of parent for extended period.
3	Severe	Serious illness, death of friend or pet, hospitalization, harsh parental discipline for extended period of time, loss of job.
4	Profound	Death of parent or close sibling, repeated sexual abuse, repeated physical abuse.

This material is provided for illustrative purposes. Workers may wish to develop such coding systems for themselves; in so doing, it is recommended that a careful definition of the terms to be used should be made for any system that is to be employed by several persons. In order to increase the usefulness and the consistency of definitions, one is well advised to state them in objective terms, be as clear as possible about meaning, and use specifiers (for example, number of times) whenever possible.

For coding information about clearly identifiable characteristics of the home, specific aspects of family life or constellation, specific self-help skills, birth history, etc., clinical teams may find the Statistical Reporting section of the 1977 AAMD manual helpful.

For research and administrative purposes, some users of this system may wish to code levels of measured intellectual functioning and adaptive behavior separately. For those purposes, the system used in previous AAMD manuals may be beneficial. They are:

Code	Level	Measured Intellectual Functioning	Adaptive Behavior
0	Not retarded	Above 70–75 IQ	No deficit
1	Mild	50–55 to 70–75	Mild deficit
2	Moderate	35–40 to 50–55	Moderate deficit
3	Severe	20–25 to 35–40	Severe deficit
4	Profound	Below 20–25	Profound deficit

MEDICAL ETIOLOGICAL CLASSIFICATION

Code　　　　　　　　　　　　**0**

00 INFECTIONS AND INTOXICATIONS
  01　Prenatal infection
    011　Cytomegalic inclusion disease, congenital (777.1)
    012　Rubella, congenital (777.0)
    013　Syphilis, congenital (090.9)
    014　Toxoplasmosis, congenital (771.2)
    018　Other (unspecified)
    019　Other (specify)

  02　Postnatal cerebral infection
    021　Viral (specify)
    022　Bacterial (specify)
    028　Other (unspecified)
    029　Other (specify)

  03　Intoxication
    031　Toxemia of pregnancy (760.0)
    032　Other maternal intoxications (specify)
    033　Other maternal disorders (specify) (760.4)
    　　　(e.g., Maternal PKU)
    034　Hyperbilirubinemia (specify)
    035　Lead
    036　Post immunization
    037　Fetal alcohol syndrome (760.71)
    038　Other (unspecified)
    039　Other (specify)

I

10 TRAUMA OR PHYSICAL AGENT
    11 Prenatal injury (specify)
    12 Mechanical injury at birth (763)
    13 Perinatal hypoxia (768)
    14 Postnatal hypoxia (specify)
    15 Postnatal injury (specify)

II

20 METABOLISM OR NUTRITION
    21 Neuronal lipid storage diseases
        211 Ganglioside storage diseases (specify) (330.1)
        212 Lipofuscin storage diseases (specify) (330.1)
        213 Other Glycolipidoses with neuronal involvement (specify)
    22 Carbohydrate disorders
        221 Galactosemia (271.1)
        222 Glycogenoses (Glycogen storage disease) (specify) (271.0)
        223 Fructosemia (Hereditary fructose intolerance) (271.2)
        224 Hypoglycemia (251.2)
        228 Other (unspecified)
        229 Other (specify)
    23 Amino acid disorders
        231 Phenylketonuria (270.1)
        238 Other (unspecified)
        239 Other (specify)
    24 Other and unspecified disorders of metabolism (277)
    25 Mineral disorders (275)
        251 Wilson disease (275.1)
        252 Idiopathic hypercalcemia (275.4)
        258 Other (unspecified)
        259 Other (specify)
    26 Endocrine disorders
        261 Thyroid dysfunction, congenital (243)
        268 Other (unspecified)
        269 Other (specify)
    27 Nutritional disorders (specify substance and time postnatal)
    28 Other (unspecified) (includes failure to thrive, postnatal)
    29 Other (specify)

III

30 GROSS BRAIN DISEASE (POSTNATAL)
    31 Neurocutaneous dysplasia
        311 Neurofibromatosis (von Recklinghausen disease) (237.7)

312 Trigeminal cerebral angiomatosis (Sturge-Weber-Dimitri disease) (759.6)
313 Tuberous sclerosis (759.5)
318 Other (unspecified)
319 Other (specify)

32 Tumors (specify)
33 Cerebral white matter, degenerative
    331 Sudanophilic leukodystrophy (330)
    332 Sudanophilic leukodystrophy of Pelizaeus-Merzbacher type (330)
    338 Other (unspecified)
    339 Other (specify)
34 Specific fiber tracts or neural groups, degenerative
    341 Huntington disease (333.4)
    342 Spinocerebellar disease (specify) (334)
    348 Other (unspecified)
    349 Other (specify)
35 Cerebrovascular system
38 Other (unspecified)
39 Other (specify)

IV

40 UNKNOWN PRENATAL INFLUENCE
41 Cerebral malformation
    411 Anencephaly (740.0)
    418 Other (unspecified)
    419 Other (specify)
42 Craniofacial anomaly
    421 Holoprosencephaly (742.2)
    422 Cornelia de Lange syndrome (759.8)
    423 Microcephalus (742.1)
    424 Macroencephaly (742.4)
    425 Crouzon syndrome (756.0)
    426 Apert syndrome (755.55)
    427 Craniostenosis (specify suture and type) (756.0)
    428 Other (unspecified)
    429 Other (specify; includes Rubinstein-Taybi; Oral-Facial-Digital; Lawrence-Moon-Biedl syndrome)
43 Status dysraphicus
    431 Meningoencephalocele (742.0)
    432 Meningomyelocele (741.9)
    438 Other (unspecified)
    439 Other (specify)

44 Hydrocephalus, congenital (742.3)
45 Hydranencephaly
46 Multiple malformations (specify)
47 Single umbilical artery
48 Other (unspecified)
49 Other (specify)

V

50   **CHROMOSOMAL ANOMALIES (758)**
Includes syndromes associated with anomalies in the number and form of chromosomes. The code numbers used in this section are from the ICD-9.

758.0 Down syndrome
Mongolism
Translocation Down syndrome
Trisomy 21 or 22, Trisomy G

758.1 Patau syndrome
Trisomy 13, Trisomy D_1

758.2 Edwards syndrome
Trisomy 18
Trisomy E_3

758.3 Autosomal deletion syndromes
Antimongolism syndrome
Cri-du-chat syndrome

758.4 Balanced autosomal translocation in normal individual

758.5 Other conditions due to autosomal anomalies
Accessory autosomes NEC

758.6 Gonadal dysgenesis
Ovarian dysgenesis
Turner syndrome
XO syndrome
Excludes pure gonadal dysgenesis (752.7)

758.7 Klinefelter syndrome
XXY syndrome

758.8 Other conditions due to sex chromosome anomalies
Additional sex chromosome
Sex chromosome mosaicism
Triple X syndrome
XXX syndrome
XYY syndrome

758.9 Conditions due to anomaly of unspecified chromosome

VI

60 OTHER CONDITIONS ORIGINATING IN THE PERINATAL PERIOD

61 Disorders relating to short gestation and unspecified low birth-weight (765)

    611 Extreme immaturity (765.0)

    612 Other preterm infants (765.1)

62 Slow fetal growth and fetal malnutrition (764)

    621 "Light-for-dates" without mention of fetal malnutrition (764.0)

    622 "Light-for-dates" with signs of fetal malnutrition (764.1)

    623 Fetal malnutrition without mention of "light-for-dates" (764.2)

    624 Fetal growth retardation, unspecified (764.9)

63 Disorders relating to long gestation and high birthweight (766)

    631 Exceptionally large baby (766.0)

    632 Other "heavy-for-dates" infants (766.1)

67 Maternal nutritional disorders (760.4)

68 Other (unspecified)

69 Other (specified)

VII

70 FOLLOWING PSYCHIATRIC DISORDER (SPECIFY)

71 Psychosis (refer to DSM III)

79 Other psychiatric disorder

VIII

80 ENVIRONMENTAL INFLUENCES

81 Psychosocial disadvantage

82 Sensory deprivation (specify)

88 Other (unspecified)

89 Other (specify)

IX

90 OTHER CONDITIONS

91 Defects of special senses (specify) (see pp. 151–152).

For Unspecified Mental Retardation, use ICD-9 Code 391.0.

DEFINITIONS OF MEDICAL ETIOLOGIES

00

Code 00 INFECTIONS AND INTOXICATIONS

This grouping includes maternal and child infectious diseases and intoxications. Subcategories are coded with additional digits and are as follows:

Code 01 Prenatal infection
This subcategory includes infectious diseases that affect the child in utero, resulting in brain damage or malformation. A history of maternal infection during pregnancy should be sought. Infections during the first trimester are particularly likely to cause malformations. It should be noted that, in rare instances, prenatal infection of the fetus may occur in absence of recognized clinical disease in the mother. There are probably many infections, particularly viral, that may affect the embryo. The following is a partial list:

Code 011 Cytomegalic inclusion disease, congenital
A disease that results from asymptomatic infection of the mother during pregnancy with the human cytomegalovirus. Manifestations vary, but common findings are hepatomegaly, splenomegaly, icterus, anemia, thrombocytopenia, purpura, and cerebral calcifications. Brain damage may be severe with microcephaly or hydrocephalus.

Code 012 Rubella, congenital
Results from German measles infection of a mother during pregnancy. Infection during the first month of pregnancy may result in abnormalities in 50% of the infants. The most common defects are cataracts, cardiac anomalies, deafness, microcephaly, and retardation.

Code 013 Syphilis, congenital
This disease results from transplacental infection of the fetus from syphilis in the mother. There are early and late forms of the disease. The early form may be marked by a variety of rashes, severe rhinitis (snuffles), moist lesions at the mucocutaneous junctions of the mouth, anus and genitalia, pseudoparalysis of limbs, and enlargement of liver, spleen, and lymph nodes. The central nervous system may be involved with low-grade hydrocephalus, convulsions, and mental retardation. The late stage (juvenile paresis) may occur at any age after infancy (usually before adolescence). The classic Hutchinson triad of this stage consists of nerve deafness, interstitial keratitis, and Hutchinsonian incisors. There may be convulsions, hemiplegia, antisocial behavior, and retardation.

Code 014   Toxoplasmosis, congenital
Maternal infection during pregnancy caused by toxoplasma gondii (a crescentic, pyriform, or oval-shaped protozoan). Symptoms vary depending on the severity of the disease and time of infection during pregnancy. Any combination of the following symptoms may be present at or a few days after birth. Fever, malaise, jaundice, lymph gland enlargement, maculopapular rash, hepatosplenomegaly, microcephaly, microophthalmia, hydrocephalus, and convulsions. Cerebral calcification and chorioretinitis are often present. There may be recovery with central nervous system sequelae of convulsions, microcephaly, hydrocephalus, chorioretinitis, and psychomotor deficit.

Code 019   Other (specify)
Other maternal infections possibly associated with congenital abnormalities, i.e., herpes simplex, coxsackie-virus Group B.

Code 02   Postnatal cerebral infection (specify)
All postnatal cerebral infections, both focal and generalized types, are classified in this category. Included are syndromes resulting from infection by viruses, bacteria, parasites, protozoa, and fungi. Postinfectious encephalitis that may follow measles, rubella, varicella, mumps, and other infections. Postvaccinal encephalitis that may result from inoculation with serum or vaccines. Other syndromes related to autoimmune and immunologic deficiency diseases that may be coded under this category. The exceptions are hemolytic (noninfection) and drug-induced disorders that are classified under intoxication. Further specification under this category can be made by using a third digit.

Code 021   Viral (specify)

Code 022   Bacterial (specify)

Code 028   Other (unspecified)

Code 029   Other (specify)

Code 03   Intoxication
Cases associated with cerebral damage due to toxic agents or conditions are classified under this division as follows:

Code 031   Toxemia of pregnancy
Classification under this category should not be made without reliable evidence of severe and prolonged toxemia in the mother.

Code 032   Other maternal intoxications (specify)
During early pregnancy, drugs or poisons taken by the mother or exposure to industrial chemicals may result in fetal damage.

Code 033 Other maternal disorders (specify)
There is evidence that chronic maternal disorders such as nephritis, diabetes, malnutrition and PKU can affect the unborn child.

Code 034 Hyperbilirubinemia (specify)
May be encountered with hepatic disease or with little or no evidence of it. The elevation in serum bilirubin that may be either of the conjugated or unconjugated type is the result of a failure of one or more steps involved in the normal pathway for excretion of bilirubin. A variety of disturbances occur and may be temporary or permanent and appear at birth or in later infancy and childhood. Severe hyperbilirubinemia produces a neurotoxicity that is known as kernicterus, one of the principal causes of neurologic abnormalities. Maternal-fetal blood group incompatibility is only one of a number of causes for the disorder.

Code 035 Lead

Code 036 Postimmunization

Code 037 Fetal Alcohol Syndrome (760.71)
Cases associated with excessive use of alcohol during pregnancy; facies and location of ears are among signs observed in infants; mental retardation and other disabilities are associated with this syndrome.

Code 038 Other (unspecified)

Code 039 Other (specify)
Permanent damage to nerve tissue may result from a wide variety of intoxicants including lead or other heavy metals, carbon monoxide, drugs, etc. Lead-based paints have been the most common source of poisoning.

I

Code 10 TRAUMA OR PHYSICAL AGENT

Cases associated with injury of the brain due to trauma or mechanical or physical agent are classified in this division. Further specification within this category follows.

Code 11 Prenatal injury (specify)
On very rare occasions encephalopathy may occur as a result of prenatal injury. This includes prenatal irradiation and prenatal hypoxia, or other trauma.

Code 12 Mechanical injury at birth (763, 767)
Attributed to difficulties of labor due to malposition, malpresentation, disproportion, or other complications leading to dystocia that may increase

the probability of damage to the infant's brain at birth, resulting in tears of the meninges, blood vessels, and brain substance. Other reasons include venous-sinus thrombosis, arterial embolism, and thrombosis. These may result in sequelae that are indistinguishable from those of other injuries, damage, or organic impairment of the brain.

Code 13   Perinatal hypoxia (anoxia) (768)
This category includes conditions resulting from prolonged anoxia from premature placental separation, massive hemorrhage from placenta previa, knotted cord, etc.

Severe birth asphyxia: one-minute Apgar score 0 to 3; pulse less than 100 per minute at birth and falling or steady; respiration absent or gasping, color poor, muscle tone absent; "White asphyxia."

Mild or moderate birth asphyxia: one-minute Apgar score 4 to 7; "blue asphyxia"; normal respiration not established within one minute, but heart rate 100 or above, some muscle tone present, some response to stimulation.

Code 14   Postnatal hypoxia (anoxia)
Anoxia may result from severe anemia, shock, poisoning, convulsions, and trauma. When possible specify the condition.

Code 15   Postnatal injury
This diagnosis calls for evidence of severe trauma, such as fractured skull, prolonged unconsciousness, etc., followed by a marked change in development. Postnatal infarction, laceration, and contusion of the brain would be included and the nature of the injury specified.

II
Code 20   METABOLISM OR NUTRITION

Disorders directly due to metabolic, nutritional, endocrine, or growth dysfunction should be classified under this category. It is further subdivided into the following:

Code 21   Neuronal lipid storage diseases
Includes a large group of disorders that show an increase in lipid content of tissues or serum. Nomenclature of these diseases is in a state of flux, and some syndromes overlap with carbohydrate disorders. For this classification they are listed as follows:

Code 211   Ganglioside storage diseases (specify) (330.1)
Includes Tay-Sachs disease (GM_2 gangliosidosis Type I), Sandhoff disease (GM_2 gangliosidosis Type II), Juvenile GM_2 gangliosidosis (GM_2

gangliosidosis Type III), Generalized gangliosidosis (GM_1 gangliosidosis Type 1), and Juvenile GM_1 gangliosidosis (GM_1 gangliosidosis Type II).

Code 212   Lipofuscin storage diseases (specify) (330.1)

Includes Jansky-Bielschowsky disease, Batten-Spielmeyer-Vogt disease, and Kuf's disease.

Code 213   Other Glycolipidoses with neuronal involvement (specify)

Includes Ceramide lactosidosis, Infantile cerebral Gaucher disease, Niemann-Pick disease, Fabry disease (autonomic nervous system lipidosis without mental retardation), Hurler disease (neuronal lipidosis, visceral mucopolysaccharidosis), Hunter disease (277.5) (neuronal lipidosis, visceral mucopolysaccharidosis), Sanfilippo disease (neuronal lipidosis, visceral mucopolysaccharidosis), and Mannosidosis (chiefly mannogalactoprotein storage).

Code 22   Carbohydrate disorders

Disorders of carbohydrate metabolism interfere with brain metabolism or supply inadequate glucose. This category is further subdivided:

Code 221   Galactosemia

Two different enzymatic defects are known to produce abnormal elevations of the concentration of galactose in blood. Galactosemia in which there is a deficiency of galactose-1-phosphate uridyl transferase activity is the most common form. The other disorder, a deficiency of galactokinase, is rare.

Code 222   Glycogenoses (Glycogen storage diseases)

A variety of disorders result from derangements of either the synthesis or degradation of glycogen and of its subsequent utilization. In one group, the liver is the principal organ involved. In a second group, cardiomegaly is the most prominent manifestation, and in the third group skeletal muscle is principally involved. Included in this category are Type I (von Gierke), Type II (Pompe disease), Type VII, Type VIII, Type IX, etc.

Code 223   Fructosemia (hereditary fructose intolerance)

The ingestion of fructose leads to abnormally elevated blood levels of fructose in two conditions. One of these, benign fructosemia, is an asymptomatic disorder resulting from a deficiency of fructokinase. The other disorder, hereditary fructose intolerance, is a serious disorder.

Code 224   Hypoglycemia

Hypoglycemia is a condition in which there is an abnormal low level of blood glucose. It is caused by a variety of conditions, and, if secondary, should not be coded under this category.

Code 229   Other (specify)
Other carbohydrate disorders are included in this category (i.e., malabsorption syndromes, Unverricht-Lafora disease).

Code 23   Amino acid disorders
This category includes enzyme disorders that affect amino acid metabolism.

Code 231   Phenylketonuria (PKU)
Phenylketonuria is an autosomal recessive defect of phenylalanine metabolism. It results from absence of the hepatic enzyme, phenylalanine hydroxylase, that converts phenylalanine to tyrosine. Mental retardation is a frequent consequence of the disease, although some cases of normal intelligence have been reported.

Code 239   Other (specify)
There are other disorders involving tyrosine, methionine, cystine, tryptophan, valine, leucine, isoleucine, etc.

Code 24   Nucleotide disorders
This group includes defects in metabolism of purines and pyrimidines. These are the basic components that are linked with the pentose sugars ribose or deoxyribose and interconnected by phosphoric acid bridges to make nucleic acids, the fundamental structural units of the gene. This category includes orotic aciduria, xanthinuria, destructive hyperuricemia, etc.

Code 25   Mineral disorders (metals)
These disorders are associated with defects in metabolism of specific metallic ions.

Code 251   Wilson disease
A recessively inherited disorder of copper metabolism manifested by progressive cirrhosis of the liver and extra-pyramidal dysfunction.

Code 252   Idiopathic hypercalcemia
Stable features of this syndrome are failure to thrive and an elevated serum calcium level in early infancy. Mental retardation is common.

Code 259   Other (specify)
Other mineral disorders should be included here. This includes pseudohypoparathyroidism, etc.

Code 26   Endocrine disorders
Includes disease associated with abnormal functioning of specific organs (pituitary, pineal, thyroid, parathyroid, pancreas, adrenal, testicle and ovary).

Code 261   Thyroid dysfunction, congenital
Hypothyroidism is the most common endocrine disorder. The disease is
divided into congenital and acquired. The congenital form is cretinism,
which in the majority of cases, is due to partial or complete absence of
the thyroid gland at birth. In the remaining cases, known as goitrous
cretinism, the thyroid gland is present but has a defect in the formation
or release of thyroid hormone.

Code 269   Other (specify)
Includes other endocrine disorders.

Code 27   Nutritional disorders (specify)
Dietary imbalances of the child can result in slow development and retardation. The imbalances arise from inadequate diet, idiosyncratic diets,
metabolic disorders, parasitism, debilitating disease, excessive intake of
vitamins, and various feeding problems. In classifying under this category,
specify substance and time postnatal. If the nutritional disorder is secondary to metabolic disorders, it should not be listed under this category.

Code 28   Other (unspecified)

Code 29   Other (specify)
Disorders not classifiable in any of the preceding metabolic, growth, or
nutritional categories are included here. This includes muscular dystrophy, Prader-Willi syndrome, etc.

III

Code 30   GROSS BRAIN DISEASE (POSTNATAL)

This category includes neoplasms and a large group of heredogenerative
disorders in which the etiology is unknown or uncertain.

Code 31   Neurocutaneous dysplasia
Hereditary conditions in which there are combined congenital lesions of
the skin and nervous system with a variety of visceral and somatic abnormalities.

Code 311   Neurofibromatosis (von Recklinghausen disease)
This disease is inherited as an autosomal dominant. Manifestations
consist of multiple tumors (neurofibromas) of the skin and peripheral
nerves, cafe-au-lait spots, cysts or erosions of bones, and tumors of
other organs including the brain. Intelligence varies from normal to
severe retardation.

Code 312 Trigeminal cerebral angiomatosis (Sturge-Weber-Dimitri disease)

The genetics of this disorder are not fully understood. A condition characterized by a "port wine stain" or cutaneous angioma, usually in the distribution of the trigeminal nerve. This is accompanied by vascular malformation over the meninges of the parietal and occipital lobes. The cortex underlying the affected meninges is also maldeveloped, showing loss of nerve cells, gliosis, and calcification that can be detected by skull X-ray. Seizures are frequent, and there may be transient or permanent hemiplegia. Intelligence varies from normal to severe retardation.

Code 313 Tuberous sclerosis (Epiloia, Bourneville disease)

Inheritance appears to be autosomal dominant, although some cases have been reported to exhibit a recessive type of inheritance. The condition is characterized by multiple gliotic nodules in the central nervous system and associated with adenoma sebaceum of the face and tumors in other organs. Retarded development and seizures may appear early and increase in severity along with tumor growth.

Code 318 Other (unspecified)

Code 319 Other (specify)

Other relatively rare neurocutaneous diseases should be included under this category and specified when possible.

Code 32 New growths (tumors)

This category includes intracranial tumors. The presence of tumors in infancy is rare but increases in frequency up to age 7 or 8 years and declines by adolescence. It is estimated that 75% of intracranial tumors in childhood are gliomas of which two-thirds are astrocytomas and medulloblastomas.

Code 33 Cerebral white matter, degenerative

This group includes clinical entities that have in common defective myelin of the central nervous system resulting in progressive destruction of white matter, and the etiology is undetermined. Those diseases for which etiologies have been established should be classified elsewhere.

Code 331 Sudanophilic leukodystrophy

The mechanisms of inheritance are uncertain. Onset of the disease may occur in infancy but more frequently in later childhood. Gait becomes impaired, and spasticity with increased reflexes appears. Cerebellar signs and seizures may appear, and mental impairment is progressive. Age at death is variable, ranging from 2 years to adolescence. Autopsy shows diffuse absence of myelin, particularly in the cerebral white matter and cerebellum.

Code 332   Sudanophilic leukodystrophy of Pelizaeus-Merzbacher type
Inheritance is thought to be an X-linked recessive gene. The most common initial symptom is bizarre and irregular nystagmus. Other signs appear: difficulty in holding up the head, increased cerebellar signs, and spasticity. Dysarthria and ataxia may become severe, and choreiform movements or a Parkinsonian facies is seen in the later stages, along with myoclonic jerks. Optic atrophy and deafness have been reported in some cases. Often the extremities become hypertonic. Intellectual function deteriorates as the disease progresses. Persons with this disease may live into adulthood.

Code 338   Other (unspecified)

Code 339   Other (specify)
Includes other general demyelinizing disorders of unknown etiology.

Code 34   Specific fiber tracts or neural groups, degenerative
This includes pyramidal, basal ganglion or extrapyramidal, and spinocerebellar disorders.

Code 341   Huntington disease
Inheritance is autosomal dominant. Onset may occur as early as 4 years, but usually later. The first symptoms may be emotional disturbance, choreiform movements seizures, or, more commonly, a progressive rigidity without definitive involuntary movements. The disease is characterized by progressive dementia, choreic movements, and death.

Code 342   Spinocerebellar disease (specify)
A group of progressive diseases characterized clinically by incoordination and ataxia and pathologically by degeneration of the structures involved with control of smooth movement. A frequent type encountered is Friedreich ataxia.

Code 349   Other (specify)
Includes other neural group disorders of unknown etiology such as Hallervorden-Spatz disease.

Code 35   Cerebrovascular system
Includes congenital vascular lesions. Although congenital, manifestations may occur at any time. Vascular lesions have been implicated in acute infantile hemiplegias and may be involved in some learning disabilities.

Code 38   Other (unspecified)

Code 39   Other (specify)
All other postnatal disease and conditions of unknown or uncertain etiologies should be specified under this category.

IV
Code 40   UNKNOWN PRENATAL INFLUENCE

This division is intended only for conditions for which no definite etiology can be established but that existed at or prior to birth. These include primary cranial anamolies and congenital defects of undetermined origin as follows:

Code 41   Cerebral malformation
This category is for congenital cerebral maldevelopments of undetermined etiology, such as anencephaly, malformations of gyri, true porencephaly, etc. Further specification follows:

Code 411   Anencephaly
This is a condition characterized by partial or complete absence of the cerebrum, cerebellum, and flat bones of the skull.

Code 418   Other (unspecified)

Code 419   Other (specify)
Includes microencephaly, etc.

Code 42   Craniofacial anomaly
This category includes a group of disorders related to cerebral-cranial-facial anomalies of unknown etiology. Further specification follows.

Code 421   Holoprosencephaly
Specific cerebral malformations with midline facial defects. The mildest form disclose only hypotelorism, at times accompanied by trigonocephaly (keel-shaped forehead), cleft palate, and microcephaly. The extreme is cyclopia, a blind proboscis in place of a nose, with a small, monoventricular brain deficient of midline structures.

Code 422   Cornelia de Lange syndrome
Diagnostic features are severe mental retardation, bushy confluent eyebrows, up-turned nose, wide upper lip, hirsutism, and skeletal abnormalities.

Code 423   Microcephalus
"True" or primary microcephaly presents a characteristic clinical picture and is transmitted as an autosomal recessive gene. The ear and nose are large, the nose joining the receding brow without a bridge; the scalp is redundant and furrowed, and the cranial vault is abnormally small. Microcephaly may be secondary to other disorders. If secondary it should be coded as a supplementary term.

Code 424   Macroencephaly
Macroencephaly refers to an enlarged head. Primary macroencephaly is a congenital anomaly of the brain, and may be familial. Patients are mentally retarded, usually epileptic and occasionally spastic. Most enlarged heads are due to hydrocephalus or space-taking lesions, which should be coded elsewhere.

Code 425   Crouzon syndrome
Major features are craniostenosis, usually of the coronal sutures, resulting in lengthening of the calvarium vertically; a characteristic facial appearance that includes facial dysotosis, hypoplasia of the maxillae, and bulging of the eyes. Mental retardation is not necessarily seen. Autosomal dominant inheritance in some cases.

Code 426   Apert syndrome
Major features are craniostenosis, usually of the coronal sutures, resulting in lengthening of the calvarium vertically; a characteristic facial appearance that includes facial dysotosis, hypoplasia of the maxillae, and bulging of the eyes; and a marked syndactyly of the hands and feet. Mental retardation varies in degree of severity. Autosomal dominant inheritance in some cases.

Code 427   Craniostenosis (specify suture and type)
Cranial sutures may close prematurely, resulting in an abnormally shaped head, increased intracranial pressure, and brain damage. Abnormal closure usually occurs before birth, but not always. Head shape depends on the pattern of suture closure. Early sagittal closure results in scaphocephaly (long narrow head). Closure of both coronal sutures results in a short, flat head or brachycephaly. Unilateral closure produces an asymmetric head, plagiocephaly. Premature closure of all sutures results in an upward growth and small circumference of the skull, oxycephaly (tower skull). Intelligence varies from normal to severe retardation.

Code 428   Other (unspecified)

Code 429   Other (specify)
Other syndromes under this category include Laurence-Moon-Biedl syndrome, Oral-Facial-Digital syndrome, Rubenstein-Taybi syndrome.

Code 43   Status dysraphicus
Includes disorders related to faulty closure of the neural tube resulting in faulty formation of midline structures, such as the spine, sternum, and palate. Further specification follows:

Code 431   Meningoencephalocele
Protrusions of the meninges and brain tissue out of the cranial cavity

into a sac covered by skin or a thin membrane. Severe mental retardation and microcephaly usually associated with this disorder.

Code 432   Meningomycelocele
External projections of the meninges along the spine. Most common in the lumbar area. Nerve tissue usually accompanies the sac and causes varying degrees of paralysis, sensory loss, and sphincter disturbances. Rarely seen without Arnold-Chiari malformation (herniation of the cerebellas tonsils and elongation and kinking of the brain stem).

Code 44   Hydrocephalus, congenital (742.3)
Hydrocephalus is an excess of cerebrospinal fluid within the ventricular and subarchnoid spaces. It is not synonymous with an enlarged head, since the latter may be due to megalencephalon or subdural fluid, whereas hydrocephalus may or may not enlarge the head. Communicating hydrocephalus implies free communication between ventricles and spinal theca, and obstructive hydrocephalus, a block to the passage of fluid. Internal hydrocephalus and external hydrocephalus indicate the site of greatest enlargement of cerebrospinal fluid spaces, whether ventricular or subarchnoid. Hydrocephalus may accompany other disorders. If the condition is secondary it should be coded as a supplementary term with the type specified.

Code 45   Hydroencephaly
In this condition the cerebral cortex, except for the inferior temporal and mesial occipital lobes, is represented only by a membrane filled with clear fluid. The size of the head at birth is normal.

Code 46   Multiple malformations (specify)
Classify under this category syndromes that have a combination of malformations but not specific enough to be coded under the above subcategories of unknown prenatal influence.

Code 47   Single umbilical artery
A disorder in which there is only one umbilical artery instead of the usual two. Approximately one-third of infants with a single umbilical artery have congenital abnormalities. Trisomy of Chromosome 18 is one of the more frequent abnormalities associated with this disorder.

Code 48   Other (unspecified)

Code 49   Other (specify)
Includes other syndromes that cannot be classified under the above categories of unknown prenatal influence.

V

Code 50   CHROMOSOMAL ANOMALIES

Syndromes associated with chromosomal aberrations are included under this category. These aberrations may be numerical, structural, or multiple (combinations involving number and structure). Possible causes of these aberrations are gene mutation, radiation, drugs and other chemicals, viruses, autoimmune mechanisms, aged gametes, existing aberrations, and a group of conditions involving thermal, temporal, geographic, and perhaps economic factors. The code numbers used are from ICD-9.

Code 758.0   Down syndrome
Clinical manifestations are brachycephalic head, an upward slant of the palpebral fissures, presence of inner epicanthal folds, speckling of the iris (Brushfield spots), thickened and furrowed tongue, extremities markedly hypotonic, simian crease, short incurved fifth digit, and wide space between first and second toes. The most common chromosomal abnormality in Down syndrome is C_2, trisomy.

Other chromosomal aberrations occasionally occurring with trisomy 21 include: trisomy D_1; trisomy 18; Triple X; Klinefelter (XXY), Turner (XO), etc.

Code 758.1   Patau syndrome
Abnormalities commonly encountered are microcephaly, prosencephalic defects, cleft lip and palate, polydactyly, flexion deformity of fingers, simian palmar creases, congenital heart defects, undescended testes; neonatal mortality rate is high. Trisomy D_1, 13.

Code 758.2   Edwards syndrome
Multiple developmental anomalies have been described. Distinguishing characteristics may include webbed neck, ptosis, hypertelorism, strabismus, digital deformities.

Code 758.3   Autosomal deletion syndrome
Cri-du-chat syndrome due to deletion of short arms of a Chromosome 5 is characterized by a weak, high-pitched cry in the neonatal period, retardation, microcephaly, microguathia, hypertelorism, epicanthal folds, downward palpebral slant, low-set ears. The deletion of short arms of a Chromosome 4 syndrome is associated with retardation, prominent glabella and nose, median cleft palate, microcephaly, hypertelorism, hypospadias, seizures.

Code 758.6   Gonadal dysgenesis
Female (gonadal dysgenesis) (XO). The clinical features of this syndrome are small stature, sexual infantilism, webbed neck, low posterior

hairline, broad chest, cubitus valgus. Mental retardation is not usual, though learning problems may be evident. Coarctation of the aorta, horsehoe kidneys, and edema of the hands and feet in neonates (Bonnevie-Ullrich syndrome) may occur. *Male.* Some features of Turner syndrome are evident (webbing of neck, short stature, cubitus valgus). Gonadal biopsy reveals seminiferous tubular hypophasia. Chromosomes are normal (46, XY), and this diagnosis should not be included in this classification.

Code 758.7   Klinefelter syndrome
Mild mental retardation may be the only clinical manifestation during childhood. At puberty eunuchoid features, gynecomastia, small penis and testes, and sterility become evident. The incidence of mental retardation increases with the number of additional X chromosomes except in a mosaic with an XX cell line.

VI

Code 60   OTHER CONDITIONS ORIGINATING IN THE PERINATAL PERIOD

Code 61   Disorders relating to short gestation and unspecified low birthweight (765)
Includes extreme immaturity and other preterm infants, without further specification, as causes of mortality, morbidity, or additional care, in fetus or newborn; includes unspecified low birthweight and short gestation associated with mental retardation.

Code 611   Extreme immaturity (765.0)
Usually implies a birthweight of less than 1,000 grams and/or gestation of less than 28 completed weeks.

Code 612   Other preterm infants (765.1)
Usually implies a birthweight of 1,000 to 2,500 grams (5 pounds, 8 ounces) and/or gestation period of 29 to 37 weeks.

Code 62   Slow fetal growth and fetal malnutrition (764)

Code 621   "Light-for-dates" without mention of fetal malnutrition (764.0).
Infants underweight for gestational age. "Small-for-dates" infants.

Code 622   "Light-for-dates" with signs of fetal malnutrition (764.1)
Infants "light-for-dates" classifiable to 621, who in addition show signs of fetal malnutrition, such as dry peeling skin and loss of subcutaneous tissue.

Code 623 Fetal malnutrition without mention of "light-for-dates" (764.2)
Infants not underweight for gestational age showing signs of fetal malnutrition, such as dry peeling skin and loss of subcutaneous tissue.

Code 624 Fetal growth retardation, unspecified (764.9)
Intrauterine growth retardation.

Code 63 Disorders relating to long gestation and high birthweight (766)
Includes exceptionally large babies and other "heavy-for-term" infants.

Code 631 Exceptionally large baby (766.0)
Usually implies a birthweight of 4,500 grams or more.

Code 632 Other "heavy-for-dates" infants (766.1)
Other fetus or infant "heavy-for-dates" or "large-for-dates" regardless of gestation period.

VII

Code 70 FOLLOWING PSYCHIATRIC DISORDER

This category is for retardation following psychosis or other psychiatric disorder when there is no evidence of cerebral pathology. If the psychiatric disorder is a concomitant manifestation, it is not classified under this category. It should be coded under additional medical information.

Code 71 Psychosis (specify type: refer to American Psychiatric Association publication, DSM-III, 1980, for appropriate usage of terms).

Code 79 Other (specify)
Includes other psychiatric disorder

VIII

Code 80 ENVIRONMENTAL INFLUENCES

Cases in which there are indications of adverse environmental conditions and in which there is no evidence of other significant organic disease or pathology are classified under this category.

Code 81 Psychosocial disadvantage
Criteria for inclusion under this category require that there be evidence of subnormal intellectual functioning in at least one of the parents and in one or more siblings (if there are siblings). These cases are usually from impoverished environments involving poor housing, inadequate diets, and inadequate medical care. There may be prematurity, low birthweight, or history of infectious diseases, but no single entity appears to have contributed to the slow or retarded development.

Code 82   Sensory deprivation (specify)
Inclusion under this category requires evidence of atypical parent-child interactions such as marked maternal deprivation or very severe environmental restrictions, such as prolonged isolation during the developmental years.

Code 88   Other environmental influences (unspecified)

Code 89   Other (specify)

IX

Code 90   OTHER CONDITIONS

This category is intended for classification of cases in which mental retardation is caused by defects in one or more of the special senses or in which there appear to be multiple biological and social conditions contributing to slow or retarded development and cases that cannot be classified under other categories. It also includes ill-defined or unknown conditions.

Code 91   Defects of special senses (specify)
For inclusion under this category, it is necessary that evidence of sensory handicaps such as blindness, deafness, etc., be the only contributing factors to the slow or retarded development (see pp. 151–152).

For Other (unspecified or unknowns), use ICD-9 Code 319.0
This category is for the classification of cases in which there is (1) no evidence of physical cause or structural defect, (2) no history of subnormal functioning in parents and siblings, and (3) no evidence of an associated psychosocial factor. To be included here are those cases of mental retardation with ill-defined or unknown etiology.

CONCURRENT MEDICAL PROBLEMS[1]

Definitions of categories included in the concurrent medical information include Special Senses, Convulsive Disorders, and Motor Dysfunctions. For definitions of terms comprising Psychiatric Impairment, readers should refer to the American Psychiatric Association publication, DSM-III, 1980. (The abbreviation NOS used in many of the definitions refers to Not Otherwise Specified.)

------

[1] Classification system and definitions are those of 1CD-9, World Health Organization, 1978.

SPEECH AND LANGUAGE ABNORMALITIES

307.0 Stammering and stuttering
 Excludes: dysphasia (784.5)
  lisping or lalling (307.9)
  retarded development of speech (315.31–315.39)

784.3 Aphasia
 Excludes: developmental aphasia (315.31)

784.4 Voice disturbance
 784.40 Voice disturbance, unspecified
 784.41 Aphonia
  Loss of voice
 784.49 Other
  Change in voice   Hypernasality
  Dysphonia   Hyponasality
  Hoarseness

784.5 Other speech disturbance
  Dysarthria   Slurred speech
  Dysphasia
 Excludes: stammering and stuttering (307.0)
  that of nonorganic origin (307.0, 307.9)

369 BLINDNESS AND LOW VISION

Note. Visual impairment refers to a functional limitation of the eye (e.g., limited visual acuity or visual field). It should be distinguished from visual disability, indicating a limitation of the abilities of the individual (e.g., limited reading skills, vocational skills), and from visual handicap, indicating a limitation of personal and socioeconomic independence (e.g., limited mobility, limited employability). The levels of impairment defined are based on the recommendations of the WHO Study Group on Prevention of Blindness (Geneva, November 6–10, 1972; WHO Technical Report Series 518), and of the International Council of Ophthalmology (1976). Note that definitions of blindness vary in different settings. For international reporting WHO defines blindness as profound impairment. This definition can be applied to blindness of one eye (369.1, 369.6) and to blindness of the individual (369.0). For determination of benefits in the U.S.A., the definition of legal blindness as severe impairment is often used. This definition applies to blindness of the individual only.
Excludes: correctable impaired vision due to refractive errors (367.0–367.9)

369.0 Profound impairment, both eyes

369.1 Moderate or severe impairment, better eye, profound impairment lesser eye

369.2 Moderate or severe impairment, both eyes

369.8 Unqualified visual loss, one eye

369.9 Unspecified visual loss

389 HEARING LOSS

389.0 Conductive hearing loss

389.1 Sensorineural hearing loss
Perceptive hearing loss or deafness
Excludes: abnormal auditory perception (388.40–388.44)
                psychogenic deafness (306.7)

389.2 Mixed conductive and sensorineural hearing loss
Deafness or hearing loss of type classifiable to 389.0 with type classifiable to 389.1

389.7 Deaf mutism, not elsewhere classifiable
Deaf, nonspeaking

389.8 Other specified forms of hearing loss

389.9 Unspecified hearing loss
Deafness NOS

343 INFANTILE CEREBRAL PALSY
Includes: cerebral:
                palsy NOS
                spastic infantile paralysis
                congenital spastic paralysis (cerebral)
                Little disease
                paralysis (spastic) due to birth injury:
                    intracranial
                    spinal
Excludes: hereditary cerebral paralysis, such as: hereditary spastic paraplegia (334.1), Vogt's disease (333.7); spastic paralysis specified as noncongenital or noninfantile (344.0–344.9)

343.0 Diplegic
Congenital diplegia, Congenital paraplegia

343.1 Hemiplegic
Congenital hemiplegia
Excludes: infantile hemiplegia NOS (343.4)

343.2 Quadriplegic
Tetraplegic

343.3 Monoplegic

343.4 Infantile hemiplegia
Infantile hemiplegia (postnatal) NOS

343.8 Other specified infantile cerebral palsy

343.9 Infantile cerebral palsy, unspecified
Cerebral palsy NOS

345 EPILEPSY
Excludes: progressive myoclonic epilepsy (333.2)

345.0 Generalized nonconvulsive epilepsy
Absences: Pykno-epilepsy
  atonic   Seizures:
  typical   akinetic
Minor epilepsy   atonic
Petit mal

345.1 Generalized convulsive epilepsy
Epileptic seizures: Grand mal
  clonic   Major epilepsy
  myoclonic
  tonic
  tonic-clonic
Excludes: convulsions: NOS (780.3), infantile (780.3), newborn
          (779.0), infantile spasms (345.6)

345.2 Petit mal status
Epileptic absence status

345.3 Grand mal status
Status epilepticus NOS
Excludes: epilepsia partialis continua (345.7);
          status: psychomotor (345.8), temporal lobe (345.8)

345.4 Partial epilepsy, with impairment of consciousness
Epilepsy:
 limbic system
 partial:
  secondarily generalized
  with memory and ideational disturbances
 psychomotor
 psychosensory
 temporal lobe
Epileptic automatism

345.5 Partial epilepsy, without mention of impairment of consciousness
Epilepsy:
 Bravis-Jacksonian NOS
 focal (motor) NOS
 Jacksonian NOS
 motor partial
 partial NOS

Epilepsy:
 sensory-induced
 somatomotor
 somatosensory
 visceral
 visual

345.6 Infantile spasms
Hypsarrhythmia
Lightning spasms
Salaam attacks
Excludes: salaam tic (781.0)

345.7 Epilepsia partialis continua
Kojevnikov's epilepsy

345.8 Other forms of epilepsy
Epilepsy:
 cursive (running)
 gelastic

Status:
 psychomotor
 temporal lobe

345.9 Epilepsy, unspecified
Epileptic convulsions, fits, or seizures NOS
Excludes: convulsive seizure or fit NOS (780.3)

GLOSSARY

This glossary is intended to provide some homogeneity to the professional language in the field of mental retardation. The condition of retardation is a complex one that requires the services of professionals from several different disciplines, each of which has a somewhat different vocabulary. Because of this situation, difficulties in communication may result in disservice to retarded individuals. This glossary is an updated version of the glossary from the 1977 edition of the AAMD Manual on Terminology and Classification.

Objectives

Our goals were:

1. To provide in a single volume a list of terms used in or relevant to the field of mental retardation and to provide definitions of those terms.
2. To indicate where appropriate equivalent terms, definitions, or criteria within a framework of common factors.
3. To provide a recommended set of terms, definitions, or criteria consistent with the AAMD classification system in mental retardation.

Procedures

This glossary is an updated version of AAMD's 1973 glossary. The basis for that glossary was a questionnaire mailed or hand-delivered to experts in the field. In addition, computerized pools of information were used, and list of over 5,000 terms was evaluated by the AAMD Committee on Terminology and Classification. This list was reduced to terms most commonly used or misunderstood or technical or professional terms. Among the sources also employed in selection of terms were:

Mental Retardation Abstracts. Washington, DC: American Association on Mental Deficiency.

Hawaii Revised Statutes Revised Word List. Pittsburgh: Aspen, 1969.

Maryland Code Word Frequency List. Pittsburgh: Aspen, 1969.

Virginia Code Word Frequency List. Pittsburgh: Aspen, 1969.

Educational Resources Information Center. *Thesaurus of ERIC Descriptors.* Washington, DC: U.S. Department of Health, Education, and Welfare, 1967, 1968.

National Library of Medicine. Medical Subject Headings—1969, *Index Medicus*, Washington, DC: U.S. Department of Health, Education, and Welfare, 1969.

American Journal of Mental Deficiency, volumes from 1970 through 1982.

Mental Retardation, volumes from 1970 through 1982.

MacMillan, D. L. *Mental Retardation in School and Society.* Boston: Little, Brown & Co., 1982.

Robinson, N. M., & Robinson, H. B. *The Mentally Retarded Child: A Psychological Approach* (2nd ed.). New York: McGraw-Hill, 1976.

In addition to using these resources, we reviewed recent programs of AAMD meetings to identify any terms that had come into common use in recent years and consulted standard and specialized dictionaries for verification of commonly used meanings of certain terms in general use.

Once a list was compiled, terms and definitions were submitted to experts in the field of mental retardation for validation and suggestions for clarification of definitions. The final list is the responsibility of the Committee on Terminology and Classification of AAMD, the organization that supported this entire project on classification and terminology.

ability grouping
grouping students into small units for instruction; usually done within classes on the basis of similarity in instructional objectives for achievement of academic skills or language development.

abstract reasoning
ability to comprehend complex relationships and to react to concepts and symbols rather than merely concrete objects; difficulty in abstract reasoning is often associated with mental retardation.

academic ability
competence in usual tasks required by schools.

academic achievement level
    level of functioning in one or more of the basic academic skills, such as reading or mathematics, as measured by standardized tests or by teacher estimation.

acrocephalosyndactyly (*See* Apert syndrome)

acrocephaly
    a disorder consisting of pointing of the head anteriorly.

acting-out behavior
    action or behavior that is very inappropriate to the social setting, usually characterized by high level of activity.

acute infantile diffuse sclerosis (*See* Krabbe diffuse sclerosis)

adaptive behavior
    the effectiveness or degree with which individuals meet the standards of personal independence and social responsibility expected of their age and cultural group. Three aspects of this behavior are maturation, learning, and/or social adjustment. These aspects of adaptation are of differing importance as qualifying conditions of mental retardation for different age groups. There are levels of adaptive behavior defined by the AAMD ABS, the Balthazar Scales of Adaptive Behavior and the Vineland Social Maturity Scale.

Adaptive Behavior Scale (AAMD ABS)
    a rating scale of adaptive behavior intended to measure an individual's routine personal, community, and social responsibility behavior as well as interpersonal behavior.

adenoma sebaceum
    skin lesions consisting of small, shiny, waxy, or reddish discrete or grouped papules, usually distributed over the butterfly area of the face and chin, sometimes accompanied by telangiectasia; adenoma sebaceum, mental retardation, and convulsions suggest the diagnosis of tuberous sclerosis.

adventitious deafness
    severe hearing impairment caused by accident or illness in individuals whose hearing was normal prior to trauma.

advocacy
activities of volunteers or representatives of organizations acting on behalf of disabled individuals; activities include efforts to obtain services, ensurance of legal and human rights, representation, and legislative and legal actions.

air conduction hearing test
administration of a pure-tone hearing test using earphones; results are compared with those of bone conduction tests to determine characteristics of hearing loss.

alexia (*See* dyslexia)

American Sign Language (Ameslan)
system for using fingers, hands, and other body parts for communication; has own grammatical rules and is frequently used with nonverbal retarded persons.

amniocentesis
the technique of aspirating amniotic fluid from the uterus of a pregnant woman for the purpose of cytogenetic or biochemical study.

anophthalmia
cogenital absence of one or both eyes.

anoxia
reduced oxygen content of the blood to a level insufficient to maintain adequate functioning of tissue, particularly brain tissue.

Apert syndrome (acrocephalosyndactly)
craniostenosis, usually of the coronal sutures, vertical lengthening of head; a characteristic facial appearance, including hypoplasia of the maxillae, bulging of the eyes, and a marked syndactyly of the hands and feet; varying degrees of mental retardation occur.

aphasia
loss of language comprehension or production that cannot be explained by hearing or motor deficits or diffuse cerebral dysfunction.

applied behavior analysis (*See* behavior modification)

aptitude
the capacity to profit from training in some particular skill.

articulation disorder
difficulty in producing certain speech sounds; frequently a problem for retarded persons, especially those with more severe degrees of retardation.

asphyxia
the interference of respiration causing extreme lack of oxygen and excess of carbon dioxide.

aspiration level
the goals set by a person for his or her own performance.

ataxia-telangiectasis
syndrome with cerebellar ataxia, telangiectasia (mainly the face, ears), extrapyramidal signs, frequent respiratory infections, and an abnormal immune mechanism; approximately one-third of the patients have mental retardation, usually late in the disease as a result of neurological involvement; it is probably a hereditary disorder with an autosomal recessive type of inheritance.

athetosis
a condition in which there are sudden jerky involuntary movements, particularly those involved with balance, posture, and intentional movements.

atrophy
a wasting of tissues, organs, or the entire body.

attendant (*also called* mental health aide)
person who is employed to provide supervision and guidance as well as some basic care and training services to individuals living in a residential facility.

attention deficit disorder (*See* hyperactivity)

audiogram
a graphic representation indicating the weakest sound heard by individuals tested at several different sound frequency levels.

audiometric zero function
zero decibel level; the lowest level at which nonimpaired persons can hear.

auditory discrimination
ability to discriminate differing sounds; tests of auditory discrimination are used to determine educational planning for stu-

dents, particularly with reference to reading, speech, and language training.

auditory motor function
expression of motor behavior guided or elicited by associated auditory stimuli or cues; responding motorically to verbal direction.

aura
a sensation of perception of stimuli not present and sometimes associated with onset of seizure activity.

autism (*also called* infantile autism)
a pervasive lack of responsiveness to other people, gross deficits in language and communication, bizarre responses to the environment, absence of delusions and hallucinations, with onset before 30 months of age.

autosomal dominant inheritance (*See* inheritance pattern)

autosomal recessive inheritance (*See* inheritance pattern)

babbling
(1) speech sounds that do not convey meaning; as found in vocalization of infants or in certain severely retarded individuals. Some retarded adults make sounds somewhat similar to those made by infants; (2) stage of speech development that precedes understandable words.

baseline
the usual level of functioning proficiency or state of an individual with respect to a particular characteristic; the frequency of occurrence of a behavior before intervention or treatment.

battered child syndrome (*also called* child abuse)
evidence of physical or psychological abuse or neglect of a child by adult(s) and potentially threatening of the child's health functioning, or life.

behavior disorder
(1) a term used to refer to observable general and social behavior abnormalities; (2) impaired or abnormal development of internalized controls or mechanisms with which individuals can effectively cope with the natural and social demands of their environment.

behavior modification (*also called* applied behavioral analysis)
precisely planned, systematic application of methods and experimental findings of behavioral science with intent of altering
observable behavior, including increasing, decreasing, extending, restricting, teaching, or maintaining behavior; some of key
concepts are:

OPERANT BEHAVIOR, behavior controlled by its consequences;

RESPONDENT BEHAVIOR (classical, Pavlovian), reflex behavior elicited or controlled by its antecedents;

POSITIVE REINFORCER, a stimulus that, when presented as a
consequence of a response, increases or maintains the response;

NEGATIVE REINFORCER, an aversive stimulus that, if removed as a consequence of a response, increases or maintains the
response;

PUNISHMENT, an aversive stimulus applied as a consequence
of a response and intended to decrease the frequency of the
response;

CHAIN, two or more performances combined into a more complex sequence, and occurring in a determinate order;

CONTINGENCY, relationship between a given response and its
environmental consequences;

CONTINGENCY MANAGEMENT, manipulation of environmental consequences of a given behavior in order to achieve a
specific behavioral goal;

DIFFERENTIAL REINFORCEMENT, reinforcement of a response under one stimulus condition but not under other
stimulus conditions (e.g., for low rate but not high rate of performance, for performance with one adult but not with other);

SCHEDULE OF REINFORCEMENT, program designed for
presentation of reinforcer; may be time (fixed or variable inter-
val) or number (fixed or variable ratio);

SHAPING, development of new behavior through systematic
plan of reinforcement for successive approximations of the behavioral goal;

TIME OUT, a period of time in which individuals in a contingency management program are removed from or denied the
opportunity to obtain reinforcers.

behavior rating scales
(1) scales for rating specific items describing an individual's behavior in a variety of situations or in dimensions of behavior; (2) measurement techniques or instruments providing classification of the level of an individual's adaptive behavior, such as the Vineland Social Maturity Scale, AAMD Adaptive Behavior Scale.

behavioral disturbance
(1) the interruption or interference of usual patterns of behavior; (2) the breaking up of a usual pattern of coping with natural and social demands of the environment; commonly symptomatic feature of some other primary disorder, trauma, or malfunction.

behaviorism
(1) a systematic position maintaining that the subject matter of psychology is observable behavior, not conscious; (2) a doctrine that the data of psychology consist of the observable evidences of organismic activity to the exclusion of introspective data or references to consciousness and mind.

bilingual student
(1) a student who speaks two languages fluently; (2) as used in many school situations, a student in a school in which English is the ordinary language of instruction, but the child comes from a home in which some other language is routinely spoken.

birth injury
a temporary or permanent trauma sustained during the birth process.

blindisms
repetitive, stereotyped movements, such as rocking, eye rubbing, waving fingers in front of eyes; blindisms are seen in many blind children as well as in certain severely or profoundly retarded or behaviorally disordered children. (*See also* stereotyped behavior)

boarding home
a community residential facility that may provide general supervision, supports, and personal care, as well as food and lodging, to semi-independent or independent persons; often used in community placement for individuals not requiring more intensive programming.

bone conduction hearing test
administration of tones to forehead with a vibrator; results are compared to air conduction test results to determine type of hearing loss.

borderline intelligence
individuals who function at the level between retardation and average intelligence; sometimes called slow learners.

Bourneville disease (*See* tuberous sclerosis)

Brachmann-de Lange syndrome (*See* de Lange syndrome)

burnout
a term used to describe loss of motivation or desire to continue working in a particular setting, as in group homes or other residential facilities.

career education
inclusion of education about the world of work in educational curricula from kindergarten throughout school years.

cerebral lipidoses
disorders in the metabolism of sphingolipids with resulting accumulation in abnormal amounts in the brain of one or more of these compounds. The cells of the gray matter are involved in cerebromacular degenerations, and those in the white matter, with demyelinization in the leukodystrophies.

cerebral palsy (Little disease)
a disorder dating from birth or early infancy, nonprogressive, characterized by examples of aberrations of motor function (paralysis, weakness, incoordination) and often other manifestations of organic brain damage, such as sensory disorders, seizures, mental retardation, learning difficulty, and behavioral disorders.

chaining (*See* behavior modification)

chemotherapy
treatment of mental, physical, and social malfunctioning by means of chemical substances or drug to arrest or lessen symptomatology.

childhood psychosis
　a pattern of child behavior characterized by markedly inappropriate recognition, understanding, or responding to people or objects in the environment.

childhood schizophrenia
　psychosis in children that may be characterized by a combination of marked isolation, inappropriate or noncommunicative speech and language, regressive behavior, delusions, or hallucinations.

chromosome abnormality
　any body in the cell nucleus that is the bearer of genes that differ in any way from the usual state or structure.

chromosomes
　microscopic intranuclear structures that carry the genes; the normal human cell contains 46 chromosomes.

chronological age (CA)
　age of an individual determined on basis of birthdate; frequently used for comparing relative status on test performance with others of same age when using tests.

class action litigation
　court action initiated on behalf of a group of individuals who have some common characteristics; many class action suits have been filed on behalf of retarded persons as a group.

clinical child psychologist
　a psychologist holding a PhD degree and specializing in diagnosis and treatment of children having psychological or developmental disabilities.

clinical evaluation
　application of generalized scientific methodology to the assessment and diagnosis of an individual, with or without using formal tests.

cluttering
　speech that is rapid, sometimes erratic in rhythm, and sometimes slurred, garbled, or repetitive and disorganized.

cognitive deficit
　an inadequate or subaverage intellectual performance or functioning.

collaborative (educational)
an educational arrangement in which several school districts cooperate to provide instruction for groups of students with low prevalence disorders, such as severe retardation.

commitment (legal)
assignment to custody or treatment by court order; this term is generally contrasted to voluntary admission procedures that are usually done through administrative processes.

community residence
a term used to describe a variety of living settings other than large state-supported residential facilities.

competency test
in legal usage, an evaluation of an individual to determine whether he or she is legally capable of making choices, hence, is legally responsible for his or her actions; incompetence may be determined for mentally ill and/or retarded persons, as well as minors.

competitive employment
working in a setting in which one competes with the general population; many mildly retarded adults engage in competitive employment.

computer-assisted instruction
teaching of units of instruction by having students interact with a computer that has been programmed to provide specific information, directions, and feedback.

concrete thinking
use of mental operations to reason without much capacity to abstract or generalize.

conductive hearing loss
hearing loss due to malfunction in sound transmissions from the auditory canal to the inner ear; may be corrected medically, surgically, or compensated for by using a hearing aid.

congenital
present at birth.

congenital toxoplasmosis (*See* toxoplasmosis, congenital)

contingency management (*See* behavior modification)

convulsive disorders (*See* epilepsy)

Cornelia de Lange syndrome (*See* de Lange syndrome)

counseling
professional guidance on the basis of knowledge of human behavior and the use of special interviewing skills to achieve
specified goals that are mutually accepted by counselor and
client.

craniofacial dysostosis
premature closure of one or more sutures of the skull with
resultant deformity of the head; may cause damage to the brain
and the eyes.

cretinism
congenital hypothyroidism, which, if untreated, results in mental
retardation, delayed skeletal maturation, dry and cold extremities, myxedema, and a large tongue protruding from an
open mouth.

cri-du-chat syndrome (cry-of-the-cat syndrome)
chromosomal disorder in which there is deletion of part of the
chromosomal material on one of the short arms of the 4–5
group; clinical manifestations are severe mental and motor retardation, microcephaly, rounded facies, hypertelorism, and in
infancy, a cry that sounds similar to that of a Siamese cat.

criterion-referenced test
a test using a standard, or criterion, that is used to determine
whether students have or have not reached an established objective; the students are compared with a predetermined standard
of performance rather than with others of their age.

cross-age tutoring
use of older and more advanced students to teach younger students, particularly to teach certain basic academic skills such as
reading; used occasionally for retarded students.

cultural deprivation (*See* deprivation, environmental)

cultural disadvantage (*See* deprivation, environmental)

cultural-familial retardation
term occasionally used to indicate a condition of unknown etiology, presumably associated with family history of borderline intelligence or mild retardation and home environment that is either depriving or inconsistent with the general culture.

custodial care
archaic term used to mean the 24-hour supervision (medical, social, physical, psychological) of a person usually provided by an institution with the purpose of maintaining the person's present condition rather than providing treatment or therapeutic function; generally contrasted to active treatment.

cystinosis (Lignac syndrome)
metabolic syndrome with excessive storage of cystine crystals in the reticuloendothelial system and other body organs; transmitted as an autosomal recessive; infant appears normal at birth. Clinical manifestations appear after 6 months of age, when growth failure, weakness, dehydration, and fever may occur; few children live beyond 8 years of age.

cytomegalic inclusion disease
an illness caused by cytomegalovirus. It may be an inapparent infection for the mother, but can, if transmitted to the fetus, cause a devastating generalized infection, including encephalitis with subsequent damage to the developing nervous system; a major complication is the damage to the central nervous system, often with severe mental retardation.

day-care program
extended care services provided on an on-going basis for individuals residing in the community and not eligible for school programs or workshops; involves social, physical, recreational, and personal-care training and activity.

decible (**also** deciBel or dB)
a unit of relative intensity of sound; used to classify degree of functional hearing.

deinstitutionalization
a term used to describe the movements of substantial numbers of residents of large state residential facilities to either smaller state facilities or to group homes located in urban, semi-urban, or rural settings.

de Lange syndrome (Brachmann-de Lange syndrome; typus degenerativus amstelodamensis; Cornelia de Lange syndrome)
severely retarded, small statured individuals with bushy, confluent eyebrows, up-turned nose, wide upper lip, hypertrichosis,
and skeletal abnormalities.

dependent mentally retarded
mentally retarded individuals who require continuing supervision or assistance in social functioning and daily living.

deprivation, environmental
insufficient quantity, variability, or discriminability of stimulation in the environment. Includes:
CULTURAL DEPRIVATION, a condition in which the general
total environment of a child is markedly inappropriate for
teaching skills needed for coping with the general environment,
even though appropriate for the subculture.
MATERNAL DEPRIVATION, a condition in which the infant
receives insufficient, inconsistent, or inappropriate stimulation
or care.
CULTURAL DISADVANTAGE, a term used in essentially the
same way as cultural deprivation.

deprivation, sensory
a condition in which one or more of the major senses (e.g., vision,
hearing) are so impaired as to reduce or restrict markedly use of
the sense; in such cases, intellectual retardation may occur if
provisions are not or cannot be made for compensation for the
reduced sensory input.

developmental delay
observed disparity between a child's actual development, particularly in language and cognition or motor skills, and the level
usually seen in children developing normally.

developmental disability
a severe, chronic disability which is attributable to a mental or
physical impairment or combination of mental and physical impairments; is manifested before age 22; is likely to continue
indefinitely; and results in substantial functional limitations in
three or more areas of major life activity.[1]

---

[1]From the Developmental Disabilities Assistance and Bill of Rights Act,
codified at 42 U.S.C. §§ 6000-81 (1976 & Supp. V 1981).

deviation IQ
IQ determined on the basis of comparison of performance of an individual on an intelligence test with the performance of others of the same age; deviation IQs have supplanted the ratio IQ (MA/CA × 100) formerly used for most intelligence tests.

diagnostic-prescriptive teaching
instruction in which assessment and evaluation are used to define specific instructional objectives and techniques; used with students having cognitive or academic deficits.

diagnostic process
comprehensive study of an individual based on findings derived from assessment, examination, and interpretation.

differential reinforcement (*See* behavior modification)

disability
functional or physical defect or impairment that can be specified and described objectively; disabilities may handicap an individual in daily living, education, or vocational performance.

dizygotic twins
twins who are not genetically identical because they came from separate eggs.

dominant gene (*See* inheritance pattern)

Down syndrome (mongolism, trisomy 21)
syndrome in which the majority of affected individuals are trisomic for chromosome number 21; clinical manifestations include epicanthal folds, oblique palpebral fissures, broad bridge of the nose, protruding tongue, open mouth, square-shaped ears, muscular hypotonia, often congenital heart disease, and varying degrees of mental retardation.

DSM-III
Diagnostic and Statistical Manual, third edition, of the American Psychiatric Association; provides a comprehensive diagnostic system for classification of disorders in psychiatry, including general classification of mental retardation consistent with AAMD's detailed system.

dysarthria

speech defect due to inadequate control of muscles used in articulation because of neurological dysfunctioning.

dyslexia

term used in inconsistent ways; generally indicates serious reading difficulty; condition characterized by an inability to read more than a few words with understanding.

early childhood education (*See* preschool education)

echolalia

the noncognitive repetition of a word or sentence just spoken by another person; senseless repetition of a word or sentence sometimes exhibited by severely retarded children, as well as by all children during early stages of language development.

ecological assessment

assessment in which stress is placed on the interaction between the individual and the environment.

educable mentally retarded (EMR)

a term used primarily by educators to refer to mildly retarded students, most of whom are capable of learning basic functional academic skills, such as reading, writing, and arithmetic, by the age of late adolescence; most EMR individuals maintain themselves independently or semi-independently as adults.

education

(1) preparation for an effective and satisfying place in society; (2) provision of structured learning experiences, based upon appropriate evaluations, through the use of a broad and varied curriculum of practical academic subjects primarily designed to develop students' ability to learn and acquire useful knowledge and basic skills and to improve the ability to apply them to everyday living; (3) education and training; the action or process of teaching or learning directed toward increased development, skill, or knowledge derived from formal or informal instruction, experience, training, and so forth; (4) a planned attempt to facilitate sensorimotor, emotional, social, and intellectual development of the individual. Emphasis is placed on the individual's ability to develop an awareness of given actions; includes activities that remedy, enhance, and compensate for the specific barriers to learning.

educational retardation

academic achievement, as measured by standardized tests, on one or more of the basic skill subjects that is markedly below that expected for chronological age level.

elective mutism

a selective refusal to speak, independent of intellectual endowment and/or neurologic status, observed in some retarded children.

electrodermal audiometry (EDA)

a procedure using measurement of skin resistance in response to sounds; used in testing very young children and severely or profoundly retarded persons.

electroencephalogram (EEG)

a measurement of the electrical activity of the brain; of value in establishing the presence of a central nervous system electrical abnormality and of particular assistance in the diagnosis of epilepsy.

electronic visual aid

any of the recently developed devices, such as the echolocation device or the Canterbury Child's Aid, which uses electronic apparatus to detect objects and emit sounds; used by blind persons, including retarded ones.

emotional lability

frequent changes or swings in mood, often accompanied by highly variable behavior.

encephalitis

inflammation of the brain resulting from the response of the cerebral tissues to a wide variety of infections and, occasionally, toxins; the diagnosis of encephalitis is usually restricted to those diseases in which there is a diffuse, nonpurulent cerebral inflammation that principally affects the gray matter; other clinical and pathological syndromes are better termed *encephalopathies*.

encephalomyelitis

a syndrome characterized by onset of neurological signs and symptoms as a result of demyelinization in the central nervous system.

encephalopathy (*See* encephalitis)

endogenous mental retardation
a term sometimes used to refer to significant impairment of intellectual functioning that is assumed to be caused by developments within or originating from within the central nervous system.

environmental deprivation (*See* deprivation, environmental)

epilepsy (convulsive disorder)
clinical disorder characterized by single or recurring attacks of loss of consciousness, convulsive movements, or disturbances of feeling or behavior; these transient episodes are associated with excessive neuronal discharges occurring diffusely or focally in the brain; the sites of neuronal discharge determine the clinical manifestations of the seizure.

epiloia (*See* tuberous sclerosis)

erythroblastosis fetalis (*See* hemolytic disease of newborns)

evaluation
the application of techniques for the systematic appraisal of physical, mental, social, economic, and intellectual resources of individuals for the purposes of diagnosis and the development of individualized program of action to be followed by periodic reappraisals as appropriate; determines the extent to which the presenting problem limits or can be expected to limit individuals' daily living and working activities.

evoked-response audiometry
a technique used for measuring hearing functioning by observing brain-wave activity in response to sounds; sometimes used with severely retarded persons.

exceptional children
(1) term sometimes used as synonym for mentally retarded; (2) term for children who deviate significantly from the average in physique, sensory acuity, intelligence, social conformity, emotional development, or learning; the term is correctly used for both high and low extremes, but most often refers to individuals with a disability.

exogenous mental retardation
a term sometimes used to refer to retardation assumed to originate from causes external to the body.

expressive language
language directed toward other(s), ordinarily spoken language or writing, but may include gestures and motoric communication; ability to communicate with others through language.

extended care
the prolonged or continued supervision, care, custody, protection, etc., of individuals; usually considered in contrast to active treatment.

family care
(1) the charge, protection, or custody given by people related by blood or marriage to one another; (2) a program and/or constellation of services provided by nonrelated persons through a recognized agency(ies) to an individual reentering the community after short- or long-term residential care and treatment directed toward enabling the individual's reorientation, readjustment, and satisfactory functioning to total life experience in the community situations; also known as aftercare, follow-up; (3) legal definitions according to state statutes.

feebleminded
obsolete term used to describe individuals of limited intelligence; has been used in England in more restricted sense to refer to a mild degree of mental retardation.

fetal alcohol syndrome
defects associated with excessive drinking of alcohol during the mother's pregnancy and manifested in the child in mental retardation, facial anomalies, heart defects, behavioral problems, or other deficiencies.

fingerspelling
use of the fingers on one hand to spell out letters of the English alphabet in order to communicate; some fingerspelling is used in sign language, but the terms are not synonymous.

follow-along
    the establishment and maintenance of a life-long relationship
    with individuals and their families, as they desire, for the pur-
    pose of assuring that anticipated changes in needs and/or needs
    arising from crises are recognized and appropriately met.

foster care (*also called* foster home care)
    a program or constellation of community services provided as in
    a family through a recognized agency(ies) to individuals requir-
    ing at least residential care and supervision on a short-term basis
    when it is impractical or impossible for them to live indepen-
    dently or with their natural family; most often regarded as sur-
    rogate family-life experience but can be more broadly inter-
    preted as supervised community semi-independent living.

foster grandparent program
    a program in which older persons, such as retired persons, inter-
    act socially with handicapped children living in residential
    facilities to the mutual benefit of both groups.

Friedreich ataxia (hereditary spinocerebellar ataxia)
    a hereditary disorder transmitted as an autosomal recessive gene
    affecting males and females equally; usual age of onset is be-
    tween 7 and 10 years, with manifestations of stumbling, ataxia,
    loss of position sense, kyphoscoliosis, pes cavus, extensor plantar
    responses, and occasional electrocardiographic changes; the dis-
    order is progressive, and death usually occurs by 30 years of age.

galactosemia
    abnormal elevation of the concentration of the carbohydrate
    galactose in the blood. Two different enzymatic defects produce
    galactosemia, but the clinical manifestations of each one are
    distinct. The more common form has an almost complete defi-
    ciency of galactose-1-phosphate uridyl transferase activity. The
    disorder is serious, leading to death in infancy or mental retar-
    dation in those who survive. The other, an uncommon disorder,
    results from a deficiency of galactokinase, is relatively benign,
    and characterized clinically only by the presence of cataracts.

gargoylism (*See* Hurler syndrome)

generalization (*See* transfer of training)

generic service system
the full range of services to all people in the areas of health, education, social service, rehabilitation employment, legal services, and housing.

genes
responsible for hereditary characteristics; are arranged at specific locations along the chromosomes of a cell.

German measles (*See* rubella)

globoid cell leucodystrophy (*See* Krabbe diffuse sclerosis)

glycogen storage diseases (GSD)
result of metabolic errors that lead to abnormal concentrations or structure of glycogen.

grand mal epilepsy
seizures characterized by generalized tonic and/or clonic movements of the extremities associated with loss of consciousness.

group homes
a generic term used to describe residential facilities for retarded persons living away from their own homes; the number of persons living together under supervision in group homes may vary from as few as 3 to as many as 50.

group living
a situation usually under supervision in which a number of unrelated individuals live together; provides mutual communication, interaction, stimulation, social support, and access to community-based programs.

group therapy
treatment by trained leadership of psychosocial problems using the interacting forces within a small unit of individuals who may have similar or differing characteristics.

halfway house
a facility designed primarily to provide a bridge between a residential facility or foster home and the community; offers living arrangements for retarded or mentally ill persons who have demonstrated a certain amount of independence and may

eventually move into independent living; can provide short-term placement as a means of determining readiness for independent living. Residents may work in the community and care for themselves and their quarters but are assured assistance in budgeting money, personalized supervision, and counseling as the need arises.

handicapped person
one who because of intellectual, physical, sensory, or emotional impairment is significantly restricted from learning, working, or adapting to the demands of the environment and society; handicap may be manifested in one or more areas of life functioning, depending on the type and degree of the disability, the demands of the environment, prosthetic devices and arrangements, and opportunities to develop skills that reduce the handicap.

haptic tests
tests relying on touch perception for assessment (e.g., of functioning) sometimes used with blind retarded persons.

hemiplegia
paralysis of one side of the body.

hemolytic disease of newborns (erythroblastosis fetalis)
an immune hemolytic disorder caused by passive transplacental transfer of a maternal antibody active against the fetus; e.g., hemolytic disease of newborns due to (a) Rh incompatibility and (b) A or B incompatibility.

hepatolenticular degeneration (Wilson disease)
a hereditary, progressive disorder characterized by slowly progressing liver disease, by dysfunction of the lenticular nucleus (in brain), or both.

hereditary spinocerebellar ataxia (*See* Friedreich ataxia)

Hertz (Hz) unit
a measurement of the frequency of sound; indicates the highness or lowness of the sound.

high birth weight
Infants weighing more than 4,000 grams at birth. Mortality increases for infants over this weight.

high risk infants
   those who have a high probability of disability as indicated by specified environmental or physical factors identified during the prenatal, perinatal, or early childhood period.

histidinemia
   abnormal level of histidine in blood due to deficiency of enzyme histidase. Some of the affected persons have had impaired speech, a few are retarded in growth, and some are mentally retarded. The metabolic defect is transmitted as an autosomal recessive trait.

holophrastic speech
   the use of a single word in place of an entire sentence or phrase; used during early speech development by all children and by some severely or profoundly retarded persons throughout life.

homebound instruction
   education provided by itinerant teachers on a short-term basis for students with temporary disabilities and longer for some severely handicapped children.

homemaker service
   direct intervention by qualified, trained persons into a home that maintains a handicapped person to assist and enable the family in coping with a handicapped family member by way of supplementing parental care, maintaining family unity, etc.; the service is not designed for long-term care, but for transitory or temporary periods of needs.

Hoover cane
   a long flexible cane that is swept in an arc in front of blind persons to aid in detection of obstacles and terrain changes; used by some blind retarded persons.

houseparents
   individuals employed to provide supervision and guidance to children, adolescents, and/or adults as surrogate mothers or fathers in a residential setting, such as an institution, group home, or halfway house.

Hurler syndrome (gargoylism, mucopolysaccharidosis)
   a disorder of mucopolysaccharide metabolism associated with characteristic facial appearance, including broad bridge of the

nose, open mouth with protruding large tongue, thickened lips, corneal clouding, coarse facial features. Hepatomegaly and hypertrichosis are present as is mental retardation. Transmitted as an autosomal recessive.

hydrocephalus
a condition characterized by enlargement of the head due to excessive pressure of cerebrospinal fluid.

hyperactivity (*See also* attention deficit disorder in DSM-III)
a degree of motor activity that is greatly in excess of that considered appropriate for the age of the child and the situation; often associated with brief attention span and high level of motoric behavior in school classrooms.

hypertelorism
abnormally large distance between the eyes and an apparent broadening of the root of the nose; not a disease entity.

hypertrophy
general increase in bulk of a body part or organ, not due to tumor formation.

hypoactive
(1) very slow, lacking, or sluggish when moving or working; (2) under, beneath, below, less than the usual use of energy.

hypoglycemia
a condition characterized by abnormally low blood sugar.

hypotonia
reduced muscle tone.

iatrogenic effects
unforeseen adverse consequences of treatment efforts precipitated, aggravated, or induced by attitudes, examination, comments, or treatments by a professional.

ICD-9
International Classification of Diseases, ninth edition; provides a comprehensive system for diagnosis of medical diseases and disorders, including a general classification system of mental retardation consistent with AAMD's detailed system.

idiopathic epilepsy
epilepsy for which the cause is unknown.

idiot

an obsolete term used centuries ago to describe all retarded persons and during the 19th and early 20th century to describe persons who would today be called profoundly or severely retarded.

idiots savant

persons with obvious mental retardation who are capable of performing remarkable feats in sharply circumscribed intellectual areas (e.g., arithmetic, calendar calculations) at a remarkably high level.

IEP (Individualized Educational Program, Individualized Educational Plan)

An educational plan devised for an individual on the basis of thorough evaluations; IEPs are mandated by PL 94-142 and must include statements of present educational functioning and performance, immediate and long-term instructional goals, educational services to be provided, criteria and procedures for determining whether goals are met, and indications of persons responsible for implementing the plan.

illiteracy

the inability to read and/or write well enough for practical use in the absence of impairment of intelligence or structural or physiological sensory defect; ordinarily attributed to failure to receive or take advantage of educational opportunities but sometimes attributed to low mental ability.

inborn errors of metabolism

deviations from normal metabolic processes dependent upon enzymes that are absent or present in abnormal amounts and are dependent upon genetic abnormalities; examples of inborn errors of metabolism with associated mental retardation are phenylketonuria, galactosemia.

independent functioning

the ability of individuals to accomplish successfully those tasks or activities demanded of them by the general community, both in terms of the critical survival demands for the community and typical expectations for specific age groups.

infantile autism (*See* autism)

Information and Referral Service
(1) a system of services through which existing resources are
identified and working relationships between and among them
are established within a community for the purposes of assisting
individuals and families to locate, obtain, and make proper use of
needed services; (2) provisions for up-to-date and complete listing of all appropriate resources serving retarded individuals.
This listing is available and quickly accessible to professionals,
parents, retarded persons, and the community. The agency
makes referrals to the needed, appropriate, and most readily
available resources.

inheritance pattern
AUTOSOMAL DOMINANT INHERITANCE, when a single
dose of the gene in the individual heterozygous for that gene
results in clinical manifestations; the trait will be found in one
parent (of either sex) and in half the sons and half the daughters
of an affected individual.
AUTOSOMAL RECESSIVE INHERITANCE, both genes must
be abnormal for the appearance of clinical manifestations; only
the homozygote is symptomatic; parents are generally clinically
normal. Theoretically, one-fourth of the offspring inherit the
abnormal genetic factor from each parent and are affected;
one-half are heterozygotes like parents, and one-fourth are
normal.
X-LINKED INHERITANCE, traits determined by genes carried
on the X chromosome may be either recessive or dominant in the
female; when a male, who has only one X chromosome, has the
specific gene, the trait is always expressed.

institution
(1) a public or private facility or building(s) providing a constellation of professional services, usually on a 24-hour residential
basis, including those directed toward the care, treatment,
habilitation, and rehabilitation of mentally retarded individuals;
is sometimes separated from the general population; (2) an organization having a social, educational, or religious purpose such
as a school, church, hospital, reformatory, etc.

intelligence quotient (IQ)
a number held to express relative level of intelligence of a person;
major standardized individual intelligence tests present IQ in

terms of standard scores that provide comparisons with the tested individual's chronological age peers.

interdisciplinary team
a group of professionals who work together, usually meeting for the purpose of determining diagnosis and for planning interventions for disabled persons; usually includes a physician, a psychologist, and a social worker, in addition to representatives of other disciplines that provide services to the individuals in a facility.

IPP (Individualized Program Plan)
used for residents of facilities providing 24-hour care; similar to the IEP used in educational settings but including more aspects of daily living and service.

IQ (*See* intelligence quotient)

ISO standard
the International Standard Organization's determination of hearing levels; slight is from 27 to 40 dB loss; mild, 41 to 55 dB loss; marked, 56 to 70 dB loss; severe, 71 to 90 dB loss; and extreme, 91 or more dB loss.

itinerant teachers
specially trained teachers who go from school to school or to homes to provide special education to homebound students or to handicapped children who are too young for school programs; work in close cooperation with the students' other teachers.

kernicterus
yellow staining of the nuclear masses of the brain and brain stem by bilirubin pigments as a result of abnormally high levels of bilirubin in the blood, as occurs in hemolytic disease of newborns.

Krabbe diffuse sclerosis (globoid cell leucodystrophy, acute infantile diffuse sclerosis)
a rapidly progressive degenerative disorder of the cerebral white matter occurring in infancy with autosomal inheritance. Affected infants appear normal at birth; clinical manifestations begin during the first months of life and consist of stiffness of the lower extremities, feeding difficulties, spells of incessant screaming. Death usually occurs before the end of the first year.

kwashiorkor
a clinical syndrome associated with mental retardation and resulting from a severe deficiency of protein with adequate or almost adequate caloric intake; occurs in children from 4 months to 5 years of age. Edema, diarrhea, dermatitis, depigmentation, and hepatomegaly are common manifestations.

labeling
applying a name to an object, person, or event; assigning a name indicating a particular classification scheme or system, or of subgroups (classes) within a classification system.

Laurence-Moon-Biedl-Bardet syndrome
a clinical syndrome characterized by mental retardation, obesity, hypogenitalism, polydactyly, and retinitis pigmentosa; mode of transmission appears to be autosomal recessive.

lead poisoning (plumbism)
increased ingestion of lead results in increased tissue burden; the residual effects of the toxic action of lead on the central nervous system are at times permanent and may even be progressive for years.

learning disabled
a broad category of students who share the common problem of having difficulty in school learning, especially in reading and/or math; some educators view learning disability as distinctly different from retardation and others do not.

least restrictive alternative (*also called* least restrictive environment)
legal term referring to the mandate that handicapped students should be provided educational services in as "normal" an environment as is consistent with their unique needs.

leukodystrophy
diffuse disorders of the cerebral white matter; there may be progressive paralytic dementias of early life due to a hereditary defect in the composition of myelin or an acquired diffuse destructive process of cerebral white matter.

life-support care
the care necessary for some profoundly retarded individuals with major biomedical problems; e.g., those requiring oxygen, special feedings.

Lignac syndrome (*See* cystinosis)

lipidosis (cerebral)
inborn or acquired disorders of lipid metabolism affecting the brain.

low birth weight (*See* Preterm)

mainstreaming
a colloquial term used by educators to refer to the integration of handicapped children into regular classes for part or all of the school day.

maternal deprivation (*See* deprivation, environmental)

measured intelligence
the ability to perceive, remember, and understand relationships and to generalize; indicated by results of a standardized general intelligence test such as the Stanford-Binet Intelligence Scale (also known as the Terman-Merrill Scale), the Wechsler Intelligence Scale for Children (WISC-R), the Wechsler Adult Intelligence Scale—Revised (WAIS-R), and the Wechsler Preschool and Primary Scale of Intelligence (WPPSI).

meningocele
a saclike mass covered by skin containing an inner layer of meninges that communicates with the meninges lining the subarachnoid space. If the mass contains meninges and also neural elements of spinal cord or nerve roots, it is classified as a meningomyelocele.

meningomyelocele (*See* meningocele)

mental age (MA)
the chronological age for which performance is "average" or "normal"; determination of MA is based on the examinee's success in passing a series of test items that are ordered in difficulty and represent age levels at which most children are successful with the items; the examinee has been successful with all test items at some level (basal age) below the assigned MA and with none at some higher level (ceiling age).

mental deficiency
(1) mental retardation; (2) sometimes used to distinguish the group of persons having demonstrable organic basis for their intellectual deficits. (*See also* mental retardation)

mental retardation

significantly subaverage general intellectual functioning existing
concurrently with deficits in adaptive behavior and manifested
during the developmental period. Levels of retardation are:
MILD MENTAL RETARDATION, a term used to describe the
degree of retardation present when intelligence test scores are 50
or 55 to approx. 70; many mildly retarded (educable) individuals
who function at this level can usually master basic academic skills
whereas adults at this level may maintain themselves independently or semi-independently in the community.
MODERATE MENTAL RETARDATION, a term used to describe the degree of retardation when intelligence test scores
range from 35 or 40 to 50 or 55; many trainable individuals
function at this level; such persons usually can learn self-help,
communication, social, and simple occupational skills but only
limited academic or vocational skills.
SEVERE MENTAL RETARDATION, a term used to describe
the degree of retardation when intelligence test scores range
from 20 or 25 to 35 or 40; such persons require continuing and
close supervision but may perform self-help and simple work
tasks under supervision; sometimes called dependent retardation.
PROFOUND MENTAL RETARDATION, a term used to describe the degree of retardation present when intelligence test
scores are below 20 or 25; such persons require continuing and
close supervision, but some may be able to perform simple self-
help tasks; profoundly retarded persons often have other handicaps and require total life-support systems for maintenance.

metabolic disease

an illness that affects, interrupts, or interferes with normal
metabolic processes.

microcephaly

hypoplasia of the cerebrum resulting in a small head; primary
microcephaly may be transmitted as in an autosomal recessive
gene; secondary microcephaly may result from exogenous lesions
due to prenatal infections, such as rubella, toxoplasmosis;
trauma such as X-ray or neonatal asphyxia; or birth injury;
associated mental retardation usually ranges from moderate to
profound.

mild mental retardation (*See* mental retardation)

minimal brain dysfunction
a term previously used to describe a condition in which a child may show behavioral or educational but not necessarily neurological signs indicative of neurological dysfunction; because the term is used in a variety of ways by different professionals, it has proven to be of limited utility. (*See also* attention deficit disorder)

modeling
a term used by social learning theorists to indicate that learning is taking place as a function of imitation of the behavior of another person.

moderate mental retardation (*See* mental retardation)

mongolism (*See* Down syndrome)

monoplegia
a condition in which one limb is paralyzed.

monozygotic twins
genetically identical twins originating from a single egg.

moron
obsolete term describing a person with mild mental retardation characterized by about IQ 50 to 75 and failure to advance beyond the mental age of about 12 years; preferred term is educable mentally retarded or mildly retarded.

mosaicism
a type of Down syndrome in which some cells have an extra chromosome and others do not.

mucopolysaccharidosis (*See* Hurler syndrome)

multiply handicapped
a classification of children in which two or more disabilities are present, e.g., mental retardation and deafness and/or blindness.

multisensory learning
a technique to facilitate learning that employs a combination of sense modalities at the same time (such as sight, tactile, and sound).

mutation
> a change in the character of a gene giving rise to new genes; this occurs rarely.

nature–nurture controversy (*also called* heredity–environment controversy)
> debate among scientific investigators over the relative contributions of heredity and environment to intellectual development, beginning with classic studies such as that of Skeels and Dye in the late 1930s; the controversy continues to date.

negative reinforcement (*See* behavior modification)

negative transfer (*See* transfer of training)

neurological dysfunctioning
> presumed or demonstrated disturbance in the functioning of the central or peripheral nervous system.

nongraded class (*also called* ungraded class)
> a small school class providing special education opportunities for handicapped pupils needing individualized learning programs along with group activities; most frequently these pupils are grouped according to general chronological age and ability (e.g., primary educable, intermediate educable) or by disability (e.g., physically handicapped, hearing handicapped, learning disabled).

nongraded system
> organized, established policies and programs without grade levels within an educational administrative unit for the delivery of education curricula to pupils; emphasizes individualized learning rather than the traditional education systems of grades kindergarten through 12.

nonverbal ability
> the power or special skill to perform an act or task, physical or mental, not involving the use of words; e.g., mechanical ability.

normalization
> a philosophical principle originating in Denmark and holding that mentally retarded persons should have made available to them patterns and conditions of everyday life that are consistent with their needs and as close as possible to the norms and patterns of mainstream society.

norm-referenced test
a standardized test with specified procedures for administration and scoring of test items and summarized statistics describing the performance on the test of a reference group of specified ages or grade levels; the performance of an examinee can be compared with that of others; scores are reported as standard scores, percentiles, grade equivalents, age equivalents, stanines, or T-scores.

norms of development
empirically derived age levels at which infants and children are typically able to perform behavior that is known to develop in a sequential pattern (e.g., locomotor, language, gross- and fine-motor skills).

occupational therapist
a specialist in restoration or development of motor skills, particularly fine-motor skills.

oligophrenia
literally, little mind or little head; mental weakness; mental deficiency; used as a synonym for mental retardation in some countries. (*See also* mental retardation)

operant behavior (*See* behavior modification)

orthotics
a professional specialty concerned with restoration of or compensation for lost function of body parts by using braces, adaptive devices, etc.

paraplegia
a condition in which both legs are paralyzed.

pediatric neurologist
a physician specializing in diagnosis and treatment of neurological disorders of children.

pediatric psychologist
a clinical psychologist specializing in psychological services for children with medical problems.

pediatrician
a physician who specializes in diagnosis and treatment of disorders of children; pediatricians also work with retarded persons of all ages.

Pelizeaus-Merzbacher disease

a rare variety of leukodystrophy characterized by early onset in infancy with prominent nystagmus and cerebellar signs, very slow rate of progression, and possibly transmitted as a sex-linked recessive trait (i.e., males in successive generations are affected through healthy females); several documented cases, however, have been females.

perception

awareness of stimuli transmitted via neurological system of organism (e.g., visual, auditory, tactile, kinesthetic sensory system); also used to indicate both the awareness of sensory stimulation and the reaction thereto.

perceptual disorder

a high-order (cerebral) impairment of the awareness of visual, auditory, or haptic stimuli.

performance test

(1) a standardized test that generally requires the use and manipulation of physical objects and the application of physical and manual skills; (2) nonverbal standardized test of intelligence.

perinatal conditions

conditions occurring around the time of the delivery of an infant.

perseveration

(1) the persistent repetition or continuation of a word, sentence, or action after it has been once begun or recently completed; (2) the tendency of any mental formation, once initiated, to remain and run a temporal course; (3) the tendency of a feeling, idea, act, or disposition to recur with or without the aid of association tendencies.

petit mal seizure

a seizure characterized by brief lapses of consciousness.

phenylketonuria (PKU)

a metabolic genetic disorder in which there is inability to metabolize phenylalanine. If untreated, results in severe brain damage and mental retardation.

phocomelia
a deformity in which one or more limbs are very short or missing; sometimes found in certain rare disorders associated with mental retardation.

phonetics
(1) the branch of linguistics that is concerned with the analysis of the sounds employed in speech; (2) speech sounds or the production or transcription of these.

phonics
in teaching reading, the phonetic value of letters of the alphabet.

physical therapist
a specialist in restoration or development of motor skills, particularly of the large muscles.

physically handicapped
persons whose nonsensory physical limitations or health problems make it difficult for them to cope with the demands of the environment to the extent that they require special services or aids.

PL 89–313
Amended Title I of Elementary and Secondary Education Act to provide grants for state-supported schools for handicapped students.

PL 91–230
the federal Elementary and Secondary Education Act; contains provisions for support for programs designed to reduce or prevent disabilities in educational settings; also Section C of the act contains legislation concerning the Handicapped Children's Early Education Program (HCEEP) for children from birth to 8 years of age.

PL 93–112, Section 504
Section 504 of the Vocational Rehabilitation Act is a civil rights provision mandating that there shall not be discrimination in providing vocational rehabilitation services under the act.

PL 94–142
Education for All Handicapped Children Act of the U.S. congress; contains provisions mandating that in order to receive funds under the act, each school system in the United States must

provide for publicly supported education regardless of the degree of severity of the child's handicapping condition.

play technique assessment
the utilization of play and dramatic objects, such as puppets, dolls, toys, and miniatures, in projective testing. Originating in play therapy with children, these materials have subsequently been adapted for psychodiagnostic testing and evaluation.

play therapy
a type of psychotherapy for children utilizing play materials and fantasy construction.

plumbism (*See* lead poisoning)

positive reinforcer (*See* behavior modification)

positive transfer (*See* transfer of training)

postencephalitic
the serious neurological and/or behavioral changes that persist after the patient has recovered from an acute encephalitis.

postmaturity (*See* postterm)

postnatal conditions
conditions that occur soon after birth.

postterm
infants born after 42 weeks of gestation (calculated from the mother's last menstrual period), irrespective of weight at birth. Often used synonymously with the term *postmature* for infants whose gestation exceeds the normal 280 days by 7 days or more.

Prader-Willi syndrome
a syndrome characterized by hypotonia, hypogonadism, and extreme obesity. Although there is usually some degree of cognitive deficit, not all affected individuals are mentally retarded.

preadmission evaluation
term sometimes used for an evaluation service conducted prior to acceptance into a program(s) and/or to determine the appropriateness and placement of an individual; may include psychosocial history, mental, physical, and psychological testing, etc. (*See also* Information and Referral Service)

prematurity (*See* preterm)

prenatal period
the time between conception and delivery of an infant.

preschool education
a training program or nursery school education in which emphasis is placed on developing self-help, motor, communication, and social skills of young children; often provided for retarded children from about age 3, but sometimes from birth until about 7 years of age.

preterm
prematurity, preferably referred to as preterm, refers to liveborn infants delivered before 37 weeks from the first day of the last menstrual period. Infants who weigh 2,500 g or less at birth are considered to have had either a shortened gestational period, a less than expected rate of intrauterine growth, or both, and are termed *infants of low birth weight*. Prematurity and low birth weight are usually concomitant, particularly among infants weighing 1,500 g or less at birth; both are associated with increased neonatal morbidity and mortality.

prevention
(1) the process of the rearrangement of forces in the society against those negative factors in life of which mental retardation is a consequence; (2) using screening and diagnostic procedures to identify high-risk children and provide interventions to prevent disability.

profound mental retardation (*see* mental retardation)

prognosis
the probable outcome of a physical, mental, or social function; based on knowledge of current status plus the known course of diseases.

proprioception
proprioceptive sensations are those that arise from the deeper tissues of the body, principally from the muscles, ligaments, bones, tendons, and joints. Kinesthesia is the awareness of muscular motion, weight, and position.

prosthetic environment
a living or educational arrangement that has been adapted educationally, physically, or in other ways in order to facilitate
maximal functioning; educational arrangements that provide for
intensive support services and residential facilities that improve
access or freedom of movement are sometimes referred to as
prosthetic environments.

prosthetics
a professional specialty concerned with replacing dysfunc-
tional or missing body parts with artificial substitutes; also, such
devices.

protein deficiency
to be lacking or in want of protein; if severe protein-calorie
undernutrition occurs in certain critical periods of mental development (probably in the late prenatal period and the first 6
months of life) it may be associated with mental retardation. (*See
also* kwashiorkor)

pseudoretardation
obsolete term formerly used to refer to a condition in which an
individual's test results indicated retarded functioning but where
the primary condition was believed to be emotional.

psychiatrist
a physician who specializes in diagnosis and treatment of mental disorders.

psychogenic mental retardation
archaic term for retardation of persons having no known
pathological signs; assumed to have a psychic experiential origin.

psychologist
a specialist in learning and behavior.

psychomotor seizures
seizures during which there are semipurposeful movements occurring during a period of altered consciousness; automatisms
include grasping movements of the hand, smacking of the lips,
irrelevant speech, and inappropriate behavior. These are focal
attacks arising from the temporal lobe.

psychopharmacological agent

drugs and other active substances used in the treatment of behavioral disorders and to influence affective, behavioral, and emotional states.

psychopharmacology

the use of drugs to influence affective, emotional, and behavioral states. Drugs used to modify behavior are generally classified into stimulants (dextroamphetamine, methylphenidate), tranquilizers (thioridazine, chlorpromazine), and antidepressents (tricyclic amines).

punishment

any stimulus presented following a discrete behavior and intended to decrease the probability of reoccurrence of the response or behavior; in behavior modification, punishment refers to only those stimuli presented that do in fact reduce the recurrence of the response.

quadriplegia

a generalized increase in muscle tone (spasticity) in all extremities; often a form of cerebral palsy.

receptive language disorder (or disability)

difficulty in the understanding of spoken language; may also refer to difficulties in understanding gestures or sign language.

recessive gene

a recessive gene only expresses itself if it is carried upon both members of the chromosome pair concerned; one abnormal gene alone produces no effect, for the normal allelomorphic gene is dominant.

recreation therapy

provision of planned, appropriate activities designed to (a) provide for individual self-expression, social interaction, and entertainment, (b) develop skills and interests leading to enjoyable and constructive use of leisure time, and (c) improve physical and mental well being.

rehabilitation

the process of improving an individual's skill or level of adjustment with respect to an increased ability to maintain satisfactory independent or dependent functioning, such as self-care, employment, etc.

residential facility (*also called* residential school or hospital)
public or private facilities, large or small, offering 24-hour service that may include short-term, long-term, diagnostic, training, or special programs and may be used in a continuum of services.

resource room
a special classroom for teaching students for part of the school day, especially for those who have a mild handicap.

resource teacher
a special educator who provides instruction during part of the school day to students who spend much of the school day in regular classrooms; the resource teacher also consults with the student's regular classroom teacher; mildly retarded students are often assigned for such services.

respite care
appropriate services in a variety of settings provided for the care of mentally retarded persons through temporary separation from their families, in or out of the home for short, specified periods of time on a regular or intermittent basis and involving other services as needed on an individual basis for the purpose of relieving the families in order to (a) meet planned or emergency needs, (b) restore or maintain their physical and mental well being, (c) initiate training procedures in or out of the home.

respondent behavior (*See* behavior modification)

Rh incompatibility
a hyperimmune state in which the mother has Rh negative blood and the fetus has Rh positive blood, which causes antibody formation in the mother. This may result in destruction of the Rh positive red blood cells and lead to pathology in the offspring, such as abortions, still births, kernicterus, or mental retardation.

Rh sensitization (*See* Rh incompatibility)

Rochester method (*See* total communication)

rubella
German measles; when occurring in a pregnant woman during the first trimester, the infection may affect the fetus by causing

congenital anomalies, including deafness, cataracts, cardiac malformations, and/or mental retardation.

schedule of reinforcement (*See* behavior modification)

Schilder diffuse sclerosis (*See* diffuse cerebral sclerosis)

school phobia
excessive fear of school.

screening program
a program in which brief assessments are used to determine the
group from which individuals with disabilities are likely to come;
for those identified in screening programs, further evaluations
are done to identify those actually having the disability; such
programs include large-scale screening testing of newborn children for metabolic disorders and kindergarten screening programs in schools.

seizure (*See* epilepsy)

selective placement
the assignment of workers to the jobs for which they are judged
best fitted or the inclusion of students in some group, class, or
category according to certain principles or criteria.

self-contained class (*See* special class)

self-injurious behavior (SIB) (*See* self-mutilate)

self-multilate
to damage or disfigure a body part by one's own action (e.g.,
biting or hitting self).

sensorineural hearing loss
hearing loss involving the central nervous system; can usually be
reduced, but not corrected, by use of hearing aid.

sensory deprivation (*See* deprivation, sensory)

severe mental retardation (*See* mental retardation)

severely handicapped
a generic term used to refer to individuals who have serious
handicaps that are predicted to continue for long-term or life;
includes a high proportion of persons at the moderately, severely, and profoundly retarded levels.

shaping (*See* behavior modification)

sheltered employment (*also called* sheltered workshop)
provision of a structured program of activities involving (a) work evaluation, work adjustment, occupational skill training, and short-term remunerative employment designed to affect placement in the competitive labor market; (b) extended, long-term remunerative selected work in a protective environment; (c) extended remunerative activities in a protective environment for individuals with severe disabilities that limit production output.

sign language
a means of communication in which gestures, usually manual, substitute for spoken words, phrases, or letters; used by deaf persons and some nonverbal retarded persons. There are several systems of sign language with some overlapping gestures among them.

slow learners
children with social and academic behavior less than usual age-level standards; individuals who function between retardation and average intelligence.

social and emotional development
the process of resolution of problems associated with self-identification, exploration and mastery, and control of environment; some problems of development are common to all persons but failure to cope with chronic or periodic stresses may require professional intervention.

social learning theory
(1) a term applied to several related theories of learning, all emphasizing the social context in which learning takes place and the importance of significant others (e.g., parents, teachers) in a child's learning; (2) a theoretical basis for many studies and educational programs for retarded students.

social responsibility
the ability of individuals to accept accountability as members of a community group and behave appropriately in terms of these expectations; social responsibility is reflected in levels of conformity, socially positive creativity, social adjustment, and emotional maturity.

social worker
a specialist with graduate school training in social work and trained to provide a variety of social services; many social workers are also psychotherapists.

spasticity
increased tonus or tension of a muscle that is associated with exaggeration of deep tendon reflexes and impairment of voluntary control.

special class (*also called* self-contained class, substantially separate class)
a class for students who have some disability (e.g., mental retardation or emotional disturbance) and are given instruction by special educators who are trained for work in the area of the disability; students are usually grouped by age span of 2 to 3 years for a single class of no more than 12 students; many moderately retarded and more severely retarded children attend special classes.

special education
a form of education involving modified or specially devised instruction for students who have difficulty learning in regular classrooms with regular curricula.

special educator
a teacher who has specialized training for working with students who have educational disability.

special needs student
a term employed in some state laws to designate students who are provided with special educational services.

speech pathologist
a specialist in the evaluation and treatment of speech and language disorders.

sphingolipidosis
inheritable disorders of the nervous system characterized by accumulation of sphingolipids, which are complex molecules prominent in nervous tissue.

spina bifida
a congenital defect resulting from failure of the neural tube to close completely during prenatal development; often associated with mental retardation.

standard error of measurement
this number indicates the degree of confidence that can be placed in a test score; e.g., if a person obtains IQ 70 on a particular test that has a standard error of 4, the chances are 2 to 1 that the "true" IQ on that test is between 66 and 74, 95 to 5 (.05 level of confidence) that the true score is between 62 and 78, and 99 to 1 (.01 level of confidence) that the true score is between 60 and 80; standard error of measurement for a particular test is obtained with a formula that takes into consideration the reliability and the standard deviation of the test. Use of the standard error of measurement can improve clinical decisions in making diagnoses.

standardized test
any test that has empirically selected test items, definite directions for administration and scoring, and data on reliability and validity; may be either norm-referenced or criterion-referenced.

Stanford-Binet Intelligence Scale (*See* measured intelligence)

stereotyped behavior
complex, repetitive movements that appear to be nonfunctional, especially repetitive hand movements, rocking, object twirling, or head banging; "blindisms." Stereotyped behavior is not uncommon among more severely retarded individuals, particularly nonverbal ones.

syndactylism
a condition characterized by webbing together of fingers and/or toes.

syndrome
the aggregate of clinical manifestations associated with any morbid process and constituting together the picture of the disease or clinical condition.

toxoplasmosis, congenital
a disease resulting from infection with toxoplasma gondii, an intracellular parasite. The congenital form (communicated to fetus from mother) is frequently manifested by a syndrome consisting of chorioretinitis, cerebral calcification, mental retardation, convulsions, and hydrocephalus or microcephaly. Postnatally acquired toxoplasmosis is a relatively common inapparent infection.

trainable retarded persons (TMR)
mentally retarded persons who are capable of only very limited meaningful achievement in traditional basic academic skills but who are capable of profiting from programs of training in self-care and simple job or vocational skills.

training
an ordered design leading to a specific end result. Training services are differentiated from educational services by their emphasis on those skills universally needed to function at a minimum level as part of society.

tranquilizer
a drug that is intended to bring tranquility by calming, soothing, quieting, or pacifying without depressing individuals.

transfer of training (*also called* generalization)
the effect of learning one concept upon the learning of another; retarded children are believed to have more difficulty in transfer of training than do their age peers.
POSITIVE TRANSFER, transfer of training in which learning or practice of one skill or task aids in learning of a second one.
NEGATIVE TRANSFER, transfer in which learning or practice in one skill or task interferes with the learning of another task.

transportation services
transporting of individuals to and from places in which they are receiving other services by public or private paid conveyance, except when furnished by the family or relative.

treatment
(1) provision of specific physical, educational, or social interventions and therapies that halt, control, or reverse processes that cause, aggravate, or complicate malfunctions or dysfunctions;
(2) a term used in research studies to mean the experimental manipulation used with subjects.

Glossary

to

syphilis
a venereal disease that can cause mental reta
whose mother contracted the disease durin
transmitted it to the fetus in the prenatal pe

target behavior assessment
direct observation and quantification of prec
havior without inference to the meaning of th

Tay-Sachs disease
a form of cerebral gangliosidosis, largely confin
Jewish ancestry derived from northeastern Eu
single autosomal recessive gene. There is an en
hexosaminidase A. The infant appears normal a
3 and 10 months of age, there is some deteriora
ment, blindness, and seizures. Patients generall
or 3rd year of life. Asymptomatic carriers can
enzyme determination of the blood. An antena
be made by enzymatic determination of fluid
niocentesis.

temporary care home
foster homes that provide short-term or emer
retarded children or adults outside their own
family emergencies or vacations.

testing and evaluation
procedures used by trained professionals to appra
ual's current status, make inferences about his or
acquire skills, or determine necessary interventio

time out (*See* behavior modification)

token economy
a system using principles of behavior modification
uals in acquiring and maintaining skills; often used
vocational training programs for retarded person

total communication
a method of teaching communication skills to nonv
with or without hearing loss; uses gestures or sig
language simultaneously for communication to th

trisomy 21 (*See* Down syndrome)

tuberous sclerosis
a syndrome characterized by adenoma sebaceum, seizures, and often mental retardation of varying degree; may be an autosomal dominant or a recessive type of inheritance.

underachiever
an individual who does not perform in specified ways as well as expected on the basis of known characteristics or previous record. Specifically, a student who does not accomplish as much in school as would be expected from his or her measured intelligence.

ungraded
a class that is not organized on the basis of grade and has no standard grade designation; includes some special classes for mentally retarded pupils.

verbal test
an intelligence test or subtest that requires the use of language to understand directions and to make the required responses. (*See also* measured intelligence)

Vineland Social Maturity Scale
a rating scale of adaptive behavior based on presence or absence of certain types of everyday behavior found to be characteristic or specified; intended to measure how individuals routinely perform rather than the maximal performance of which they are capable.

visual perception (*See* perception)

Wechsler Adult Intelligence Scale—Revised (*See* measured intelligence)

Wechsler Intelligence Scale for Children—Revised (*See* measured intelligence)

Wechsler Preschool and Primary Scale of Intelligence (*See* measured intelligence)

Wilson disease (*See* hepatolenticular degeneration)

X-linked inheritance (*See* inheritance pattern)

APPENDIX A

Age 3 years and above: PROFOUND

(**Note.** All behavior at greater degree of impairment would also indicate PROFOUND deficit in adaptive behavior for persons 3 years of age or above.)

Independent functioning: Drinks from a cup with help; "cooperates" by opening mouth for feeding.

Physical: Sits unsupported or pulls self upright momentarily; reaches for objects; has good thumb-finger grasp; manipulates objects (e.g., plays with shoes or feet). Note: some persons who are profoundly retarded in other areas have moderate to good motor skills, including ambulation.

Communication: Imitates sounds, laughs, or smiles back (repeats "Ma-ma," "buh-buh" responsively); no effective speech; may communicate in sounds and/or simple gestures; responds to gestures and/or signs.

Social: Indicates knowing familiar persons and interacts nonverbally with them.

---

3 years: SEVERE
6 years and above: PROFOUND

Independent functioning: Feeds self finger foods; "cooperates" with dressing, bathing, and with toilet training; may remove clothing (e.g., socks) but not necessarily as an act of undressing as for bath or bed.

Physical: Stands alone or may walk unsteadily or with help; coordinates eye-hand movements.

Note. These illustrations were prepared by one of the committee members (S.A.W.) for use in her classes at Boston University.

Communication: One or two words (e.g., "Mommy," "ball") but predominantly communicates through vocalization or simple gestures.

Social: Responds to others in predictable fashion; communicates needs by gestures, noises, or pointing; plays "patty-cake" or plays imitatively with simple interaction; occupies self alone with "toys" for a few minutes.

---

3 years: MODERATE
6 years: SEVERE
9 years and above: PROFOUND

Independent functioning: Tries to feed self with spoon but has considerable spilling; removes socks, pants; "cooperates" in bathing; may indicate wet pants or "cooperate" at toilet.

Physical: Walks alone steadily; can pass ball or objects to others; may run and climb steps with help.

Communication: Uses 4 to 10 words; may communicate many needs with gestures (e.g., pointing).

Social: Plays with others for short periods, often as parallel play or under direction; recognizes others and may show preference for some persons over others.

---

3 years: MILD
⸍ 6 years: MODERATE
9 years: SEVERE
12 years and above: PROFOUND

Independent functioning: Feeds self with spoon (cereals, soft foods) but may still spill or be messy; drinks unassisted; can pull off clothing and put on some (socks, underclothes, boxer pants, dress); tries to help with bath or hand washing but still needs a lot of help; indicates toilet accident and may indicate toilet need and uses toilet when taken there.

Physical: Climbs up and down stairs but not alternating feet; runs and jumps; balances briefly on one foot; can pass ball to others;

transfers objects; does 4- to 6-piece form-board puzzles without aid.

Communication: Speaks in 2- or 3-word sentences (Daddy go work); names simple common objects (boy, car, ice cream, hat); understands simple directions (put the shoe on your foot, sit here, get your coat); knows people by name. (If nonverbal, may use as many as 10 to 15 gestures to convey needs or other information.)

Social: Interacts with others in simple play activities, usually with only one or two others unless guided into group activity; has preference for some persons over others.

---

6 years: MILD
9 years: MODERATE
12 years and above: SEVERE
15 years and above: PROFOUND

Independent functioning: Feeds self with spoon and/or fork, may spill occasionally; puts on clothing but needs help with small buttons and jacket zippers; tries to bathe self but needs help; can wash and dry hands but not very efficiently; toilet trained but may have accidents, wet bed, or may need reminders and help with cleaning and clothes.

Physical: Hops or skips; climbs steps with alternating feet; rides tricycle (or bicycle over 8 years); climbs trees or jungle gym; plays dance games; throws ball and may hit target.

Communication: Has speaking vocabulary of over 300 to 400 words and uses grammatically correct sentences. If nonverbal, may use many gestures for communication. Understands simple verbal communications, including directions and questions ("Put it on the shelf." "Where do you live?"). May have some articulation problems. May recognize advertising words and signs (Ice cream, STOP, EXIT, MEN, LADIES). Relates experiences in simple language.

Social: Participates in group activities and simple group games; interacts with others in simple play ("Store," "House") and expressive activities (art, dance).

9 years: MILD
12 years: MODERATE
15 years and older: SEVERE

Independent functioning: Feeds self adequately with spoon and fork but may need help cutting meat; can butter bread; can put on clothes and button and zipper clothes; may tie shoes; bathes self with supervision; is toilet trained; washes face and hands without help.

Physical: Can run, skip, hop, dance; uses skates or sled or jump rope; can go up and down stairs alternating feet; can throw ball and hit target.

Communication: May communicate in complex sentences; speech is generally clear and distinct; understands complex verbal communication, including words such as "because" and "but." Recognizes signs and words but does not read prose materials with comprehension.

Social: Participates in group activities spontaneously; engages in simple competitive exercise games (dodge ball, tag, races); has friendship choices that are maintained over weeks or months.

Economic activity: May be sent on simple errands and make simple purchases with a note; knows money has value but does not know values; may use coin machines.

Occupation: May prepare simple foods (sandwiches); can help with simple household tasks (bed making, sweeping, vacuuming); can set and clear table.

Self-direction: May ask if there is "work" to do; may pay attention to task for 10 minutes or more; makes efforts to be dependable and carry out responsibility.

---

12 years: MILD
15 years and over: MODERATE

Independent functioning: Feeds, bathes, dresses self; may select daily clothing; prepares easy foods (e.g., eggs) for self or others; combs/brushes hair; may shampoo or roll up hair; may wash and/or iron and store own clothes.

Physical: Good body control; good gross- and fine-motor coordination.

Communication: Carries on simple conversation; uses complex sentences. Recognizes words, reads sentences, ads, signs, and simple prose material with comprehension.

Social: Interacts cooperatively and/or competitively with others.

Economic activity: Can be sent on shopping errand for several items without notes; makes minor purchases; adds coins to dollar with fair accuracy.

Occupation: May do simple routine household chores (dusting, garbage, dishwashing); prepare simple foods that require mixing.

Self-direction: May initiate everyday activities; attends to task 15 to 20 minutes (or more); is conscientious in assuming responsibility for simple household tasks.

---

15 years and adult: MILD

(**Note.** Individuals who routinely perform at higher levels of competence in adaptive behavior than illustrated in this pattern should NOT be considered as deficient in adaptive behavior. Since by definition individuals are not retarded unless they show significant deficit in *both* measured intelligence and adaptive behavior, those individuals who function at higher levels than illustrated here cannot be considered to be retarded.)

Independent functioning: Exercises care for personal grooming, feeding, bathing, toilet; may need health or personal care reminders; may need help in selection or purchase of clothing.

Physical: Goes about hometown (local neighborhood in city, campus at residential center) with ease, but cannot go to other towns alone without aid; can use bicycle, skis, ice skates, trampoline, or other equipment requiring good coordination.

Communication: Communicates complex verbal concepts and understands them; carries on everyday conversation, but cannot discuss abstract or philosophical concepts; uses telephone and communicates in writing for simple letter writing or orders but does not write about abstractions or important current events.

Social: Interacts cooperatively or competitively with others and initiates some group activities, primarily for social or recreational purposes; may belong to a local recreation group or church group, but not to civic organizations or groups of skilled persons (e.g., photography club, great books club); enjoys recreation (e.g., bowling, dancing, TV, checkers) but either does not enjoy or is not competent at activities (e.g., chess, bridge, tennis) or hobbies requiring rapid, involved or complex planning and implementation.

Economic activity: Can be sent or go to several shops (without a note to shopkeepers) to purchase several items; can make change correctly, but may not use banking facilities; may earn living but has difficulty handling money without guidance.

Occupation: Prepares simple meals; performs everyday household tasks (cleaning, dusting, dishes, laundry); as adult can engage in semiskilled or simple skilled job not requiring complex thinking or judgment.

Self-direction: Initiates most of own activities; is conscientious about work and assumes much responsibility but needs guidance on jobs requiring responsibility for important decisions (health care, care of others, complicated occupational activity).

APPENDIX B

ILLUSTRATIONS OF DECISION-MAKING IN IDENTIFICATION AND LEVELS

The IQ of approximately 70 has been selected as a cut-off point for mental retardation. Discussion of the decision to use the IQ of approximately 70 is provided throughout this book, particularly in Chapters 2 and 4. The decision to classify any individual as retarded is crucial in the life of that individual and requires sound clinical skills in those making such decisions. All standardized tests should be administered with strict adherence to directions, scoring of test items should be done with extreme carefulness. One should not alter test administration instructions or scoring, but discuss any conditions that may have affected scores or performance when reporting one's interpretation of test results. Consideration should be given to the characteristics of the measures used, including validity, standard error of measurement, and type of content. Many individuals are referred because retardation is considered to be a probability, but when evaluated the individuals are determined not to be retarded. In such cases, there is a good probability that the individual is in need of some type of special service and will need to be provided services or referred to another service agency.

DECISIONS IN BORDERLINE CASES

I.   Bill, age 5, was evaluated after selection during kindergarten screening. Family is "poverty level" and has 6 children. Mother reported that Bill feeds self and dresses self except for shoe tying, that he tries to help around the house and with younger children (e.g., makes bologna sandwich for little sister); she says he watches TV a lot, but not Sesame Street; she has little time for reading to children or taking them to museums, etc. and says the home is busy and noisy. Psychologist reported Binet IQ of 68, with range of 4 testing levels, and Vineland of 78. He conversed with the psychologist freely, asked many questions about objects in room. He can count to 5 and recognizes words that are the names of commercial items, saying he learned them from TV.

DECISION: NOT RETARDED. Adaptive behavior within normal limits. Monitor progress in kindergarten & 1st grade.

II.   Maria, age 10. Family moved to mainland from Puerto Rico 10 months ago. Home language is Spanish and Maria plays with Spanish-speaking children around home, with English-speaking ones at school. She has learned to converse in English, but is not fluent. Cannot read in English except for signs and some functional words, names, and some basic sight words she has learned in the two months she has been in school. Is well coordinated physically, plays competitive exercise games at school and home (e.g., sandlot baseball). Plays simple card and board games at home. Above 90th percentile on 8 ABS Part One domains.

Performance IQ on WISC-R was 70, with Block Design of 8, Picture Arrangement of 7, Coding of 7. Binet IQ (administration in English) was 61. Two errors on Bender-Gestalt with

Koppitz scoring. Goodenough-Harris standard score of 76. On standardized arithmetic test, level was 4.5 on computation, 1.9 on arithmetic reasoning test requiring reading.

DECISION: NOT RETARDED. Although difficult to test because of language barrier, she understood enough English to follow simple directions of tests. Although Binet IQ is clearly within retarded range, all scores that are less dependent on English were not. There is strong probability that she will function at higher level when she has mastered English, but she should be monitored by teachers and given re-evaluation if indicated.

III. Camilla, age 8, youngest of 3 children. Parents have been concerned about her development since Camilla was 4 years old, primarily because of slow language development and slowness in development of self-help skills. Mother works parttime, but has spent a lot of time with Camilla from infancy, reading to child, playing with her, and attempting to stimulate language. Camilla now feeds herself with spoon and sometimes uses fork. Gross motor skills appear to be good, but fine motor skills are delayed. Camilla has good articulation, uses short sentences with correct grammar, but vocabulary is limited for age (e.g., failed vocabulary task on Binet for 6-year level) and is below developmental norms in language development. Has short attention span for age and requires many trials to master new material. Binet IQ was 70. Criterion-referenced test indicates recognition of about 25% of basic sight words; she recognizes functional words in context (LADIES, STOP, etc.) for very common words, but not such terms as ENTER HERE. Counts to 20 and understands concept of 4 objects. Repeated kindergarten and standardized achievement tests at school have consistently been 1½ to 2 grades below expected for age. In class and in everyday life, she appears to perform at a lower level than indicated by latest standardized test scores.

DECISION: RETARDED. Currently she is functioning at retarded level in both adaptive behavior
and measured intelligence. Level of
retardation: MILD.

IV. Cheryl, age 12. Medical diagnosis at age 3 was "Cerebral Palsy, Severe." Self-help skills are minimal, although she tries to feed self with spoon (modified) and "helps" to extent physically possible when dressing. Speech is very difficult to understand but she comprehends and responds to compound and complex sentences. Uses communication board well and understands Bliss symbolic communication. On the WISC-R, subscale weighted scores were: Information—7, Comprehension—7, Arithmetic—8, Similarities—6, Picture Completion—9, Vocabulary—7; weighted score of 10 is average and *SD* is 3 for subtests so she does not show retardation in subtests that could be administered. Columbia Mental Maturity Scale score was 83. Receptive vocabulary on PPVT was 88. Raven Progressive Matrices was 23rd percentile.

DECISION: NOT RETARDED. Although markedly retarded in
adaptive behavior skills, the
psychologist did not classify her
as retarded on the basis of the
subscales of WISC-R that could
be administered, other tests,
and receptive language level.
She will need special services
and probably will be classified as
eligible for special education on
basis of "Orthopedic Handicap"
or "Physical Handicap."

V. Kevin, age 16. Medical diagnosis at age 4 was "Cerebral Palsy, Severe." Can indicate agreement and disagreement (Yes, No) by head movements and noises, but does not talk. Self-help skills limited to attempts to feed self with spoon and attempting to remove some clothing. Speech/Language therapist reported language skills to be below 18 months level. Psychologist reported that he seemed not to understand object permanence (Piaget scheme). Attempts to administer standardized scales such as Binet and WISC-R were unsuccessful. In educational programs he has mastered simple communication board with 3 objects, has learned 4 signs for communication (drink, eat, thank you, please). Large number of trials with guidance and modeling required for acquisition of any new skill.

DECISION: RETARDED. Level of retardation: PROFOUND.

VI.   Sally, age 11. Referred by teacher because of "inability to do class work." Sally's school records indicate difficulty with academic work since first grade. Now reads some functional words and about 150 basic sight words and has simple word attack skills (e.g., phonics), but poor reading comprehension for age. Stanford Achievement Test in Fall of this year indicated: Reading Comprehension—2.3, Word Recognition—3.1, Arithmetic Computation—3.4, Arithmetic Reasoning—2.2. Adaptive behavior is reported to be about level of normal child of seven years. Vineland Social Maturity Scale SQ is 64. WISC-R Verbal IQ is 65, Performance IQ is 76, Full Scale IQ is 69.

DECISION: RETARDED. Level of retardation: MILD.

VII.   David, age 4. Reported by social workers to have been a neglected child. Removed from parents to foster home 3 months ago. Foster mother reported that he had "made tremendous progress" in new home. Is very quiet and does not talk much to strangers; was difficult to test, but did cooperate during testing. Has been in a preschool program for 3 months and teachers report progress. Vineland Social Maturity Scale has gone from 46 to 58 since moving to foster home. AAMD Adaptive Behavior Scale shows functioning now at between 50th and 70th percentile (norms for retarded) on most of the sub-scales of Part I, around 80th to 90th percentile on Part II domains. Binet IQ is 54, with test range of 6 levels. He has language, but uses simple words to communicate his wants and observations. Language level estimated to be at about 28 to 30 months level now. Monitor next year.

DECISION: RETARDED. Level of retardation: MILD. He is at lower limits of Mild level and could have been classified as either Mild or Moderate under current system. The history, current behavior in foster home, ability to make rapid progress, and standard error of measurement of Binet were all considered in making this decision on level of retardation.

VIII. Devane, age 4. Lives with parents and one older sibling. His APGAR rating at birth was 4. Has attended preschool since age 2½. Mother reported that he uses a spoon for self feeding (with much spilling), and can remove his socks and underpants; he is partially toilet trained but still has some daytime accidents; he speaks single words and occasional two word sentences or holophrastic phrases. Participates in play with guidance, but seems to prefer parallel play. Binet IQ was 54; was very cooperative during testing and appeared "upset" at failures. Language level estimated to be at about 23 months level by speech/language therapist.

DECISION: RETARDED. Level of retardation: MODERATE. On basis of overall current functioning, language, standard error of measurement of Binet.

IX. Lynn, age 23. In educational programs since age 6. Feeds and dresses himself, but needs help in selection of clothing to wear and must be "checked" to ensure everything is appropriate before going out. Goes about home community without getting lost, but cannot take buses alone. Can go to store 2 blocks away on errand, but takes note for storekeeper and does not know if he has been given correct change. Is reliable in helping with simple household

chores such as bed making, table setting, running vacuum cleaner,
helping at simple chores in kitchen. WAIS scores were below
norms. Binet IQ was 38; psychologist reported that he did not
respond to some verbal tasks, which had to be marked "Fail" and
she did not know whether he could have responded correctly. His
speech is barely understandable, with many articulation problems,
but he responds to directions and requests. He functions adequately in a sheltered workshop on simple tasks requiring stuffing
bags, simple assembly, and attaching stickers in correct places. He
understands that he is paid for work and talks about using the
money he makes, but must be supervised in making purchases with
his money. Vineland Social Age was 5.8 years.

DECISION: RETARDED. Level of retardation: MODERATE.
He is at the borderline of Moderate/
Severe. Decision is based on all data
combined.

X.   Carol, age 23. Has been in educational programs since age 6 in
separate school consortium supported by several school districts.
Has had speech and language therapy, in school and privately.
Feeds self with spoon and dresses self, but mother buys clothing
"easy for her to get on" because she has difficulty with some
clothing. Goes to next door neighbor's house alone, but gets lost if
more than a block or two from home. Attempts to help at home
and does set table, but must do so by setting "a place for Mom, one
for Dad, one for me." Counts by rote to 20, but cannot select 3
objects from a group. Has learned to recognize the word LADIES,
but may call some other word with somewhat similar configuration
by the same name. She likes to talk, using simple, repetitive statements or questions such as "Can you get me a job? "My Mom has a
new dress." Still has some echolalia. During testing she was
cooperative, but had rather short attention span. Binet IQ was 38,
with 5 levels used. She has been tested many times, with IQs
reported of 32, 31, 40, 33, and 30 for previous tests over the past 15
years. Has attempted training in two different sheltered workshops,
but "made no progress." All ABS domains (Part One) below
50th percentile.

DECISION: RETARDED. Level of retardation: SEVERE. At borderline between Severe and Moderate, but functioning seems more like that of Severely than Moderately retarded persons.

XI.   Benny, age 15. Developmentally slow since birth. Has been in school programs since age 5 and Mother had home visits from Developmental Center since Benny was age 1. Ambulation is good, but fine motor skills are not. Feeds self and dresses self except for zippers. Toilet trained, but occasionally has accidents. Likes outdoor activities such as going into swimming pool, climbing, and running races. Can talk, but is repetitive and has a limited vocabulary. Likes to watch TV and play games involving throwing and catching ball. Plays such games cooperatively with relatives, but does not initiate other games spontaneously. Enjoys going to stores with parents, but has no concept of making purchases other than handing the clerk money and waiting for change; however, he likes to have money and shows it to others when he has any. He also shows others cards he receives from relatives and does so repeatedly to same person. Progress at school has been very slow, but he has learned some simple routines such as putting away materials, following directions. Recognizes sign for major fast food shop and some cereal names (when seeing them in context). Can work and enjoys simple form boards. Binet IQ of 23. Attempt to test for academic achievement was unsuccessful as basal level of test was too high for him. Vineland was 4.0 years.

DECISION: RETARDED. Level of retardation: SEVERE. With the IQ of 23 he could be classified as Severe or Profound, but his general functioning overall seems more consistent with the Severe level than the Profound one.

XII.   Frank, age 15. Developmentally slow since birth. Has been in school program since age 4; Mother had visits from staff at Developmental Center since Frank was 1 year old. Ambulation good, but fine motor skills poor. Feeds self with spoon, but needs help with knife and fork. Can remove most of his clothes, but cannot completely dress himself. Does not talk or point to objects but responds to simple verbal requests such as "Please sit down." Likes to run and to play in swimming pool, but does not engage in interactive play. Goes about town with parents, but does not interact with others he meets except in minimal way such as smiling or laughing. Does not recognize his own name in print, but does respond to name when called. Favorite activity seems to be rocking back and forth, both when standing and sitting. Will sit in front of TV set, but does not stay more than a few minutes and appears to be watching movements on screen rather than characters. Binet IQ of 23; tasks requiring verbal responses were marked "Fail" and a basal age was not established at the 24 months level because he was unable to pass Picture Vocabulary; testing required 6 levels because he passed some motor tasks at higher level.

DECISION: RETARDED. Level of retardation: PROFOUND.

INDEX

AAMD Adaptive Behavior Scale, 6, 25, 42, 43, 45; *defined* 157

AAMD Ad Hoc Committee on Data Banks, 86

AAMD Committee on Terminology and Classification, 3, 6, 7, 155

Ability grouping: *defined* 156

Abortion, therapeutic, 97

Abstract reasoning: *defined* 156

Academic ability: *defined* 156

Academic skills, 25, 26

Academic achievement level: *defined* 157

Accessory autosomes NEC, 133

Acrocephalosyndactyly (*See* Apert syndrome)

Acrocephaly: *defined* 157

Acting-out behavior: *defined* 157

Acute infantile diffuse sclerosis (*See* Krabbe diffuse sclerosis)

Adaptive behavior: assessment, 42–46; clinical judgment, 55; deficits in, 1, 11, 25, 26; *defined* 1, 157; interview process, 44; levels by age, 46, 203–208; maladaptive, 44, 72, 98–110; measurements, 25, 42–46; mental retardation levels, 46; rating scales, 43–44, 112

Adaptive Behavior Inventory for Children, 44

Adenoma sebaceum, 142; *defined* 157

Adolescence, adaptive behavior standards in, 25

Adrenal glands, 140

Adventitious deafness: *defined* 157

Advocacy: *defined* 158

Age, and adaptive behavior standards, 25, 203–208

Aged gametes, 147

Air conduction hearing test: *defined* 158

Akinetic seizures, 153

Alcoholism, maternal, 63, 64

Alexia. (*See* dyslexia)

Amentia: *defined* 143

American Sign Language (Ameslan): *defined* 158

Amino acid disorders, 94, 131; *defined* 140

Amniocentesis: 62, 197; *defined* 158

Anemia, 95, 135, 138

Anencephaly, 132, 144

Anophthalmia: *defined* 158

Anoxia, 63, 65, 68, 138; *defined* 158

Antianxiety agents, 105, 108

Anticonvulsants, 93, 105, 108–110

Antidepressants, 105, 107–108

Antimongolism syndrome, 133

Antipsychotics, 105, 106–107

Apert syndrome, 132; *defined* 145, 158

Aphasia, 151; *defined* 158

Aphasis, developmental, 151

Aphonia, 151

Applied behavior analysis (*See* behavior modification)

Aptitude: *defined* 158

Arnold-Chiari malformation, 146

Arterial embolism, 138

Articulation disorder: *defined* 159

Asphyxia, 65, 138; *defined* 159

Aspiration level: *defined* 159

Assessment, 21, 23; of family environment, 51–53; psychological, 38–41; safeguards, 53–57, 81

Astrocytomas, 142

Ataxia, 143

Ataxia-telangiectasis: *defined* 159

Athetosis: *defined* 159

Atonic seizures, 153

Atrophy: *defined* 159

Attendant: *defined* 159

Attention deficit disorder, 99 (*See also* hyperactivity)

Audiogram: *defined* 159

Audiometric zero function: *defined* 159

Auditory discrimination: *defined* 159–160

Auditory motor function: *defined* 160

Aura: *defined* 160

Autism, 14, 15, 99–100; *defined* 160

Autoimmune: deficiency, 136; mechanisms, 147

Autosomal chromosome abnormality, 133, 147, 180

Autosomal deletion syndrome, 133; *defined* 147

Autosomal dominant inheritance: *defined* 180

Autosomal recessive inheritance: *defined* 180

217

Autosomal translocation, balanced, 133

Babbling: *defined* 160; (*See also* speech disorders)
Bacterial infection, 130, 136
Balthazar Scales of Adaptive Behavior, 43, 44, 157
Basal ganglion disorder, 143
Baseline: *defined* 160
Batten-Spielmeyer-Vogt disease. (*See* juvenile amaurotic idiocykaryotyping)
Battered child syndrome: *defined* 160; (*See also* child abuse)
Bayley Scales of Infant Development, 40
Behavior (*See* adaptive behavior)
Behavior disorder: *defined* 160
Behavior management, 111–112
Behavior modification, 120; chaining *defined* 161; contingency management *defined* 161; differential reinforcement *defined* 161; negative reinforcement *defined* 161; operant behavior *defined* 161; positive reinforcer *defined* 161; punishment *defined* 161; respondent behavior *defined* 161; schedule of reinforcement *defined* 161; shaping *defined* 161; time out *defined* 161
Behavior rating scales: *defined* 162
Behavioral disturbance, 98–110; *defined* 162
Behaviorism: *defined* 162
Bielschowsky disease. (*See* juvenile amaurotic idiocykaryotyping)
Bilingual student: *defined* 162
Bilirubin, 137
Biochemical screening, 97
Biosocial factors, 68–70
Birth: asphyxia, 138; injury *defined* 137, 162; trauma, 137; weight, 61–61, 69, 133, 148
Blindisms: *defined* 162
Blindness, 41, 100, 150, 151–152; *defined* 151–152
Bliss symbols, 117
Blood incompatibility, 137 (*See also* Rh incompatibility)
BMT Instrument, 44
Boarding home: *defined* 162
Bone conduction hearing test: *defined* 163
Bonnevie-Ullrich syndrome (*See* gonadal dysgenesis)
Borderline intelligence: *defined* 163

Borderline retardation, 6
Bourneville disease (*See* tuberous sclerosis)
Brachmann-de Lange syndrome (*See* de Lange syndrome)
Brachycephaly, 145, 147
Brain damage, 99, 135, 138
Brainstem evoked potentials, 96
Brushfield spots, 147
Burnout: *defined* 163

CA (*See* chronological age)
Cafe-au-lait spots, 141
Cain-Levine Social Competency Scale, 44
Calcification (*See* cerebral calcification)
California Preschool Social Competency Scale, 44
Camelot Behavioral Systems Checklist, 44
Carbohydrate disorders, 131, 138; *defined* 139–140
Carbon monoxide, 137
Cardiac anomalies, 135
Cardiomegaly, 139
Career education: *defined* 163
Cat cry (*See* cri-du-chat)
Cataracts, 135
Cattell Infant Intelligence Scale, 40
Ceramide lactosidosis, 139
Cerebellar ataxia, 142
Cerebral calcification, 135, 136, 142
Cerebral lipidoses: *defined* 163
Cerebral malformation, 132; *defined* 144
Cerebral palsy, 14, 92, 95, 96, 99; *defined* 163; infantile, *defined* 152; intelligence testing in, 41
Cerebral white matter, degenerative, 132; *defined* 142
Cerebrovascular system, 132, 143
Chaining. (*See* behavior modification)
Chemotherapy: *defined* 163
Child abuse, 66, 71
Childhood, adaptive behavior standards in, 25, 203–208
Childhood psychosis: *defined* 164
Childhood schizophrenia: *defined* 164
Choreiform movements, 143
Chorioretinitis, 136
Chromosome abnormality: 61–62, 63, 64, 93; categories, 133; *defined* 147–148 (*See also* inheritance pattern)

Chromosomes: *defined* 164; sex, 133
Chronological age (CA): 30, 32–34; *defined* 164
Cigarette smoking, 63, 64
Cirrhosis of the liver, 140
Class action litigation: *defined* 164
Classification: clinical applications, 91–122; history of, 5; misuses of, 20–21; purposes of, 2; research applications, 89–90; service system applications, 79–82; systems, 17–20
Cleft palate, 144, 147
Client Centered Evaluation Model, 44
Clinical child psychologist: *defined* 164
Clinical evaluation: *defined* 164
Clinical judgment, need for: 55, 208–209
Cluttering: *defined* 164
Cognitive deficit: *defined* 164
Cognitive-developmental theory, 34–38
Collaborative (educational): *defined* 165
Columbia Mental Maturity Scale, 41
Commitment (legal): *defined* 165
Communication problems, 96
Communication skills, 25, 26, 117–118; in adaptive behavior levels, 203, 204, 205, 206, 207
Community residence: *defined* 165
Competency test: *defined* 165
Competitive employment: *defined* 165 (*See also* work)
Competitive Employment Screening Test and Remediation Manual, 44
Computer-assisted instruction: *defined* 165
Concrete thinking: *defined* 165; operations level, 36
Conductive hearing loss, 152; *defined* 165
Confidentiality, 86
Congenital: *defined* 165
Congenital abnormalities, 136
Congenital hypothyroidism, 92, 94
Congenital malformations, 60, 64, 144
Congenital toxoplasmosis (*See* toxoplasmosis, congenital)
Contingency (*See* behavior modification)
Contingency management (*See* behavior modification)
Contusion (laceration), 138
Convulsions, 65, 135, 136, 138, 153–154
Convulsive disorders, 150; classification, 153–154 (*See also* epilepsy)

Cornelia de Lange syndrome (*See* de Lange syndrome)
Counseling: *defined* 166
Coxsackie-virus Group B, 136
Craniofacial anomaly, 132, 144
Craniofacial dysostosis, 132; *defined* (Crouzon syndrome) 145, 166
Craniofacial malformation, 144, 166
Craniostenosis, 132, 145; *defined* 145
Cretinism, 94; *defined* 141; 166; goitrous, 141
Cri-du-chat syndrome, 133; *defined* 147, 166
Criterion-referenced test: *defined* 166
Cross-age tutoring: *defined* 166
Crouzon syndrome (*See* craniofacial dysotosis)
Cry-of-the-cat syndrome (*See* cri-du-chat syndrome)
Cultural deprivation: *defined* 168 (*See also* deprivation, environmental)
Cultural disadvantage: *defined* 168 (*See also* deprivation, environmental)
Cultural-familial retardation, 48; *defined* 167
Custodial care: *defined* 167
Cutaneous angioma, 142
Cyclopia, 144
Cystine, 140
Cystinosis: *defined* 167
Cytogenetics, 93, 158 (*See also* chromosomal abnormalities)
Cytomegalic inclusion disease, congenital, 130; *defined* 135, 167
Cytomegalovirus, 135

Day-care program: *defined* 167
De Lange syndrome, 132; *defined* 144, 168
Deaf, intelligence testing of, 41
Deaf mutism, 152
Deafness, 29, 135, 143, 150, 152, 157; sign language, *defined* 158
Decible: *defined* 167
Deinstitutionalization: *defined* 167
Dementia, 12, 143
Demyelinization, 171
Dental abnormalities, 95
Dental hygiene, 95
Deoxyribose, 140
Dependent mentally retarded: *defined* 168

Deprivation, cultural: *defined* 168
Deprivation, environmental, 70–75, 149; *defined* 168
Deprivation, maternal, 70–75, 149; *defined* 168
Deprivation, sensory, 70–73, 150; *defined* 150, 168 (*See also* blindness; deafness)
Dermatoglyphic peculiarities, 93
Destructive hyperuricemia, 140
Developmental appraisal, 38
Developmental deficits, 11
Developmental delay: *defined* 168
Developmental disability: *defined* 168; legislative definition of, 14
Developmental Disabilities State Plan, 82
Developmental period: defined, 1, 11
Deviation IQ: *defined* 169
Diabetes, maternal, 65, 137
Diagnosis, medical, 91–94
Diagnostic coding, examples of, 127, 128
Diagnostic-prescriptive teaching: *defined* 169
Diagnostic process: *defined* 169
Diet, 95, 149 (*See also* nutritional disorders)
Differential reinforcement (*See* behavior modification)
Diplegia, 152
Disability: *defined* 169
Disadvantage, cultural: *defined* 168
Dizygotic twins: *defined* 169
Dominant gene (*See* inheritance pattern)
Down syndrome (mongolism, trisomy 21), 22, 62, 93, 94, 95, 133; *defined* 147, 169
DSM-III, 2, 7, 10, 99, 123–126, 127–129, 133, 149, 150; *defined* 169
Drug-induced disorders, 136–137
Drugs, 63, 101, 147 (*See also* psychopharmacological agents)
Dysarthria, 143, 151; *defined* 170
Dyslexia: *defined* 170
Dysphasia, 151
Dysphonia, 151
Dysphoria, 98
Dystocia, 137

Early adolescence, in adaptive behavior standards, 25, 203–208

Early childhood, in adaptive behavior standards, 25, 203–208
Early childhood education (*See* preschool education)
Early intervention, 73–74
Echolalia: *defined* 170
Ecological assessment: *defined* 170
Economic activity, in adaptive behavior levels, 206, 207, 208
Edema, 65, 148
Educable mentally retarded (EMR): 113; *defined* 170
Education, 111–117; *defined* 170 ms 263
Education for All Handicapped Children Act, The, (*See* PL 94–142)
Educational facilities, 101
Educational management, 111–117
Educational retardation: *defined* 171
Edwards syndrome, 133; *defined* 147
Elective mutism: *defined* 171
Electrodermal audiometry (EDA): *defined* 171
Electroencephalogram (EEG), 92; *defined* 171
Electronic: communication aid, 117; visual aid *defined* 171
Emotional disturbance, 98–110, 143 (*See also* psychiatric disorders)
Emotional lability: *defined* 171
Employment, sheltered *defined* 196 (*See also* work)
Encephalitis, 60, 65, 136; *defined* 171; postvaccinal, 136
Encephalomyelitis: *defined* 171
Encephalopathy, 137, 171 (*See also* encephalitis)
Endocrine disorders, 131; *defined* 171
Endogenous mental retardation: *defined* 172
Environmental deprivation (*See* deprivation, environmental)
Environmental influences, 70–75, 134; *defined* 149–150
Enzyme disorders, 61, 139
Epicanthal folds, 147, 148
Epilepsy (nonconvulsive), 153; (convulsive), 14, 92, 93, 99, 145, 153; *defined* 153–154, 172; grand mal, 153; petit mal, 153; progressive myoclonic, 153 (*See also* seizures)
Epiloia (*See* tuberous sclerosis)
Erythroblastosis fetalis (*See* hemolytic disease of newborns)
Eunuchoid features, 148

Evaluation: *defined* 172; services, 82–89
Evoked-response audiometry: *defined* 172
Exceptional children: *defined* 172
Exogenous mental retardation: *defined* 173
Expressive language: *defined* 173
Extended care: *defined* 173
Extra-pyramidal dysfunction, 140, 143

Fabry disease, 139
Facial dysotosis, 145
Facies, 137
Fairview Development Scale, 44
Fairview Social Skills Scale for the Mildly and Moderately Retarded, 44
Familial cretinism, 61
Family environment, 47–53, 70–72; assessment of, 51–53
Family care: *defined* 173
Family planning, 71, 72, 73, 97
Feebleminded: *defined* 173
Fels Parent Behavior Rating Scale, 52
Fetal alcohol syndrome, 64, 130; *defined* 137, 173
Fetal growth, 134; slow *defined* 148
Fingerspelling: *defined* 173
Focal seizures, 154
Follow-along: *defined* 174
Formal thinking operations level, 37
Foster care, 51, 75; *defined* 174
Foster grandparent program: *defined* 174
Foster home (*See* foster care)
Friedreich ataxia, 143; *defined* 174
Fructokinase, 139
Fructose, 139
Fructosemia, 131; *defined* 139
Fungal infections, 136

Galactokinase, 139
Galactose, 139
Galactosemia, 61, 131; *defined* 139, 174
Ganglioside storage diseases, 131; *defined* 138
Gargoylism (*See* Hurler syndrome)
Gaucher disease, 139
Gene defects, 61
Gene mutation, 147
General intellectual functioning: *defined* 1, 11
Generalization (*See* transfer of training)
Generic service system: *defined* 175

Genes: *defined* 175
Genetic disease, 61, 91
German measles (*See* rubella)
Gesell Developmental Schedules, 41
Gestational disorders, 134; *defined* 148–149 (*See also* prematurity, postmaturity)
Gliomas, 142
Gliosis, 142
Globoid cell leucodystrophy (*See* Krabbe diffuse sclerosis)
Glucose, 139
Glycogen storage diseases (GSD), 61, 131; *defined* 139, 175
Glycogenoses (*See* glycogen storage disease)
Glycolipidoses, 131; *defined* 139
Gonadal dysgenesis, 133; *defined* 147
Grand mal epilepsy, 153; *defined* 175 (*See also* epilepsy)
Gross brain disease, postnatal, 131, 141–143; *defined* 141
Group homes: *defined* 175
Group living: *defined* 175
Group therapy: *defined* 175
Growth, disorders of: *defined* 138–141
Gynecomastia, 148
Gyri malformation, 144

Halfway house: *defined* 175–176
Hallervordern-Spatz disease, 143
Handicapped person: *defined* 176
Haptic tests: *defined* 176
Hearing loss, 96, 152 (*See also* deafness)
Heavy-for-dates, 134, 149; *defined* 149 (*See also* gestational disorders)
Heavy metals, 137
Hemiplegia, 135, 142, 143; congenital, 153; *defined* 176; infantile, 153
Hemolytic disease of newborns, 136; *defined* 176
Henderson Environmental Learning Process Scale, 52
Hepatic disease, 137
Hepatolenticular degeneration: *defined* 176
Hepatomegaly, 135
Hepatosplenomegaly, 136
Hereditary fructose intolerance (*See* fructosemia)
Hereditary spinocerebellar ataxia (*See* Friedreich ataxia)
Heredogenerative disorders, 141
Heroin, 63

Herpes simplex, 136
Hertz (Hz) unit: *defined* 176
Hexosaminidase, 199
High birth weight: *defined* 176
High risk infants: *defined* 177
Hirsutism, 144
Hiskey-Nebraska Test of Learning Aptitude, 41
Histidinemia: *defined* 177
Holophrastic speech: *defined* 177
Holoprosencephaly, 132; *defined* 144
Homebound instruction: *defined* 177
Homemaker service: *defined* 177
Home Observation for the Measurement of the Environment, 52
Hoover cane: *defined* 177
Horseshoe kidneys, 148
Houseparent: *defined* 177
Hunter disease, 139
Huntington disease, 132; *defined* 143
Hurler disease: *defined* 177–178
Hutchinsonian incisors, 135
Hutchinson triad, 135
Hydrocephalus, 96, 133, 135, 136, 145; *defined* 146, 178
Hydroencephaly, 133; *defined* 146
Hyperactivity, 99, 100, 102; *defined* 178
Hyperbilirubinemia, 130; *defined* 137
Hyperextension, 96
Hyperflexion, 96
Hyperkinetic (*See* hyperactivity)
Hypertelorism, 147, 148; *defined* 178
Hypertrophy: *defined* 178
Hypoactive: *defined* 178
Hypoglycemia: 62, 65, 131; *defined* 139
Hypoplasia of the maxillae, 145
Hypospadias, 147
Hypothyroidism, 141
Hypotelorism, 144
Hypotonia: *defined* 178
Hypoxia, 131; *defined* 178

Iatrogenic effects: *defined* 178
ICD-9, 2, 7, 10, 23, 123, 126, 127, 128, 133, 134, 147, 150; *defined* 178
Icterus, 135
Idiopathic epilepsy: *defined* 178
Idiopathic hypercalcemia, 131; *defined* 140
Idiot: *defined* 179
Idiots savant: *defined* 179

IEP: *defined* 179
Illiteracy: *defined* 179
Immunologic deficiency, 61
Inborn errors of metabolism, 61, 136; *defined* 179
Incidence, 75–77, 79
Incoordination, 143
Independent functioning: in adaptive behavior levels, 204, 204, 205, 206, 207; *defined* 179
Individualized Educational Plan (*See* IEP)
Individualized Educational Program (*See* IEP)
Individualized Program Plan (*See* IPP)
Infancy, in adaptive behavior standards, 25
Infantile autism (*See* autism)
Infantile cerebral Gaucher disease, 139
Infections, 95, 130, 134; hidden, 95; prenatal, 60–61, 130, 135–136; postnatal, 65, 130, 136
Information and Referral Service: *defined* 180
Inheritance pattern: autosomal dominant inheritance *defined* 180; autosomal recessive inheritance *defined* 180; *defined* 180; recessive gene *defined* 193; X-linked inheritance *defined* 180
Institution: *defined* 180
Intelligence: assessment of, 27–41; average, 31; borderline, 16, 22; dull normal, 16; error of measurement in, 56; levels, 13, 23, 32, 39–40; subaverage, 11; temporal variation in, 55; tests, 11, 23, 24, 28–32, 40–41, 55–57; quotient (IQ), 11, 13, 22–25, 27–41, 55, 76, 208; *defined* 180–181; untestable, 127
Interdisciplinary team: *defined* 181
Interstitial keratitis, 135
Intestinal parasitic disease, 95
Intoxication, 130, 134; *defined* 136
Intracranial tumors, 142
IPP: *defined* 181
IQ (*See* intelligence)
Irradiation, 63
Irritability, 95
ISO standard: *defined* 181
Isoleucine, 140
Itinerant teachers: *defined* 181

Jackson Characteristics of the Treatment Environment, 52
Jansky-Bielschowsky disease, 139
Jaundice, 136
Juvenile gangliosidosis, 138
Juvenile paresis, 135

Kernicterus: *defined* 137, 181
King, Raynes, and Tizard Child Management Survey, 52
Klinefelter syndrome, 133, 147; *defined* 148
Knowledge Availability Systems Center (KASC)
Krabbe diffuse sclerosis (globoid cell leukodystrophy, acute infantile diffuse sclerosis): *defined* 181
Kuf disease, 139
Kwashiorkor: 67; *defined* 182 (*See also* protein deficiency)

Labeling, 7, 20–21; *defined* 182
Labor, complications of, 65, 137
Laceration, 138
Language development, 96, 101, 118 (*See also* communication skills)
Language therapy, 96, 112, 118
Large-for-dates, 149
Late adolescence, in adaptive behavior standards, 25
Lawrence-Moon-Biedl syndrome, 132, 145; *defined* 182
Lead encephalopathy, 66
Lead intoxication, 130, 137
Lead poisoning, 63; *defined* 182
Learning disabilities, 15, 16, 66, 68, 143; *defined* 182; legislative definition of, 15
Learning disabled, 16; *defined* 182
Learning process
Least restrictive alternative: *defined* 182, 280
Leisure skills, 119–120, 122
Leiter International Performance Scale, 41
Lesions, 135, 141, 143, 145
Leucine, 140
Leukodystrophy: *defined* 182; Pelizaeus-Merzbacher, 132, 143; Sudanophilic, 132, 142–143
Life-support care: *defined* 182
Light-for-dates, 134; *defined* 148

Lignac syndrome (*See* cystinosis)
Lipidosis (cerebral): *defined* 183
Lipochondrodystrophy (*See* gargoylism)
Lipofuscin storage diseases, 131; *defined* 139
LISREL, 87
Literacy, 75
Little disease, 152; *defined* 163
Living arrangements, 110–111
Low birth weight, 72 (*See also* gestational disorders; prematurity)
LSD, 64
Lymph gland, 136

MA (*See* mental age)
Macroencephaly, 132; *defined* 145
Mainstreaming: *defined* 183, 281
Major epilepsy, 153
Malabsorption syndromes, 140
Maladaptive behavior (*See* adaptive behavior)
Malformations, multiple, 133
Malnutrition, 67, 73–74; fetal, 134, *defined* 148–149; maternal, 64, 65, 71, 73–74, 137 (*See also* nutritional disorders; protein deficiency)
Mannogalactoprotein storage, 139
Mannosidosis, 139
Manpower development center
Maple syrup urine disease, 61
Maternal infection (*See* prenatal infection)
Maternal deprivation, 72–73; *defined* 168 (*See also* deprivation, environmental)
McCarthy Scales of Children's Abilities, 32, 41
Measles, 136 (*See also* rubella)
Measured intelligence, 12; *defined* 183 (*See also* intelligence)
Medicaid, 80
Medical management, 91–97
Medulloblastomas, 142
Megalencephalon fluid, 146
Meningocele: *defined* 183
Meningoencephalocele, 132; *defined* 145–146
Meningomyelocele, 96; *defined* 146 (*See also* meningocele)
Mental age (MA), 30, 32–34, 55; *defined* 183

Mental deficiency: *defined* 183 (*See also* mental retardation)

Mental Measurements Yearbook, 87

Mental retardation: adaptive behavior and, 26, 42–46, 130; associated with sociocultural or psychosocial disadvantage, 70–75; of biologic origin, 59–70; categories, 125, 126, 129; classification difficulty, 59; defined, 1, 11, 184; incidence of, 75–77, 89–90; intelligence measurement and, 22–25, 31, 32–33; legislative definition of, 14; levels of, 13, 32, 129; mild, 13, 37, 93, 125, 126, 129, *defined* 184; moderate, 13, 38, 125, 126, 129, *defined* 184; prevalence of, 75–77, 89–90; prevention of, 72–75; profound, 13, 36, 37, 92, 125, 126, 129, *defined* 184; severe, 13, 37, 92, 125, 126, 129, *defined* 184; typology, 59; unspecified, 125, 126, 134, 150

Mercury poisoning, 63

Merrill-Palmer Scale of Mental Tests, 41

Metabolic disease: *defined* 184

Metabolism, disorders of, 94, 131; *defined* 138–141

Methionine, 140

Microcephalus, 132; *defined* 144

Microcephaly, 64, 92, 135, 136, 144, 147, 148; *defined* 184

Microencephaly, 144

Microguathia, 147

Microophthalmia, 136

Mineral disorders, 131; *defined* 140–141

Minimal brain dysfunction, 99; *defined* 185 (*See* also hyperactivity)

Minnesota Developmental Programming System, 44

Modeling: *defined* 185

Money, concept of, 26

Mongolism (*See* Down syndrome)

Monoplegia, 153; *defined* 185

Monozygotic twins: *defined* 185

Moos Family Environment Scale, 51

Moron: *defined* 185

Mosaicism: *defined* 185; of sex chromosome, 133

Mother-child relationship, 48, 69, 71

Motor dysfunction, 118–119, 150; ataxia, 143; cerebral palsy, 152–153; diplegia, 152; hemiplegia, 153; monoplegic, 153; paraplegia, 152; quadriplegic, 153; spasticity, 152; tetraplegic, 153

Motor impaired, 118; intelligence testing of, 41

Motor skills, 118–119 (*See also* physical development)

Mucopolysaccharidosis, 139 (*See also* Hurler syndrome)

Multiple malformations: *defined* 146

Multiply handicapped: *defined* 185

Multisensory learning: *defined* 185

Mumps, 136

Muscular dystrophy, 141

Mutation: *defined* 186

Myelin, 142

Myoclonic seizures, 143, 153

Nature-nurture controversy: *defined* 186

Needs assessment, 84

Negative reinforcement (*See* behavior modification)

Negative transfer (*See* transfer of training)

Neglected child (*See* deprivation, environmental)

Neoplasms, 141

Nephritis, 137

Nervous system, 12, 13, 16, 126

Neural groups, degenerative, 132; *defined* 143

Neurocutaneous diseases, 142

Neurocutaneous dysplasia, 131; *defined* 141

Neurofibroblastamatosis (*See* neurofibromatosis)

Neurofibromatosis (von Recklinghausen disease), 131; *defined* 141

Neurologic testing, 93

Neurological dysfunctioning, 100; *defined* 186

Neuronal lipid storage diseases, 131, 138

Neuronal lipidosis

New growths (*See* tumors)

Niemann-Pick disease, 139

Non-English speaking, intelligence testing of, 41

Nongraded class: *defined* 186

Nongraded system: *defined* 186

Nonverbal ability: *defined* 186

Nonverbal, intelligence testing of, 41

Normalization: *defined* 186

Norm-referenced test: *defined* 187
Norms of development: *defined* 187
Nucleic acids, 140
Nucleotide disorders: *defined* 140
Nutrition, 95, 131
Nutritional disorders, 65, 95, 131, 134; *defined* 141
Nystagmus, 143

Obesity, 97
Occupation, in adaptive behavior levels, 206, 207, 208
Occupational therapist: *defined* 187
Occupational therapy, 95
Oligophrenia: *defined* 187
Operant behavior (*See* behavior modification)
Optic atrophy, 143
Oral-Facial-Digital syndrome, 132, 145
Organic brain dysfunction, 100, 101
Orotic aciduria, 140
Orthopaedic treatment, 96
Orthotics: *defined* 187
Otitis media, 94, 95
Ovarian dysgenesis, 133
Ovary, 140
Overactivity (*See* hyperactivity)
Oxycephaly, 145

Pancreas, 140
Paralysis, 146, 152
Paraplegia, 152; *defined* 187
Parasitism, 136, 141
Parathyroid, 140
Parent-child interactions, 47, 66, 68, 150 (*See* also deprivation, maternal)
Parkinsonian facies, 143
PASS-3, 52
Patau syndrome, 133, 147
Pediatric neurologist: *defined* 187
Pediatric psychologist: *defined* 187
Pediatrician: *defined* 187
Pelizaeus-Merzbacher disease, 132; *defined* 143, 188 (*See* also leukodystrophy)
Penis, 148
PEP (*See* protections in evaluative procedures)
Perception: *defined* 188
Perceptual disorder, 66; *defined* 188
Performance test: *defined* 188

Perinatal conditions, 63, 69; categories, 134; *defined* 148–139, 188; hypoxia, 138; injury, 137; malnutrition, 148, 149
Perkins-Binet Intelligence Scale, 41
Perseveration: *defined* 188
Petit mal seizure, 153; *defined* 188 (*See* also epilepsy)
Phenylalanine hydroxylase, 140
Phenylketonuria (PKU), 61, 92, 94, 131; *defined* 140, 188; maternal, 130, 137
Phocomelia: *defined* 189
Phonetics: *defined* 189
Phonics: *defined* 189
Physical defects, 95
Physical development: in adaptive behavior levels, 203, 204, 205, 206, 207
Physical therapist: *defined* 189
Physical therapy, 95, 119
Physically handicapped: *defined* 189
Piaget, 35–38
Pica, 100
Pineal gland, 140
Pituitary gland, 140
PKU (*See* phenylketonuria)
PL 89–313; *defined* 189
PL 91–230; *defined* 189
PL 93–112, Section 504: *defined* 189
PL 94–103, 14
PL 94–142, 10, 15, 54, 81, 113, 114; *defined* 189–190
PL 95–602, Title V, 14, 82, 854
Placenta previa, 138
Plagiocephaly, 145
Plastic surgery, 96
Play technique assessment: *defined* 190
Play therapy: *defined* 190
Plumbism (*See* lead poisoning)
Poisoning, 136, 138; lead, 63, 66; mercury, 63 (*See* also intoxication)
Polydactyly, 147
Pompe disease, 139
Porencephaly, 144
Port wine stain, 142
Porteus Mazes, 41
Positive reinforcer (*See* behavior modification)
Positive transfer (*See* transfer of training)
Postencephalitic: *defined* 190
Postimmunization: infection, 136; intoxication, 130, 137

Postmaturity, 134; (*See also* gestational disorders; preterm)
Postnatal cerebral infection, 130, 136
Postnatal conditions, 65–70; *defined* 141–143, 190
Postnatal hypoxia (anoxia), 131, 138
Postnatal infarction, 138
Postnatal injury, 66, 131, 138
Postnatal malnutrition, 67
Postterm, 134; *defined* 190
Prader-Willi syndrome, 141; *defined* 190
Preadmission: *defined* 190
Prematurity, 62–63, 68–69, 93; *defined* 148; (*See also* gestational disorders; preterm)
Prenatal: factors, 60–65; hypoxia, 62, 137; infection, 60–61, 135–136; injury, 63, 131, 137; irradiation, 63, 64, 137; malnutrition, 63, 64; period *defined*, 191; unknown influences, 132, *defined* 144–146
Preoperational-intuitive level, 36
Preoperational-transductive level, 36
Preschool education: *defined* 191
Preterm, 133, 148; *defined* 191 (*See also* gestational disorders; prematurity)
Prevention, 72–75, 91; *defined* 191
Prognosis: *defined* 191
Program Analysis of Service Systems, 52
Program plan, 84–85
Progress Assessment Chart, 44
Project on Technical Planning in Mental Retardation of AAMD, 5
Proprioception: *defined* 191
Prosthetic environment: *defined* 192, 294
Prosthetics: *defined* 192
Protections in evaluative procedures (PEP), 54–55
Protein deficiency, 64; *defined* 192 (*See also* kwashiorkor)
Protozoic infections, 136
Pseudohypoparathyroidism, 140
Pseudoparalysis, 135
Pseudoretardation: *defined* 192
Psychiatric disorders, 98–102; categories, 134; *defined* 149, 150
Psychiatrist, 119; *defined* 192
Psychogenic mental retardation: *defined* 192
Psychologist, 119; *defined* 192
Psychomotor deficit, 136
Psychomotor seizures: *defined* 192
Psychopharmacologic agents, 63, 102–110; *defined* 193; table of, 105

Psychopharmacological management, 102–110
Psychopharmacology: *defined* 193
Psychosis, 99, 100, 134; *defined* 149; disintegrative, 99, 100
Psychosocial disadvantage, 48–51, 59, 70–75, 134; *defined* 149
Psychosocial influences, 48–51, 63, 68–70
Psychosocial stressors, 125, 127, 128–129
Psychotic disorder (*See* psychosis)
Ptosis, 147
Punishment (*See* behavior modification)
Purines, 140
Purpura, 135
Pyramidal disorders, 142 (*See also* extra-pyramidal dysfunctions)
Pyrimidines, 140

Quadriplegia, 153; *defined* 193

Radiation, 64, 147
Rashes, 135
Receptive language disorder: *defined* 193, 298
Recessive gene, 61; *defined* 193 (*See also* inheritance pattern)
Recreation therapy, 119; *defined* 193
Rehabilitation: *defined* 193–194
Residential facility, 113; *defined* 194
Resource room: *defined* 194
Resource teacher: *defined* 194
Respite care: *defined* 194
Respondent behavior (*See* behavior modification)
Rh incompatibility: *defined* 194 (*See also* blood incompatibility)
Rhinitis, 135
Rh sensitization (*See* Rh incompatibility)
Ribose, 140
Rigidity, 143
Rubella, 60, 65, 130, 135, 136; *defined* 135, 194–195
Rubenstein-Taybi syndrome, 132, 145

Sandhoff disease, 138
Sanfilippo disease, 139
San Francisco Vocational Competency Scale, 44
Scaphocephaly, 145
Schedule of reinforcement (*See* behavior modification)

Schilder diffuse sclerosis (*See* diffuse cerebral sclerosis)
Scholz disease (*See* leukodystrophy)
School phobia: *defined* 195
Screening program: *defined* 195
Sedatives, 105, 108
Seizure, 92–93, 142, 147, 153–154; akinetic, 153; atonic, 153; focal, 154; grand mal, 153, 175; major epilepsy, 153; minor epilepsy, 153; myoclonic, 153; petit mal, 153, 188; psychomotor, 154 (*See also* epilepsy)
Selective placement: *defined* 195
Self-contained class (*See* special class)
Self-direction, in adaptive behavior levels, 206, 207, 208
Self-help skill, 25
Self-injurious behavior (SIB) (*See* self-mutilate)
Self-mutilate: *defined* 195
Senses, defects of special, 134
Sensorimotor skills development, 25
Sensorimotor stage of development, 35, 37
Sensorineural hearing loss, 152; *defined* 195
Sensory deprivation (*See* deprivation, sensory)
Service-system: evaluation, 82–89; management, 79–81; planning, 81–82
Severely handicapped: *defined* 195
Sexual infantilism, 147
Shaping (*See* behavior modification)
Sheltered employment, 121; *defined* 196 (*See also* work)
Shock, 138
Sign language: *defined* 196
Simian crease, 147
Skull fracture, 138
Sleeping problems, 97
Slow learners, 16; *defined* 196
Small-for-dates, 149 (*See also* gestational disorders; prematurity)
Social and emotional development: *defined* 196
Social and Prevocational Information Battery, 44
Social learning theory: *defined* 196
Social responsibility: *defined* 196
Social skills, 25, 119–120; in adaptive behavior levels, 203–208
Social worker: *defined* 197
Socialization, 251

Socioenvironmental factors, 70–75
Spastic infantile paralysis, 152
Spasticity, 142, 145; *defined* 197
Special class, 113; *defined* 197
Special education, 115; *defined* 197
Special educator: *defined* 197
Special needs student: *defined* 197
Special senses, defects of: *defined* 150
Speech disorders, 96, 151; aphasia, 151; babbling *defined* 160; categories, 151; delays, 101, 118, 151; dysphasia, 151; elective mutism *defined* 171; lisping or lalling, 151; slurred, 151; stammering and stuttering, 151 (*See also* communication skills; voice)
Speech pathologist: *defined* 197
Speech therapy, 96, 112, 118
Sphingolipidosis: *defined* 197
Spina bifida: *defined* 198
Spinal sclerosis (*See* Friedreich ataxia)
Spinocerebellar disease, 132; *defined* 143
Splenomegaly, 135
Standard error of measurement: *defined* 198
Standardized test: *defined* 198
Stanford-Binet Intelligence Scale, 10, 23, 30, 31, 32, 40, 41, 56, 57
Statistical reporting, 128, 129
Status dysraphicus, 132; *defined* 145
Stereotyped behaviors, 99; *defined* 198
Sterility, 148
Stimulants, 105, 106
Strabismus, 147
Sturge-Weber-Dimitri disease (*See* trigeminal cerebral angiomatosis)
Sudanophilic leukodystrophy, 132; *defined* 142, 143
Supplemental Security Income (SSI), 80
Syndactylism, 145; *defined* 198
Syndrome: *defined* 198
Syphilis, 60, 130; *defined* 135, 199

Target behavior assessment: *defined* 199
Tay-Sachs disease, 61, 97, 138; *defined* 199
Teachers, 119
Temporary care home: *defined* 199
Terman-Merrill Scale, 183
Testes, 147, 148
Testicle, 140
Testing and evaluation: *defined* 199 (*See also* assessment)
Tetraplegia, 152

Thrombocytopenia, 135
Thrombosis, 138
Thyroid dysfunction, 92, 131, 140; *defined* 141
Time, concept of, 26
Time out (*See* behavior modification)
Token economy: *defined* 199
Total communication: *defined* 199
Toxemia, 65, 130, 136
Toxic substances, 63, 64, 65, 66, 136
Toxoplasmosis, acquired, 60
Toxoplasmosis, congenital, 60, 65, 130; *defined* 136, 200
Trainable retarded persons (TMR), 113; *defined* 200
Training: *defined* 200
Tranquilizer: *defined* 200
Transfer of training: *defined* 200
Transfer, negative: *defined* 200
Transfer, positive: *defined* 200
Translocation Down syndrome, 133
Transportation services: *defined* 200
Trauma or physical agent, 65, 66, 131, 137; prenatal, 65, 131, 137; postnatal, 65, 66, 131, 138
Treatment: *defined* 200
Trigeminal cerebral angiomatosis (Sturge-Weber-Dimitri disease), 132; *defined* 142
Trigonocephaly, 144
Triple-X syndrome, 133, 147
Trisomy 13, 133
Trisomy 18, 133, 146, 147
Trisomy 21 (*See* Down syndrome)
Trisomy 22, 133
Trisomy C_2, 147
Trisomy D_1, 133, 147
Trisomy E_3, 133
Trisomy G, 133
Trisomy condition, 62, 133, 146, 147 (*See also* chromosomal abnormality)
Tryptophan, 140
Tuberous sclerosis, 132; *defined* 142, 201
Tumors, 132, 141, 142; *defined* 142
Turner syndrome, 133, 148
Typus degenerativus amstelodamensis (*See* de Lange syndrome)
Tyrosine, 140

Umbilical artery (single), 133; *defined* 146
Underachiever: *defined* 201
Ungraded: *defined* 201
Unverricht-Lafora disease, 140

Valine, 140
Varicella, 136
Venous-sinus thrombosis, 138
Verbal test: *defined* 201
Vineland Social Maturity Scale, 42, 44, 45, 157; *defined* 201
Viral infections, 130, 136, 147
Vision, low, 151–152 (*See also* blindness; deprivation, sensory)
Visual impairment, 151
Visual disability, 151
Vocational skills, 25, 26
Vocational training, 26 (*See also* work training)
Voice: change in 151; disturbance, 151; hoarseness, 151; hypernasality, 151; hyponasality, 151; loss of, 151
Voght disease, 152
Von Gierke disease, 139
Von Recklinghausen disease (*See* neurofibromatosis)

WAIS (*See* Wechsler Adult Intelligence Scale)
Webbed neck, 147
Wechsler Adult Intelligence Scale-Revised, 23, 41, 183 (*See also* intelligence)
Wechsler Intelligence Scale for Children-Revised, 23, 41, 57, 183 (*See also* intelligence)
Wechsler Preschool and Primary Scale of Intelligence, 41, 183 (*See also* intelligence)
Wechsler scales, 30, 32, 56
Wilson disease, 131, *defined* 140 (*See also* hepatolenticular degeneration)
WISC, WISC-R (*See* Wechsler Intelligence Scale for Children-Revised)
Work, 120–122
Work training, 121–122
WPPSI (*See* Wechsler Preschool and Primary Scale of Intelligence)

Xanthinuria, 140
X-linked inheritance, 143; *defined* 180 (*See also* inheritance pattern)
X-rays, 92
XO syndrome, 133, 147
XXX syndrome, 133, 147
XXY syndrome, 133, 147
XYY syndrome, 133